RECALL TO LIFE —

The Jewish Woman in America

Recall to Life –

The Jewish Woman in America

Anita Libman Lebeson

SOUTH BRUNSWICK

NEW YORK • THOMAS YOSELOFF • LONDON

Library of Congress Catalogue Card Number 77-88278

Thomas Yoseloff, *Publisher*
Cranbury, New Jersey 08512

Thomas Yoseloff Ltd
108 New Bond Street
London W1Y OQX, England

SBN 498 07480 3

Printed in the United States of America

FOR HERMON LEBESON
AD OLAM

CONTENTS

CONTENTS

PREFACE

Every book weaves its own history. The beginning of a book may coincide with a flash of insight, with a dramatic episode, with a moment in time waiting to be forever held in memory, with an obligation to others, with the fulfillment of a long-cherished purpose. It may be a dream made real. It may be time made to stand still or time recaptured. It may be identification with protagonists long dead who seem to have captured immortality. It may be the awareness of the erasures which obliterate life. It may be the knowledge that history is a continuum—"a river that maketh glad the heart."

Recall to Life was born in the war-rubbled streets of London. Postwar London was scarred and pitted, its ancient grandeur crushed, precious landmarks demolished. A city of enchantment was made desolate. In "London: Things Seen and Unseen," we had sought out its Jewish sections—Stepney, Bethnal Green, Whitechapel—and tried to describe the ruins: "Wiped out by diabolical marksmen. Lost to time and history. Forever to remain unseen except with the mind's eye. Waiting to be recalled to life by poets and writers, remembered in elegies, immortalized in monuments and stained glass windows. . . . The generations will come and go . . . the Eternal People will endure. No bombs will erase them. No tyrants put them to death. They will remain, the seen and the unseen, imperishable, immortal, abiding."

So over the years the notes began to accumulate. Libraries disgorged their secrets. Biographies leaped to life. Events and participants were joined. Facts and footnotes filled many boxes. Yet beyond all this was the persistence of impressions that defied words. The communication of a mood that alternated between despair and exultation; between what has been wrought and what may still be achieved; the ultimate choice between life and death; between faith in immortality or acquiescence in total annihilation—these were the contradictions which had to be reconciled.

Many were the friends to whom I turned for clarification. It is impossible to acknowledge them all. A few who have been especially helpful must be singled out.

Rabbi Philip L. Lipis read the entire manuscript and made invaluable suggestions which were incorporated into the many-times rewritten text. Rabbi Edgar E. Siskin was generous in his interpretation of the spheres of influence which the three main branches of Judaism had pre-empted. Both Rabbi David de Sola Pool and Tamar Pool were inexhaustible sources of information and inspiration. Rabbi Isidore S. Meyer was frequently consulted and always helpful. Mr. Abraham Berger and Miss Dora Steinglass made the resources of the Jewish Division of the New York Public Library readily available. Miss Fanny Lindey generously shared the accumulation of years of notes and published articles on Jewish organizational activities. The late Fanny Goldstein of the Boston Public Library showed me her personal scrapbooks—the accumulation of years of dedicated research.

Dr. Dora Edinger, Mrs. Elsie Schwarz of the Chicago Public Library, and Mrs. Matalie Cohen of the Plotkin Library of North Shore Congregation Israel were among those who supplied valuable information.

From Mrs. E. Solis-Cohen I received numerous notes and printed items which helped in the interpretation of the personality of Mrs. Solomon Schechter and some of her close associates. Mrs. Alfred S. Alschuler, Sr., shared from her family archives much hitherto unavailable information about Hannah Solomon and other members of her family, as well as some autobiographical material included in this book.

Justin Turner was indefatigable in collecting and forwarding many biographies of Californians. Richard Press of the Deering Library of Northwestern University assembled many volumes of publications which were indispensable. The late Samuel Caplan of Congress Weekly provided a forum in the pages of the magazine which he so ably edited. Various staff members of the American Jewish Congress furnished important data. Mrs. Adele H. Nusbaum of B'nai B'rith Women was similarly helpful. Sara Jacobson of HIAS responded to all requests for information.

Particularly helpful was Sarah Elkin Braun, who was instrumental in securing autobiographical notes and informal family histories of many otherwise-forgotten Shunammites whose shining lives needed to be recalled. Another generous collector of hitherto unavailable material was Leah Mishkin, Librarian and Curator of the Saul Silber Memorial Library of the Hebrew Theological College.

Max Siegel, literary agent and staunch friend, followed the evolution of this book with keen interest, reading its several versions with patience and encouragement.

Without my husband, Hermon Lebeson, who shared

in the travels to many distant libraries, translated books
and articles from the Hebrew and Yiddish, read and
reread the manuscript with care, evaluating and rein-
terpreting controversial data, this book would not have
been written. My debt to him can never be adequately
acknowledged. It was a shared undertaking—and to him
this work is dedicated.

ANITA LIBMAN LEBESON
Evanston, Illinois

RECALL TO LIFE —

The Jewish Woman in America

1

Time unrolls. Man is the scribe. We see recorded history largely through his eyes. Woman who is
his life's companion is a self without a shadow. This is
not her conscious renunciation. Nor is man the usurper
by choice. Each has his own role and destiny. Woman is
the forgotten actor in the human drama, the anonymous
co-author of the plot which involves all mankind.

Historians, sociologists, cultural anthropologists have
recently described an "overemphasis on the importance
of the male."[1] This is found in every age and every section of our world. The role of woman in social history
is now being considered, analyzed, described. We are
taking a giant step forward and Buddha's instructions
about women, "Don't see them, Ananda," are no longer
universally applicable.[2]

This is a book whose protagonists are women. They
are the neglected and often forgotten heroines whose lives
helped to shape their times. There are learned and literate
women among them and those whose only literacy was

of the heart. Yet they all had one trait in common—they believed themselves to be custodians of a precious way of life. They had purpose in life. They had a commitment to God. They kept the faith.

It is hard to find a place in time to begin our story. Properly both space and time wear mourning from the year seventy when a nation was conquered, a great city made desolate, and coarse and ruthless hands erased a God-fearing people from their ancient home. Centuries of dispersion, degradation, hopeless wandering, lamentation and yearning, of hearts turning toward Jerusalem and prayers celebrating the ancient days, succeeded each other.

No people in history ever carved the geography of their lost homeland on their hearts—save the Jews. A land was torn from them. Yet these wanderers knew its contours, cherished its wells and springs, blessed its snow-capped mountains, celebrated the harvests it once yielded and the trees that gave shade to their ancestors. Every Jew had a passport to the land from which he was exiled. In his heart he knew where he belonged. In life, in death. There is a funeral dirge chanted by Sephardim "in which the mourners pray that the deceased, after passing the Cave of Machpelah, may come upon the guardian cherubim and receive from them a 'ticket' or 'passport' . . . to the Garden of Eden."[3] It was a lasting covenant they had made with God. Man could not undo it.

Man tried. The annals of Jewish history deplete our souls.

It was a miracle that the remnant of Israel survived. "Endowed with an inner strength that bordered on the mysterious, Jewish life displayed an incredible capacity for recovery and renewal."[4] How they lived through their ordeals, how they became crypto-Jews driven into hiding, how they emerged to reaffirm their faith, how they strengthened each other and sheltered the refugees, how they sought and found inner strength—all of this reverberates through history. We have their prayers, eloquent petitions storming the very gates of heaven, crying for deliverance. We have the sagas of some of their wanderers describing scattered communities of Jews. We have their enduring prose and their poignant poetry charged with love of God and love of their lost homeland. We have their maps—for they were incurable students of geography. We have their astronomical charts—for they were inveterate astronomers. We have their portolani—for they were obsessed with navigation and traced on maps the known and the unknown seas and harbors. Their maritime knowledge, their maps and instruments made Jewish scholars greatly sought after. Protection replaced prejudice where Jewish skills existed. Savants basked in the sun of royal favor.

In March of 1492 two related events occurred. In that month the Spanish Edict of Expulsion was announced. And Columbus, sponsored and befriended by Don Isaac Abravanel and other influential Jews, was happily engaged in the outfitting of his ships. "Jews had an important part given them in the American drama," writes John Boyd Thacher. "The last sound Columbus heard as he was preparing to sail from the old world was the wailing of the Jews." This melancholy dirge was the drumbeat of Jewish history.

Don Isaac Abravanel exhorted his fellow Jews: "Let us surmount every trouble for the honour of our nation and our religion. . . . If they leave us with life, we will live; if they deprive us of it, we will die; but never let us violate our holy law."

So was launched the era of great discovery. So was begun a new chapter in Jewish history. The Western Hemisphere awaited its weary pilgrims.

The South American chapter of the history of the Jews has been simply stated. Professor Renard says: "In 1500 Alvarez Cabral was driven by a storm to the coasts of Brazil, which the government peopled with exiled Jews and convicts." Among the secret Jews and those who professed Judaism openly there were planters, merchants, tobacco growers, sugar refiners, brokers, storekeepers, peddlers, soldiers—and their wives and children. Men left ample records. Women cast no shadows on the pages of recorded history.

Jews came to South America both singly and in family groups. Gaspar *Judeo,* (the Jew) was a member of Cabral's epochal voyage of discovery. One of the most colorful Brazilian pioneers was a Lisbon marrano, Fernando de Loronha or Noronha. The little rockbound island off the coast of Brazil which he discovered is named the Island of Fernando Noronha. Leland De Witt Baldwin in *The Story of the Americas* notes the fact that while orthodox Catholics and "old" Christians, "that is, without Jewish or Moorish blood," were preferred as explorers and settlers, nevertheless many of diverse origins were included in the crews . . . Columbus . . . may have been a Jew himself. More than one voyager took along Jewish interpreters of Arabic in the hope that the Grand Kahn could speak Arabic."

In a classic work on the history and civilization of Brazil, *The Masters and the Slaves,* by Gilberto Freyre we read: "São Paulo was probably the nucleus of the Brazilian population with the largest strain of Semitic blood." "The tentacles of the Holy Office," he goes on, "had not reached as far as that, although they were already closing upon Bahia and Pernambuco, where all that was lacking was for the bonfires to be prepared." Paulo Prado corroborates this: "In São Paulo they were not persecuted by the formidable instrument of the Inquisition . . ."[5]

Sugar culture produced a feudal economy from the start. The *Casa Grande* was for the prosperous lord of the manor. The hovel for the slave laborer. The family was "the colonizing unit. This was an economic and a social organization that at times ran counter not only to Catholic sexual morality but to the Semitic tendencies of the Portuguese adventurer toward trade and barter as well."[6] We know that among the dwellers in the Big Houses on the plantations were Jewish women and children who were among Brazil's earliest pioneers. A basic fact about the early Judaism of the pioneer is that "the nexus binding the Jewish group together is a common historical experience rather than a confession of creed."[7] Whether these manorial dwellers were professing Jews or crypto-Jews, they were bound together by enduring ties.

The enterprising Fernando de Loronha was a dynamic entrepeneur and prosperous shipowner. He led an expedition of New Christians to Brazil. Of his five ships which we can identify by name, one was called the *Judea*. The historian Calmon writes that under Loronha Jewish colonization in Pernambuco and Bahia was of foremost importance. Of the earliest settlers, Jews were in the majority. When the second armada set sail for Brazil in May of 1501, the southernmost point which these sea-weary navigators touched must have looked like the promised land to them. They thought of Canaan. When they made their landfall their settlement was appropriately called Cananea. At Cape Frio a fort was built by these new settlers and New Christians—the first in Brazil.

It took forty days for Pedro Alvares Cabral after leaving Lisbon to make his landfall in Brazil. "When on April 22, 1500, Nicolau Coelho stepped ashore for the first time on Brazilian territory he was accompanied by Gaspar da Gama."[8] The first land grant was issued to a New

Christian. "Fernão de Noronha was thus the first donatario
in Brazil."[9] From ships' logs and other contemporary records we learn that his was a profitable venture. We know
that Noronha's settlers were productive and that dyewood
and other products were carried back to Portugal. Sugar
cane was planted and the sugar industry became a thriving
one. But what we lack are the details of daily life, the
shape and form of their shelters, their thoughts and feelings, their hopes and dreams. We have only occasional
faint glimpses of the plots of their lives.

What of their imperishable moments? When the walls
of a family go up and a place of shelter and privacy is
created shutting out the wild beasts and lurking enemies,
does not the heart quicken with pride, and hope dwell
beneath the roof? After the hazards and acute discomforts
of the Atlantic crossing and constant surveillance by the
agents of the Inquisition and denunciations by mercenary
spies, how good it must have been to shut the door on
lurking danger, to be upheld by the safety of one's family
circle.

There were always the hazards of fortune and of providence. Here is one of many examples. One of the first
five sugar mills in Brazil was "De Santiago." It belonged
to Jews. Diogo Fernandes and several co-religionists owned
this "large mill with good land, excellent water and much
timber . . ."[10] It was completely destroyed in a war with
the natives. The governor of Pernambuco reported this
loss to the king of Portugal, stating that as a result of
this loss, Diogo and his wife and seven daughters and
two sons had become totally impoverished. He described
the Indian attack, praised Diogo's capabilities and knowledge of the sugar industry and "suggested a royal favor
for Diogo."[11] Always there were catastrophes impending.
Sometimes there was partial deliverance.

There is practically no mention of Jewish women in

the documents and books that are extant. Their presence
is assumed when families are taxed, when children's
schools are provided and teachers engaged, when the
distribution of supplies and charity practices are mentioned in records. We have scholarly translations of two
Congregational Minute Books of Brazil—Congregation
Zur Israel of Recife and Magen Abraham of Mauricia.
Since these are the first records of organized Jewish communities in the New World and since the New York
Jewish community is "but an offshoot of that of Recife"
the works of Dr. Arnold Wiznitzer are of prime importance.[12]

It is a slender volume which records that historic day,
the first of Kislev, 5409, November 16, 1648, when forty-
two regulations were devised and enacted for the guidance
of the congregation. Transported to Amsterdam, to the
Livraria Ets Haim, "it seems that the manuscript of the
Minute Book remained in the Archives of Amsterdam
unnoticed by historians from 1654 to 1911." Among the
earliest provisions was the selection of Trustees of the
Talmud Torah and of the Treasurer of the Ets Hayyim
School. Only men were present at these meetings. One
wonders whether the criteria for the selection of the Ruby
or Rubi, the teacher of the younger children, may not
have been indirectly influenced by the wives and mothers.
The Ruby served as a substitute for the hazzan "when the
latter was prevented from being present at the synagogue."
There was a ritual bath for the women of the congregation. But no Gentile women were permitted to use the
tevilah "without the prior consent of the Mahamad (the
Executive Committee) . "Under the penalty of excommu-
nication and a fine of fifty florins. This is the only regu-
lation in the Minute Book that makes reference to wom-
en."[13] It is possible that little girls were admitted to a
"Talmud Torah School for smaller children," for the

Ets Hayyim (Gemara) School was designated "for older boys."

It is interesting to note that private giving of alms was specifically prohibited. The Synagogue Sedaka fund required that all contributions and disbursements for charity be in the hands of the Mahamad. The Sedaca paid for (and here is another evidence of women in the community) "dowries and trousseaux of poor orphan girls . . ."[14] All *promessas,* pledges to charity, which include the dowries and funds to orphans, free-will offerings, both for the needy in Brazil and those in the Holy Land were payable quarterly.

The free years, when Jews could profess and practice their faith in the province of Brazil were the years of the Dutch occupation. When in 1624 an important foothold by the Dutch was established in Brazil, it brought many Jews into the open after long, drab, frightening years underground. But when the Portuguese reconquered some of these outposts, despair took over once more. So the seesaw military operations continued. Every Jew rejoiced in Dutch military victories and was plunged into depression when the Portuguese showed strength. There were years when the sugar crops failed and many Jews were debt-ridden. The years from 1642 to 1644 were especially bleak. Conditions in Europe were ominous. The worst excesses committed against the Jews since the Crusades, the Chmielnicki massacres, were unleashed (1648-1655) . Frightened and hopeless refugees once more took to the roads, to the high seas.

On January 27, 1654, the Portuguese commander entered Recife. New Holland was lost to the Dutch. "The synagogues were destroyed, the stones of the Jewish burial ground overturned, and the Jewish settlement ended."

Portuguese officials made an inventory of all that had been left behind. All Jewish property was confiscated.

There were dwellings, big and small. There was a "Rua dos Judeos," a Jewish square, a Jewish beach. There were "some big houses . . . on the same side of the river, facing the street of the Jews, that had served them as a Synagogue, built with stone and calk . . ."

So the first chapter of Jewish history in the New World ended—and every female protagonist of this 150-year narrative remains to this day an anonymous participant—a shadow member of a silent chorus—a Shunammite! Like her namesake in the Bible, a heroine in a forgotten plot. Yet not quite anonymous. For on crumbling stones in lonely cemeteries one finds records of lives nobly lived, of the bereaved recounting their sorrows, and of their unyielding belief that God will somewhere complete the unfulfilled days so tragically cut short.

History and biography are chipped in granite.

There are such data. Writes Salo W. Baron in 1956: "Tombstone inscriptions have long been a major source of Jewish history . . . scholars interested in tracing the early history of Jewish communities have diligently gathered whatever material of this type has survived the ravages of time. . . . In fact, it is but a few years ago that, in his *Portraits Etched in Stone,* Dr. David de Sola Pool was able to present a first contributions to the knowledge not only of the persons buried there, but also of the entire community in which they lived."[15] So the Esthers and Sarahs and Abigails who lived and died are recalled to life. Their virtues are remembered and their sorrowing kin share their grief with us. "Here Lyeth Interr'd the Body of the Charitable Sara Late Wife of Mordecay Massiah who departed this life. . . . Aged 34 years 1 Mo and 15 Days . ." There are "charitable" Rachels and "honest" Esthers. Charity was a prized virtue. Of one widow it was said: "She was a Good Wife A Tender Mother & Very Charitable."[16]

On the eve of momentous days, on the American continent, an unmarried woman was saluted for all eternity
as follows:

> Here lies till happy Resurrection
> A maid Possessed of every perfection
> cutt off in the prime of youth and life
> Er'e her Virtues could Shine as wife
> Her loss much regreted by all
> Her Friends afflicted at her fall
> This Consolation thear thought Imploy
> Her Soul perfect felicity doth Injoy
> Sarah Pereira Henriques departed this
> Life . . . being . . . 36 years & 4 months.[17]

Here is the Jewish belief in immortality and in resur-
rection indelibly stated. Here too is the last line of Psalm
16 paraphrased: "in thy presence is fullness of joy."

The records of the Inquisition and of the grave erased
anonymity both in the New World as well as in the Old.
The following Inquisition entry, eloquent in its cruel
recall, names some New World heroines:

> Year 1601
> Process against Lenor de Caceres, only child of Antonio
> Diaz de Caceres, and Miss Catalina Cueva de Carbajal,
> his wife, also her mother and sisters, for Judaism . . . .

Not quite anonymous, some of these female residents
of the newly discovered lands. Not quite lands of promise.

Unhappily it is to the records of the so-called "Holy
Office" that we must turn to glimpse some of the household practices, the rites and customs which were evidence
of Judaic observances leading to torture and trial, imprisonment or death. Although some of the victims of
the Inquisition were also Lutherans and others were non-

conformists, the chief prey hunted by black-robed clerical sleuths were "Judaizers." High on the list of "crimes" was the observance of the Jewish Sabbath; wearing of fresh clothing and jewelry and fresh undergarments on Friday afternoon as well as cleaning homes; lighting of candles at an earlier hour on Friday afternoons and permitting them to burn out; observance of ritual slaughter of animals; avoidance of certain types of meat and fish; fasting on Yom Kippur and asking forgiveness of each other on that day; the eating of unleavened bread and the use of new utensils on Passover; the blessing of children without making the sign of the cross, and many like offenses.

So Ana Rois, wife of Heitor Antunes who arrived in Bahia with her husband and four daughters and three sons, on December 28, 1557, was denounced with her children and four granddaughters, her husband having mercifully died before the Inquisition got around to him.[18] Maria Lopes, married to the one-time chief surgeon of Lisbon who was later appointed chief surgeon of Brazil, came on the same ship with the Antunes family. "All of the Judaizers in Bahia . . . were obviously wealthy people, owners of sugar mills, merchants, surgeons, innkeepers, and farmers." They were not spared the tortures of the Inquisition. The Inquisitorial commission published in 1591 an Edict of Faith, a Monitory Letter, and a Term of Grace for the city of Bahia and the surrounding territory. Confessions of sins, self-denunciations and denunciations of others were invited on the promise of mitigating treatment at the hands of the Inquisitorial gentry. Panic ensued. Denunciation of self and neighbor followed. In their fright they reached far into the past. One man denounced Beatriz Antunes, her sister Dona Leonor and their mother Ana Rois, "alleging that they claimed to be descendants of the Maccabees, an aristocratic Jewish family." We learn that "the Judaizers of Bahia had secret

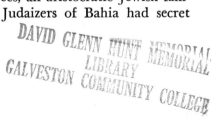

synagogues, rabbis, and perhaps a Sefer Torah . . ."[19]

Not only the secret and the arcane, remotely connected with Jewish antiquity, was practiced and cherished. Fairy tales circulated identifying the Indians of Brazil as descendants of the lost tribes of Israel. A private shorthand sprang up among the initiates. "Take one step at a time, for matzoth is fragile," they would warn each other. Secret signs of caution were common. What loomed ahead was so frightening, so cruel, so utterly hopeless, that it called forth every resource of fortitude and courage to face life as a secret Jew.

In the "List of Brazilian Jews Executed by the Inquisition" in Lisbon during the years 1644-1748 is Dossier 2218. The name of one victim is Theresa Pays de Jesus![20]

At an auto-da-fe of July 30, 1709, in Lisbon, 13 Brazilian Jews were tried of whom four were women. In July 26, 1711, of fifty cases involving Judaizers, 26 were men and 24 women.[21] Nine of the 24 women were married to men who were arrested and sentenced. "The other 15 were widows or daughters of manufacturers or sugar cane farmers, physicians, and lawyers. None was sentenced to death."[22]

2

In 1654 refugees from Brazil reached the haven of New Amsterdam. An immigrant, Jacob Barsimson, had previously come from Holland on August 22, 1654. He was known as a Jewish merchant, one of the Jews whom the Brazilian Jews found on their arrival—and not too openhanded. For when the twenty-three refugees, "big and little" insolvent and stripped of their possessions on the high seas, unable to pay for their passage, appealed to Jacob, "he would not lend them a single stiver." Nor were the Christian city fathers disposed to be charitable. It was a bleak and desperate time, a time of heartache and uncertainty for the little pilgrim band of men and women and children.[1]

Of their vicissitudes much has been written. David and Tamar de Sola Pool's detailed account in *An Old Faith in the New World* is an empathic narrative of the sorrows of these Jewish pilgrims. Names of men as petitioners and litigants abound. But here and there, from the ooze of anonymity which usually covers the activities

of early Jewish women, a few begin to emerge. One of
the small band of immigrants appeared in court to represent Rycke Nounes "whose goods were sold, over and
above her own freight debt, in order to obtain with that
money some support for her." Her petition was granted.
She was one of the founding mothers of Shearith Israel.
One other female name appears in those first records—
that of Judicq de Mereda. We may assume that with the
men the women joined in their ancestral worship, leading
Governor Stuyvesant to complain that "they have many
times requested of us the free and public exercise of their
abominable religion . . ." Yet it was not until 1728 that
"a burst of vigorous new life in the congregation" led to
the purchase of land and the plans for the erection of a
house of worship. Their numbers had increased. The old
cemetery lot was filled. It was necessary to proceed with
"the Building of a Sinagoga and for a Burying place . . ."
Jews in distant places were listed as contributors, among
them a Jewess from the Barbados. A special "banco" was
reserved in the women's gallery for the women of the
Gomez family. A ritual bath used by women (rebuilt in
1759) adjoined the synagogue.

On the seventh day of Passover, the anniversary of its
consecration, special prayers are said and the names of
early builders of the congregation are recalled. Three
women are included in this roster of honor: Rachel Luiza,
Bilhah Abigail Franks, and Simhah de Torres.

From September of 1654, when the little band of Jews
came to New Amsterdam, it was but a decade until New
Amsterdam fell to the English and was renamed New
York. The rights and privileges which the early Jewish
settlers had wrested from the Dutch were continued. Restrictions wherever met were vigorously protested. Largely
conditions in the New World mirrored those in the Old.[2]
Rights had to be defined and interpreted by law courts.

This involved trading privileges as well as voting rights. Jews shared in the affairs of the larger community as when seven residents contributed to the building of a steeple on Trinity Church in New York. Involvement with new environment in no way diminished their memories of the old. Ties with European kin were nurtured and zealously maintained. Business dealings were transoceanic in scope and often long distance marriages were proposed and discussed and arranged. There was a universe of discourse between Jews in America and their European kin.

From letters which were exchanged, from household inventories, from wills which were drawn up, from occasional references to Jewish settlers found in the diaries and papers of Christian friends and neighbors and officials, a tapestry is woven with glimpses of a way of life which has faded leaving but faint traces of people and events. Yet these are our tools. Although much of the evidence, historical and sociological, about the participation of women in Jewish communal life is indirect, inferred and implied, we do occasionally find a record of more than vicarious importance. When in 1685, "the first known regular reader of services," Saul Pardo, arrived in New York to become the spiritual leader of Shearith Israel, he managed not only to perform all of his religious duties but to became a highly prosperous merchant. The home he built for his wife, Esther and their children, a son Josiah and three daughters, Abigail, Sarah and Hannah, was valued at the then high figure of a hundred pounds. His successor, Abraham Haim de Lucena, also combined the twin careers of hazzan and merchant. One of the most interesting genealogical records is traced through Rachel de Lucena. We read in *An Old Faith in the New World*:[1]

"De Lucena's wife, Rachel, bore him a daughter, Rebecca. She became the wife of Mordecai Gomez in 1741. Their daughter Eve Esther became the wife of Uriah

Henricks in 1762. Through this daughter and granddaughter, Abraham Haim de Lucena became the pro-
genitor of leaders in the congregation in every generation
down to our day."[3]

Fragmentary as these facts may be, it is possible to re-
construct the past, to put flesh on the bare skeleton. The
record reveals date, place, occupation, triumph, tribula-
tion, accomplishment or failure. When we read that
fifteen Jewish families arrived in Newport in 1658 bringing with them the first three degrees of Masonry "and
worked them in the house of Campanall," we are given
a whole series of montages of social and fraternal life.
Women figure in this activity if only as hostesses and
providers of refreshment. Boston's first tax list shows
that "Ye Jew" Rowland Gideon and his wife Bathsheba
were taxpayers in 1674. Asser Levy of New York, butcher
and solid citizen, headed, a well-equipped household
which, among other items, boasted an inventory which
included thirteen tablecloths, twenty-four napkins, household silver and goblets, a Sabbath lamp, "a parcel of old
books," and many pictures. Yet he was one of the three
Jews arrested as a debtor when, as part of the original
band of twenty-three pilgrims who came to New Amsterdam, their passage money could not be paid. Such success stories abounded.

Life is not made of artifacts. Sabbath candles imply
Sabbath observance but they do not capture the soft glow
of candlelight filtering through almost transparent fingers
as the Sabbath is invoked by the swaying and devout
homemaker. Tablecloths and silver imply hospitality and
the practice of amenities. But they do not begin to convey
the hazards of life. Medical help is scarce and often unavailable. Mothers die in childbirth and infants are
snuffed out because there are no medicines. The pitfalls

of daily living are always greater than the sum of its pleasures. New homes in the freer air of America give shelter but they do not assuage the pangs of separation and loneliness. Many a sigh is heard whose anguish needs only reunion with dear ones to relieve it. Memories are fragile but infinitely dear. They span both space and time.

Such letters and private papers as have survived the centuries reveal only that the capacity of men and women to suffer and to rejoice remains unchanged. Fluctuations of mood alternate from the heights of exaltation to the shallows of despair. The love of parents for their children is a perennial glow. Dreams of security are spun into lullabies. Young people go off adventuring into war and on long journeys of exploration. And girls, beautiful or plain, with or without dowries, are catapulted into matrimony with men they scarcely know into a life they cannot even envisage.

Such is the fabric of our history.

Most Americans are familiar with the privations of pioneering life. They know that early Americans lived in a perpetual state of siege. The toll of life was heavy. Often graves had to be concealed so that the stalking enemy would not be informed of the dwindling ranks in the stockades. The weather could be an ally or a destroyer. Food supplies could be depleted through drought or insect damage. Shelters could be wiped out by marauding activities of hostile Indians or by bolts of lightning. Epidemics could decimate the population. Jews were as vulnerable as their Christian neighbors. They accepted life with whatever resources, moral and physical, were theirs. Yet to them there fell additional burdens— always the lot of a minority living within the framework of a host culture, a dominant culture that sometimes was hostile, often was detached, at times totally oblivious, at other times bent on evangelizing and missionary activities whose aim was to sell salvation and obliterate cultural differences.

What were these differences which set Jewish men and women apart? They were both temporal and spiritual. They were also other-worldly. Some Jews came to North America after generations of underground profession of their faith. They had been tenacious in adversity and under persecution. They could do no less in the open. Adjustment was always hard. But how much more difficult to learn to live again with dignity and pride, to profess what had been arcane and forbidden, to assert that in Judaism lay their hope and their salvation in this world and in the next. Harsh laws may be vehemently rejected within the heart. But blandishment and persuasion are not as easily spurned. Proximity and neighborly relations often lead to intermarriage. The genealogies of Jews record the sad depletion of ranks, the losses of countless Jews and their descendants. One need only consult the records of many early congregations like Shearith Israel to be aware of the escape hatch of intermarriage.

Language was a barrier. Among the earliest Jewish settlers in America were those who spoke Spanish and Portuguese and those who were at home in Yiddish, German, and Dutch. Some knew English. But many whose earliest business ventures included a peddler's pack or basket trudged from outpost to outpost with the barest knowledge of English. Not only did they have to make sales, but they had to be fed and sheltered by their customers. This led to complications which at times involved law suits as healthy appetites and normal physical hungers were assuaged.

Dietary laws were a problem for those who observed them. Sometimes Jews were reminded by Christian friends to bring their sharp knives for ritual slaughter of animals.

The Sabbath was observed in strange and lonely places. Prayers were recited in forest shelters and the Psalms chanted along dusty footpaths or beneath some spreading oak or elm. *"Es iz schwer zu sein a Yid,"* the slogan of later generations, could well have been the theme song of early Jewish pilgrims in America.

These facts are borne out in strange ways. The fact that Jews were multilingual and came from many distant places is verified by the cemetery inscriptions. Five languages were used—Hebrew, English, Portuguese, Spanish, and Latin. In New York, in Newport and in London this was true. Says Rabbi Pool in his *Portraits Etched in Stone:* "The languages on the tombstones not only give evidence as to the vernacular of New York Jews in early colonial days; they also bear testimony as to the land of origin of these pioneer settlers."[4] Other interesting facts are deduced by Dr. Pool and some describe early female pioneers. On nomenclature: ". . . the Jewish women of those days turned more readily to sophisticated names, though the majority bore classical Biblical names. They ring the changes on fifteen Biblical names with Sarah the first favorite occurring twelve times. . . . Next in popularity are Rachel (ten times), Esther (eight times), Rebecca (seven times), and Deborah, Jochebed, and Miriam (four times each) . . . among thirty-eight women's names there are no less than twenty which are not of Jewish tradition." Among the names which betray geographic origins are Reyna, Bianca, Amelia, Justina, Phoebe, Rose. Jochebed, the mother of Moses, becomes Jossy or Joice. "But," adds Dr. Pool, "let none interpret it to the disparagement of the daughters of Israel. The rabbis stressed the merit of the women of Israel as one reason why the Hebrews were found worthy of redemption from Egypt. . . ."[5]

Many generalizations are drawn by Dr. David de Sola Pool from his study of the epitaphs of early American

Jews. A serious problem which early New York Jews faced, and this was equally true of other early American Jewish communities, was that of inbreeding. "There was too little matrimonial choice in the small town of New York. Sometimes a wife or a husband was found and brought from Newport, R. I., or Philadelphia, the only two Jewish communities within a distance of a few days' travel. At other times, marriages seem to have been arranged with Jewish families at more remote points in the United States, in Central America, or even in Europe. Sometimes the problem was drastically solved by marriage outside of the community. But to a large extent, marriages in the New York Jewish community soon became more or less close cousin marriages."[6]

One of the earliest tombstone biographies was that of "the blissful" Sarah Bueno de Mesquita. Another Sarah was Sarah Rodriguez de Rivera. She was described as a "modest worthy and honored woman" who died in childbirth—"and she had hard labor and in her labor in giving birth her soul fled and she died in her agony also the fruit of her body after her . . ." Hard as it was to be a Jew, it was much harder to be a Jewess! Sometimes just the age of the occupant of the grave is eloquent, as in the case of Rebecca Gomez who died in her twenty-eighth year, or of Miriam Lopez de Fonseca "reverent and virtuous" who died in her forty-fifth year "in bliss and glory" on the eve of Rosh Hashanah. Or "the blissful honored and virtuous" Esther Rachel, wife of Mordecai Gomez. When a spinster of 77, Reyna, or Malkah Gomez died, she was saluted as "the honored maiden." Equally extolled was Grace Hays, stepmother of Bilhah Abigail Levy Franks, as a "modest woman." Modesty they cherished as well as charity. Esther Gomez was saluted as "the beloved and charitable." And Sarah Pinto who died in 1785 at the age of 87 was described as a "Virtuous mother in

Israel." In the same year Elkalah Mendes Seixas, wife of
the eminent patriot and rabbi, Gershom Mendes Seixas,
died in her 36th year, "And she went to seek the Lord . . ."

So out of crumbling stones and carved inscriptions we
rebuild lives, recapture eternal values and verities, are
overwhelmed by the tragedies of early death and are reminded that bereavement is not mitigated by calendar
years nor are virtues forgotten when the story of a life
is completed. Virginity was extolled in young women and
old—for not to find a mate merely reflected lack of opportunity. Charity and modesty and goodness of heart
were the prime virtues. A woman's vocation could be
fulfilled in marriage or in good works. To be a spinster
meant the refusal to escape, to intermarry. It meant wil-
lingness to walk a solitary path because she had elected
to keep the faith.

All of this makes us treasure every letter, diary, or
private confession which occasionally comes down to us
giving us a rare and precious view of the interior of a
woman's heart, the secrets of the dark and hidden corridors of her mind.

One such treasure we have. *Glückel of Hameln By
Herself* is a work of penetrating insight and of undeviating honesty. She lived in Germany between the years
1646 and 1724, a time of migration and terror for the
Jews of Europe. The portrait is recognizable, for it describes the immigrant woman who came to America, holding up a true likeness for posterity. The fears and frus-
trations and dangers she records are applicable to her
co-religionists in Europe. Yet the folkways and mores
which surround Glückel, the arranged marriages based on
convenience, dowry, status of bride's family and scholarship of groom's, the identification with all synagogue
concerns, the sharing of private joys and communal sorrows—all of these aspects of European Jewish life had

their counterpart in the New World. The motif of life
for Glückel and her contemporaries is recognizable. Her
invocations to God and Patriarchs were Jewish invocations. Her faith was a powerful support. There was no
mistaking her allegiance, her orientation, her dedication
to Judaism. Separated as she was by thousands of miles
from her New World sisters, she manages to convey to
us a very special and unique mirror-image of a Jewish
woman who was in the historic stream of Jewish life.
There was a total commitment to her faith.

Martin Buber has said it better than any one else in
our time: "Are we still truly Jews? Jews in our lives? Is
Judaism still alive? . . . Let us recognize ourselves: We,
in whom, and in whom alone, that mysterious affirmation
and negation of civilization—affirmation and negation in
one—was implanted at the origin of our existence, we are
the keepers of the roots [italics added]."[7] From Glückel's
day to ours, the historic stream of Jewish life has been in
the hands of "the keepers of the roots," women as well
as men.

Glückel's world was one of sorrows and tribulations,
of wars and insecurity and infant mortality and cruelty
and exploitation, of pogroms, military conscription of little children, kidnapping and forced conversion, degradation, discrimination, insecurity, perpetual flight, lack of
protective homeland, lack of concerned government, occu-
pational restrictions, forbidden marriage. Hers was a
world of perpetual partnership with trouble, hunger and
privation, yet her voice speaks to us of undying love, of
the wonder of little children, of exaltation and inspiration and firm faith. It is a self-portrait. But it is also a
portrait of the immigrant Jewess from Europe transplanted to America.

Glückel was born in Hamburg two years before the
end of the Thirty Years War, a time which brought untold

sorrows to the Jews of Central Europe. Jewish refugees from Poland in 1648 fled like sheep pursued by hungry wolves, the Cossacks, led by the infamous Chmielnicki and his murdering hordes. She was but eight years old when the Jews arrived in New Amsterdam. News from the New World trickled through to the Old. She was married at fourteen, bore thirteen children of whom one died in infancy, and after thirty years of marriage she lost her husband. "During the dreadful, grief-laden nights that followed Reb Chaim Segal's death . . .," she began to write down the story of her life. She begins: "In the year of Creation 5451 I began writing this with an aching heart."[8]

Night after night Glückel of Hameln searches her heart and empties her memories into little notebooks which have been miraculously preserved. The years of her life reveal not only her personal griefs, joys, bereavements, deprivations. They mirror her times, show the condition of the Jews, detail the lives of women, bring us the intrigues and plots, the strange and awesome workings of Providence when to survive as a Jew was as stupendous a miracle as was ever witnessed. "This, dear children," she writes, "will be no book of morals . . . we have our holy Torah. . . . The best thing for you, my children, is to serve God from your heart, without falsehood or sham, not giving out to people that you are one thing while, God forbid, in your heart you are another. Say your prayers with awe and devotion. . . . Moreover, put aside a fixed time for the study of the Torah . . ."[9]

Glückel's memoirs were discovered in 1896. They were translated from the original Yiddish text by "a member of the Glückel clan." She was the famous Bertha Pappenheim, Freud's "Anna O.," whose identity was inadvertently disclosed by Ernest Jones. Kobler has described Bertha Pappenheim as "one of the most amiable women

in modern Jewish history."[10] Certainly she does credit to
Glückel. Martin Buber called Bertha Pappenheim the
"White Flame" and she richly deserved the name. The
"white flame" was lit by Glückel many generations before.

Glückel's little notebooks throb with life. The life
drama portrayed by her is similar to the grim facts recorded in stone in Europe and in America. She was their
contemporary—and ours. What she discovered in herself
was echoed in the lives of many Jewish immigrant wom-
en in America.

Our emerging American feminine protagonists gradually shed their anonymity. They become vocal and eloquent as the decades and generations unroll. They are
personalities in their own right. They cry out to be remembered. Individual differences become startlingly
clear. It is fascinating to watch the transformation of
values, the emergence of new goals in the challenge of
pioneering in the New World. Adaptability has always
been necessary to survival. In one respect Jewish pioneers
in America were most fortunate. Christian pilgrims
brought Hebraism to America. They were astute enough
to recognize the Jews as the historic vehicle of that tradition which they revered and under which many of their
early compacts and agreements were consummated. "The
covenant of grace is the very same now that it was under
the Mosaical dispensation. . . ."[11]

The penetration of Hebraism in early America continues to overwhelm historians of both Jewish life in
America and of the life of the great community which
surrounded Jews.[12] In names of individuals and in names
of communities, in diaries and letters, in charters of self-
government, in sermons, the Old Testament was a significant source of influence. From seaboard settlements to

the hinterland one finds overwhelming evidence of the identification of pioneers with the ancient Biblical characters, with their prophetic vision and dream.

Often the aversion and suspicion and hostility which Jews had known in Europe gave way to blandishment and moral suasion in America. This was not only true in seaboard communities but may be traced westward. As our frontiers were pushed over mountain passes and arterial rivers, intrepid Jews along with their Christian neighbors pursued the course of inevitable expansion. When an ox train of eleven families reached Easton, Pennsylvania, Meyer and Rachel Hart were there. Joseph Simon was in Lancaster before the town was laid out. He was followed by a Dr. Isaac Cohen from Hamburg. A generation of native Jews was growing up in New York, Rhode Island, Georgia, Pennsylvania, and elsewhere. Immigrants from Europe were being drawn by the magnet of the New World. It was a time of hope, of opportunity, of dreams and their fulfillment.

It is not our purpose here to review the history of Jews in America, nor to encompass in detail the many activities of Jewish women from the earliest days to the present. What we are concerned with is to seek out and discover the contribution that Jewish women have made within the framework of Jewish life in America as Jews. We note briefly the careers of "the lost women" who through intermarriage and subsequent identification with the Christian community gave themselves and their descendants a new identity. Nor, as happened in later years, do we describe those women who through their talents and creative abilities gave of themselves in full measure to general causes and patriotic ideologies worthy as they may be. We seek to trace the continuity of Jewish faith and life as it was manifested by committed women aware of their ancient heritage to which they gave their undying allegiance.

"Most of the women," writes David de Sola Pool, "who lie at rest in this God's acre have as little 'biography' as a child for whom life has scarce begun. For what life, other than one of routine domestic propriety, did women lead in 1725, or even in 1825? No public office, no community service, no business distinction was theirs, and living traditions of the personalities of a century ago or two centuries ago are as rare as they are apt to be unreliable."[13] Yet even "routine domestic propriety" like "the stone which the builders rejected" became the cornerstone of the structure of Jewish life in America.

When Salo Baron speaks of "the intensity of Jewish family life, which made all parents strain their resources to the utmost to nurture their children to maturity . . .,"[14] he is attesting to the key role of women. Professor Baron stresses "the great measure of communal responsibility which included the care of the sick, orphaned, and aged." In those areas we know that women had an important and continuing role.

It is with such women that we are concerned. These the protagonists we "Recall to Life."

3

The erection of the first synagogue in New
York was news of magnitude. Women in the New York
Jewish community as well as women at a distance made
generous contributions. One woman donated ten pounds
to buy a Torah. Another, Mrs. Lunah Burgos of Barbados,
sent forty pounds to build a wall around the cemetery.
By 1730 when the Mill Street synagogue was dedicated,
its president was an Ashkenazi, Jacob Franks, who had
married an energetic and articulate woman, Bilhah Abigail Franks, daughter of Moses Levy. Jacob Rader Marcus
has made some of her letters available to us. They enlarge
her portrait, that of a woman whose enthusiasm for the
erection of the first sanctuary in North America is matched
only by her total absorption in her role as wife and
mother. The birth of their eldest, Naphtali—meaning hart
or stag—led Abigail to call him "Heartsey." In his teens
he sent to London to enlarge and expand his education under the tutelage of his father's brothers. In 1737
she wrote her son a long letter largely of condolence on

the death of his uncle. She wrote: "For my part when I
find a person has soe great a cause for griefe I can say
but little by way of releife, knowing nature has its call
upon these occasions and nothing but time and reasson
to aswage the dolor."

Her letter continues with various personal and household and domestic details. "Our little congregation affords
variety of news and tatle . . ." An apology for her spelling:
"You'll observe I sit down to write in a hurry by the
incorrectness of my letter, for I put things down just as
they occur to my memory."[1] She sent a gift of pickles to
her son. They were spoiled. "I can't tell what should be
the reason the pickoles should be spoilt, unless the vinegar
runs of . . ." She complained that her son does not write
enough. "I shall be very glad of some of y'r long epistles,
and allsoe that you would send us some little amusements
wich you have bin very remiss off late." She asks for books,
"allsoe 2 bottles of the best Scotch snuff for my own use,
and 2 pr. specticles of the very best . . ." On the whole a
most contemporary letter. "Her children were her life,"
writes Marcus. "Unflinchingly loyal to her faith . . ." he
goes on, "yet her closest friends were Christians and she
was a welcome guest in their homes. She wrote of herself
as a 'patriot'; this land was 'our country,' but she could
never reconcile herself to intermarriage . . ."

On the seventh of June, 1743, she writes to congratulate
"Dear Heartsey" in London on his marriage and to express her sense of "severe affliction" at the elopement of
his sister Phila. "Good God, wath a shock it was when
they acquainted me she had left the house and had bin
married six months . . . I had heard the report of her
goeing to be married to Oliver Delancey, but . . . I gave
noe heed to it . . . Oliver has sent many times to beg
leave to see me, but I never would . . . I dread seeing him
and how to avoid I know noe way, neither if he comes

can I use him rudly . . ."² Many a modern parent's
dilemma.

Bereavement, separation from children, love and marriage, devotion to faith and earnest desire for the continuity of one's people unassailed by intermarriage, inability to accept the hard reality of marriage out of the
faith—of such things was life made in the early days. "My
spirits was for some time soe depresst that it was a pain
for me to speak or see any one . . . but I shall never have
that serenity nor peace within . . ." What greater eloquence can summarize the depression which followed her
daughter's elopement?

Such letters are treasures in all their untarnished eloquence. They are invaluable because they are revealing,
erasing the barriers of time between ourselves and our
ancestors, exposing the unchanging human situation in
the midst of changing times. Mobility to which, perforce,
Jews were committed meant constant enforced moving
about the earth in search of sanctuary. In the midst of
change they sought continuity. We find people expressing
the eternal verities in immutable and familiar words. In
life and death, in separation and reunion, in affluence and
poverty, in licit and illicit romance, in depression and
exaltation, in envy and generosity, in moral grandeur and
moral depravity—the setting and costume may differ but
the capacity to feel and to react, to appeal and to reject,
to grant or to withhold favors—all of these remain unchanged.

Here is a father disposing of his property in 1763.
Judah Hays in his will states at the outset that he leaves
to his wife "absolutely all my plate and linnen and all
my household furniture." He disinherits his daughter
Rachel "to whom I give only five shillings, as she married
contrary to my will and disire." A similar situation is
reflected in the case of the daughters of Samuel Jacobs, a

Canadian merchant whose daughters were convent-edu-
cated and whose predilections for Christian friends led
to the inevitable, the desire to marry out of the faith.
In 1786, Jacob's daughter Polly writes from St. Dennis:
"Dearest Father: I am in such a situation that it would
be impossible for me to tell you what my heart subscribes.
Let me then, with candor and truth and the help of the
education you have given me, request of you the tenderness to look on your Polly as your child, to give your
blessing, not your curse. . . . It is true I have acted in
this affair very ill in not telling you my mind, but as I
suffer by your taking all away from me, don't make me
mesarable by rejecting me as not your child."³ These plots
are ever old, ever new.

Preparation for holidays and Holy Days were not to
be taken lightly. Thus letters from parents to their children are exchanged in which reminders are frequent of
the Hebrew calendar dates of upcoming holidays as well
as invitations to come home for the celebrations.

Aaron Hart writes to one of his sons in March, 1790:
"I see no way for you to keep *Pesah* at William Hanry
thear fore you had batter come over hear the Sunday before than you neat not due any thing to your house to git
the *hamez* our of your house . . ."⁴ Late eighteenth-century
Jewish life in Virginia is described in meaningful detail
by an astute and observant woman, Rebecca Alexander,
who married Hyman Samuel. She writes in Yiddish to
her "Dear and Worthy Parents" in Europe: ". . . We are
completely isolated here. We do not have any friends . . .
There is no cemetery in the whole of Virginia. In Richmond, which is twenty-two miles from here, there is a
Jewish community consisting of two quorums . . ." Rachel
continues: "One can make a good living here, and all
live at peace . . . There is no rabbi in all of America to
excommunicate anyone. This is a blessing here; Jew and

Gentile are as one. There is no *galut* here. In New York and Philadelphia there is more *galut*." So there were bright spots in lonely places.

After Passover Rachel and Hyman Samuel plan to move their family to Charleston, South Carolina. In a subsequent trans-Atlantic letter Rachel explains the planned move to her parents: ". . . I know quite well you will not want me to bring up my children like Gentiles. Here they cannot become anything else . . . [In Charleston] there is a blessed community of three hundred Jews. You can believe that I crave to see a synagogue to which I can go."

Like all mothers, Rachel is extremely proud of her children's accomplishments. "My children cannot learn anything here, nothing Jewish, nothing of general culture. My Schoene, God bless her, is already three years old. I think it is time that she should learn something, and she has a good head to learn. I have taught her the bedtime prayers and grace after meals in just two lessons. I believe that no one among the Jews here can do as well as she."

We see faith burgeoning. Family pride in evidence. Gradual contact and friendship and esteem with non-Jewish neighbors developing. Appreciation for the glorious advantages of freedom and self-expression in America emerging. Communal organizations being built. Travel and trade expanding. Yet ever and always the threads of kinship with relatives in Europe and the West Indies continuing to hold firm. The education of children is always paramount. Employment of teachers is a serious business with letters crossing and recrossing the Atlantic which discuss references, qualifications and teaching conditions. Changes are not infrequent and the administration of Hebrew schools invariably presents innumerable problems.

More and more we find in books, in letters, in diaries of Christians, evidence of interest in Jews and Judaism.

One such observer was Peter Kalm, who traveled in North America in 1748 and 1749. He writes on November 2, 1748:

> Besides the different sects of Christians, there are many Jews settled in New York, who possess great privileges. They have a synagogue and houses, and great country seats of their own property, and are allowed to keep shops in town. They have likewise several ships, which they freight, and send out with their own goods . . . I was frequently in company with Jews . . . I was in their synagogue last evening for the first time, and this day at noon I visited it again, and each time I was put in a particular seat, which was set apart for strangers or Christians. . . . Both men and women were dressed entirely in the *English* fashion; the former had all of them hats on . . . The galleries, I observed, were appropriated to the ladies, while the men sat below . . . The *Rabbi* stood in the middle of the synagogue, and read with his face turned towards the east; he spoke, however, so fast, as to make it almost impossible for anyone to understand what he said.

Interfaith friendships flourished in many places. Records of such contacts begin often with curiosity and end with an abiding and pervasive mutual esteem. Such a diarist was Ezra Stiles, graduate of Yale and later its president, who came to Newport in 1755, studied Hebrew and visited the synagogue on more than one occasion. In his diary he describes the first Bar Mitzvah he witnessed. He notes too the predisposition of "a young Jewess in Town, born here, one Miss Polack," who was deeply impressed by Christian exhortations at school. "This at length alarmed her Friends & they kept her at home." The Jewish custom of blessing children was noted in the Stiles diary: "It is customary with the Jews for Parents to lay their hands on the Heads of their Children and give them their Blessing . . . This is frequently done at Meals and Friday Evening after Supper . . ." This love and tender yearning over children is described again and again. Concern for little children is shown in the many and detailed provisions drawn up for the administration of synagogue schools, for the qualifications and salary of the schoolmaster, for the stipulation in detail of his duties. On the last day of Passover in 1731 a parochial school was dedicated to the children of the congregation Shearith Israel. Five years later the reader of the congregation, David M. Machado undertook "to keep a publick School in due form for teaching the *hebrew Language,* either the whole morning or afternoon as he shall think most proper, and any poor that shall be thought unable to pay for their children's learning they shall be taught gratis."[5]

Bits and pieces of information attest to the priority given to the education of young children, to their behavior in synagogue and parochial school, to their general demeanor. It also carried over into generous support of public schools. Several years after Meyer Hart reached Easton, Pennsylvania, his county tax was larger than any other taxpayer's. Five years after he had made the covered wagon journey his name led the list of contributors to the public school building fund. His son Michael, who because of a speech defect was called "the stuttering Jew," enlisted in the army in August of 1776 and was made a corporal. In Lancaster, Pennsylvania, Joseph Simon's home was used as a place where Jews met for worship and study, a kind of private synagogue being maintained there. It was in that home that Michael Gratz, indefatigable entrepreneur, merchant and land speculator, met and married Miriam Simon, daughter of Joseph, and a firm bond between the Gratz family and the Simons was forged. It was with Miriam Simon Gratz that Barnard Gratz left his "dear little Rachel" after the death of her mother. In Miriam's letter to her brother-in-law there is a warmth of feeling which must have endeared her to all who knew her then as it does us today. "I believe I have lugged all the children in," writes Miriam to her brother-in-law, Barnard Gratz. ". . . Don't, my good Brother, condemn me for thinking highly of my blessed children . . ." This from the mother of Rebecca Gratz.[6]

Jacob Mordecai, native-born son of a German-Jewish immigrant, who eventually settled in Warrenton, North Carolina, father of three little orphaned girls, sent them to relatives in Richmond after their mother's death. He maintained a stilted and correct correspondence with his children and expressed his pleasure at their diligence, "perseverance and attention" in their studies. He assures the little girls that "your pleasures will increase with your knouledge of things" "Be good girls, mind your reading and writing, that you may be able to send me letters often . . ." And again "I please myself with the progress you make in your studies, the attention you pay to cleanliness, and a neat disposition in your dress . . ."[7]

Little Rachel Gratz writing to her father, Barnard, during the Revolutionary War acknowledges his instructions "about minding my schooling." She continues: "I have just begun to cipher and I am very much delighted at it. I am in Averdepois weight and can cast up anything."

Hebrew and Hebraism were part of early school curricula in non-Jewish schools. A book published in Philadelphia in 1726 contained the Hebrew alphabet. Earlier (in 1693) William Bradford had used Hebrew words in a book he had printed. In 1720 Judah Monis received the degree of Master of Arts at Harvard. Two years later, having become a convert to Christianity, he was appointed a Hebrew teacher at Harvard. Christian clergymen and some laymen studied Hebrew. Jewish boys whose parents

were attached to synagogues were early enrolled in Hebrew school with competent or incompetent teachers—
depending on luck or chance as to who was available
either at home or imported from abroad. But so far early
American Jewish history has not produced the name of
a biography of a *matmida* (a female Jewish scholar).
Women picked up many customs, rites, and household
procedures governing *kashruth* and home observances by
a process of osmosis from their mothers and grandmothers.
Prayers were memorized by women or read aloud in the
home and in the synagogue. Women were custodians of
a religious way of life, of a tradition. Preparation for the
Sabbath, for Holy Days and holidays was in their hands—
subject to stern and unyielding demands, rules and regulations decreed by synagogue trustees. Inspection of kitch-
ens and utensils and food was at times carried out by these
officials when laxity or gossip made some household or
housekeeper suspect. Obedience to the law was inbred.
Proximity to observant neighbors and social pressure exercised additional controls. Life was regulated by the religious calendar. It centered around the rites of passage
that were familiar and cherished. Social ostracism, synagogue fines, public and private condemnation were the
lot of the deviant. Compromise there may have been in
isolated homesteads, or along the trails and roads of the
"hawkers and walkers." But by and large the circumference of a synagogue surrounded like-minded people
practicing ancient folkways with dedication and consecration and decorum. It was an umbrella under which all
Jews took shelter.

Women owned their own Bibles and prayerbooks, often
cherished family treasures containing genealogical data.
Thus Leah, daughter of Jacob de Olivera, one of the
original settlers of Georgia in the year 1733, had when
she married Joseph Tobias later of Charles Towne, South

Carolina, a large leatherbound Bible. The death of her
husband was the first entry in that book.[8] That they in-
structed their little children from whatever available
sources they had may be noted. This was the traditional
role of the mother. It is best expressed in a tender poem,
a fragment from the Cairo Genizah, from a manuscript
discovered by Elkan N. Adler and exquisitely translated
by Nina Davis. Called "The Ages of Man," it shows woman's role in the education of her son:

> "Arise and prosper," say ye unto him
> Of five years, whose desires rise apace
> Like the awakening sun on regions dim
> He hath his mother's breast for resting place . . .
>
> How urge ye him of ten years with intent
> Toward instruction? Yet a little space,
> And he will grow and find his chastisement.
> Speak unto him with tender tone of grace:
> Joy shall he rouse,
> For them that bare him, for his father's house . . .
>
> At thirty years into a woman's hands
> He falleth; rise and look on him and see . . .
> . . . .the want shall be
> Now of his life
> Only the wants of children and of wife.[9]

This preoccupation with children, with their future,
their education, pervades many documents and letters
of the early period of American Jewish history. Childless
couples lavished their love on adopted children and on
the children of their neighbors. So we read: "Having no
children of their own, Aaron and Rachel Levy found
happiness in bestowing their affection upon the ten children of Michael and Miriam Gratz . . . The oldest of

these children, Simon, was adopted by Aaron Levy as his son."[10] Having provided for his wife, Rachel, during her lifetime, Aaron Levy made numerous specific bequests. Among them he left to Rebecca Gratz "My gilt Silver Oval Sugar Bowl with lid and Silver Bowl without lid . . ." To Jacob Gratz he left "all my English Books Except the Prayer Books." To Benjamin Gratz "all my Hebrew Books & English Prayer Books." We may assume that Rachel Levy was apprised of these bequests and approval of them. The will was drawn in June of 1802. But we are totally unaware of the extent of Rachel's uses of the books in Hebrew and English which went to the grandchildren of Joseph Simon.

Women were preoccupied with their husbands as well as with their children. In 1796 we find a poignant letter addressed by a woman to the trustees of Shearith Israel, pleading for the release of her husband who had apparently been jailed on the complaint of the congregation. "I beg you will take into Consideration my present Situation & Distress I am in at this present time from the Behaviour of my husband," writes Mrs. G. Philips in 1796. "I acknoledge he deserved Some punishment, but as you have punished him with Confinement I hope it will bee the Means of his Better Conduct in future . . ." This being "his first offense," she goes on, "I do promise in future to keep him from going to Synagoge any more . . .[11] We do not know the measure of her husband's transgression but we sympathize with his wife's abject concern.

The mosaic is pieced. From the Sheftall Diaries, 1733-1808, we get further glimpses of early Jewish history, seeking out for special attention the little notices that involve women. The founder of the family, Benjamin Sheftall, was an Ashkenazi who was "a moving force in the creation of an organized Jewish community in Savannah."[12] The record begins simply: "The Names of the Jews that arrived in Savannah in Georgia on the eleventh day of July 1733." The name of Dr. Nunes led the list. It was followed by that of his mother. There were forty-two settlers named on the original list. "These persons were the first of our nation that came to this country [Georgia]—At the same time they brought with them a Safertora . . ." Thirteen women's names are on that first list. Later another group joined these pioneers. The first vital statistic reads: "1733 July 25th—Mrs. Ledismo was brought to bed with a son named Ralph." Similar accouchement notices follow at regular intervals. Women died in childbirth and babies succumbed to fatal illnesses. One baby boy "died very young ocationed by his nurse givin him acrons to eate, through her ignorance." The little boy was named Sheftall Sheftall, a name to recur in later history. Heartbreak followed on heartbreak as death struck mothers and infants. But grief could not be long indulged in pioneer settlements. So notices of second marriages succeeded obituaries: "1738 November the 20th—Benjamin Sheftall was maryed to Hannah Solomons his 2 wife." Laconic entries conveyed elaborate plots: "1786 October the 4th—Miss Rachel Jacobs was maryed to Cushman Polock. This lady arrived from Philadelphia some short time before for the purpose." There were divorces as well. The following terse notice has a modern ring: "On Thursday the 22nd day of August 1799, David Leion and his wife Hannah—late Hannah Minis, parted as man and wife never to live together again, they disagreeing for a length of time before they parted."[13]

Finally we close with an obituary written by a son of his mother. "On Saturday, the 14th day of November in the year 1811 at 8 o clock in the evening, death closed the life of our Mother in the 57 year and 11 months of her age . . . Few Females who have appeared on the Stage of action ever surpassed, if equaled our Mother in urbanity and uniform deportment of manners, to strong and intuitive perception. She united an accurate judgement alive to every sensibility for her species, she possessed that great benevolence of character that ever exerts itself for the alleviation of distress. Nothing was more consolatory to her than to wipe the tear from the cheek of affliction, nothing more calculated to tranquilise her mind than a conviction of having performed some charitable deed by which misfortune was stripped of its acrimony. Intercourse & observation peculiarly fitted her for the civilized and enlightened circles. She eminently possessed every qualification that adorns the Female character. In the domestic sphere her conduct was characterized by kindness, virtue and affection, every thought of her heart was for her children, their sufferings were hers. Our Mother survived our Father 2 short years. They lived together in the full enjoyment of harmony. She sank under the calamity of his loss. 10 affectionate children lament the loss of this most endeared, affectionate parent."

One could go on spinning tales, unfolding biographical dramas, depicting the little and big crises of vanished lives. Old papers, crumbling notebooks, faded documents, rodent-bitten family papers all clamor to be used. Time is a vast eraser rubbing out sharp outlines and leaving faint traces of character and personality. Anonymity is a thick fog into which one generation after another passes. To penetrate that fog, to recall to life, to re-create ghostly figures and endow them again with the breath of life— that is an unattainable goal. Yet there are moments when the miracle takes place and ancient woes become present sorrows and old joys gladden the living heart and one's long-departed sisters throng our rooms. Their voices long

stilled tell us: "This is how it was then. So we lived and
so we died. And that was the sum of our earthly experience."

And we who share the same human situation today are
quick to reach out a sisterly hand and answer: "So it is
with us also."

4

Is there a thing of which it is said,
   "See, this is new?"
It has been already in the ages before us.
There is no remembrance of former things,
Nor will there be any remembrance of later things yet to
   happen
Among those who come after.

—Koheleth

Briefly, all too briefly, we have recalled former times.
Reverently we have traced the epitaphs on crumbling
tombstones. Impressed by one inescapable fact that there
is a door marked Exit for every living soul and that the
chronicler stands at the threshhold evoking the past,
describing the present, peering with myopic eyes into the
future. He is aware that there is verily nothing new under
the sun, that anonymity and fame are but reverse sides
of the same coin. The rhythm and pattern of life is unchanging. The light that our progenitors shed illumines

our days also. We—as did they—set our goals high. We stumble and fall and shake the dust from our garments and go on again. And we recall our predecessors, strengthened in the knowledge that as they survived wars and extermination and pogroms and degradations and personal bereavement and sorrow and ill health and blindness and acute physical agony, so will we be given strength to endure—until the ultimate deliverance—"the fullness of joy."

It was the men who delivered the sermons, exhorted the multitudes, evolved the law and its interpretation, decreed the folkways and mores to implement daily life. They wrote the books, studied the stars, made the maps and the instruments for navigation, led the pilgrimages of escape. They wrote most of the letters, kept the chronicles, inventoried possessions, made the wills, listed business assets and losses. They governed and administered synagogues. They made long business journeys and petitioned governments and advanced moneys for exploration and sought lands of refuge and led many an exodus in search of sanctuary.

What of the women? The Jewish woman accepted the masculine decrees which governed her lot with an inner grace which betokened an inner strength. She adapted herself to the lesser role, the silent role in communal affairs, the accepting role in religious doctrine, the illiterate role in a world and a way of life in which literacy was the highest good. She toiled endlessly in market place and home to liberate her husband and her sons for a life of scholarship. Her place in the synagogue was symbolic. She sat in balconies behind lattice-worked grilles or curtained-off spaces, invisible, often unable to read a line in her prayerbook, depending on some woman reader who could both follow and translate the words on the holy page. Or if "educated," she could read a truncated version of the prayers especially prepared for her "small" mind, the "teitch-humesh" designed for her.

These geographically separated Orthodox prayer sections for women are still in use in synagogues in our land and in many parts of the world—in Amsterdam and London and Jerusalem and New York and Chicago. Sitting there, one feels surrounded by those early worshippers, sharing in their rejection and their isolation, recalling that the silent role is often the heroic one. Whence came their strength and their moral grandeur? How did they manage to extract from their hearts those eloquent prayers and petitions which upheld them from Sabbath to Sabbath? From poverty and insecurity and physical danger and mental assault? Perhaps theirs was the religion which found solace in doing and being and implementing and inspiring and transforming their homes into islands of holiness and serenity. Was this not their great oblation?

Slow was the ascent from anonymity to the wearing of a name. As the centuries rotated—impeded by religion and custom and man-made laws—women forsook their cocoons and emerged as creatures who made their own flight, butterflies with untried wings!

Each woman's activities may be described by a series of concentric circles. From earliest times her major labors were home-centered. Next she was drawn to the synagogue where she could feel and express her inner yearning for closeness to God, for understanding of self and family. For some women the "great society," the host culture beckoned like a flame. They were attracted to that flame like ephemerida to a candle glow. Among them were the "lost girls" who could not resist missionary blandishments. There were the insecure souls who seemed to feel that in those glittering circles beyond home and synagogue there was the magic of acceptance and the resolution of old slights and rejections.

There were the incurable romantics who rebelled against entering into involuntary marriage with cousin or imported groom. There were the isolated maidens far from other Jews and synagogues who met and mated with the sons of their Christian neighbors. Finally, there were the spinsters—Jewish women who were wooed but declined offers of marriage for the sake of the preservation of their inner integrity and their avowed commitment to their ancient faith. Examples abound. Strange and fascinating plots are discovered. Heroines emerge. Women whose will and personality, whose talent or genius expressed itself in writing, on the stage, in the arts, in social service, forged a place for themselves. As pilgrim's wife, as matriarch or wage earner, as spur to husband and children, as a dedicated votary to causes for amelioration of the underprivileged and deprived, as anonymous member of the chorus or the spotlighted headliner—in all of these roles we find the Jewish women.

New World synagogues were the dispensers of charity to indigent neighbor and stranded traveler. In all of these activities women were involved. Providing food and shelter, sewing for widows and orphans, sitting up with the sick, preparing the bodies of the deceased for burial, collecting dowries and planning weddings for brides without family or kin, taking in the aged and the sick into their homes, performing the midwife's role and caring for mother and infant, adding orphans to the family circle, both relatives and strangers—these were but a few of the philanthropic and charitable enterprizes that fell to the women of the congregation. The home and the synagogue flowed into each other. For at first worship was conducted in private homes, in simple log cabins, in lonely outposts where a *minyan* (a quorum of ten men) was seldom encountered. The consecration of a house of worship was a dedicated undertaking. Distant congregations shared in the privilege of contributing to building funds. When the Jews of Newport appealed to their fellow Jews in New York, the following response was made:

"Conformable to your desire a *Nedaba* was made in our synagogue the Seventh day of *Pesach* . . ." The Jews of Newport acknowledged the gift of £149 6ᵈ and wrote to the donors:

"We Devoutly join with you in Prayer 'That our God may Graciously enable his people to do *Mitzvoth*'" (good deeds).

Women made gifts to synagogues as well as men. Women also appear on the synagogue rolls as recipients of charity. One widow was voted "Six Shillings pr. week in case there is any surplus after the officers are paid." This generous offer was refused after a short time and the recipient "declined taking her allowance from the *Tzedakah* for the future, with thanks for what already received." Rachel Campenel, widow of Asher, the sexton, was voted a pension of twenty pounds per annum "in consideration of her age & infermities . . ." Another widow was allowed a subsidy for four weeks only. At one meeting it was "Resolved that Mrs. Hannah Louzada should be dispatched to Lancaster & that her son Benja. should be maintained here by the congregation . . ."

Poor people were often boarded out and the congregation paid their board bills. Women were busy as seamstresses. We read in the synagogue minutes: "That three Corse Shirts be made & sent to Aaron Pinto as he is almost naked . . ." Sheets were provided for the sick. Itinerants were temporarily sheltered, fed, provided with clothing where needed and an occasional stipend from the Sedaka fund. But the main tool of philanthropic administration was the dispatching of widows or orphans or stranded travelers or mendicants to other communities. This technique of "ticket to elsewhere" crops up again and again.

In fairness we might add that the demands upon community, congregation and individual homes were so pressing, the family crises so recurrent, the need to shelter one's kith and kin because of the frequent tragedies that befell, so demanding that problems presented by strangers had to be met by sending applicants to other congregations.

Life under pioneering conditions was rugged. It took courage and endless ingenuity to solve one's daily problems. It took heroic measures to keep their ranks from dwindling. Cherished children brought up within the orbit of synagogue and religious home slipped away from the fold through intermarriage. It was only rarely that the process was reversed. Here is one example: On November 13, 1749, Anna Barnett wrote to the Adjunta of Mikveh Israel in Philadelphia:

Gentlemen

Permit one who has not the Happiness to be Born a Jewess & Favoured Imediatly from the God of Israll as you are to Request your Attention to my Particular Case & trust that Nothing has been or Shall be Wanting on my part to Render me Worthy of being Admitted . . . to become a Jewiss [sic] this I ask not as a Favour, but as a Right feeling as I do . . . I am Ready & willing to Submit to Such Ceremonies as are Necessary to Optain this my demand the Greatest of all my Wordly wishes & may the God of Abraham Isaac & Jacob take you under his Holy Protection. . . .

It is not known exactly who Anna Barnett was, although it is theorized that she may have been the wife of Nathan Barnett who died in 1797. Blau and Baron point out that often pleas for conversion were based on expediency, a civil marriage having preceded the plea.[1] Such requests were reluctantly granted at some times, refused at other times.[2] It should also be noted that the prevailing point of view of Christians toward the Jews in their midst was one of desire to persuade them to Christianity. An example is a poem by an anonymous author which appeared in the *Christian Spectator* in February of 1823, titled "On the Depressed State of Jewish Females." It begins:

> Daughters of Zion! from whose humbled brow
> The glory hath departed . . .

Another poem by a Mrs. Crawford begins with this plea:

> Hebrew maiden, veil thy beauty,
> Lest my heart a rebel prove,
> Breaking bands of holy duty,
> For the silken chains of love.[3]

Massachusetts-born Hannah Adams, cousin of the two Adams Presidents and the first American woman to make a profession of writing and of history united within her person that ambivalence which combines rejection of Judaism with love of those who professed it. She was born in Medfield in 1755. By the time she died in 1831, she left a number of books dealing with religion, New England and the Jews. Her two-volume *History of the Jews* appeared in 1812. Possibly because her own life was marred by misfortune, ill health, grinding poverty, monotony, anxiety, insecurity, she was drawn to a people whose catastrophic battle for survival is one of the grimmest and most miraculous chapters in human history. In Jewish history she found "a dreary wilderness, unenlivened by one spot of verdure."[4] In contemplating the drama of Jewish survival she was aware of the many transgressions of "the Christian world enveloped in darkness and ignorance; and the professed disciples of the benevolent Redeemer violating the fundamental precepts of the gospel . . ." In Jewish history "a wonderful object arrests our attention, and the feelings of indignation and compassion are suspended by astonishment while we contemplate . . . a helpless race of men, whom all nations have endeavored to exterminate, subsisting during ages of relentless persecution . . ." She became thoroughly fascinated by the history of the Jews and by their heroism. It was said of her: "if you want to know Miss Adams, you must talk to her about the Jews." For "she venerated the antiquity of their origin . . . She felt for them as a suffering and persecuted people . . . she considered them as a standing monument of that religion, which she regarded as the *first and best of God's gift to men."*

It is interesting to note that just as Hannah Adams was the first woman in America to be a professional writer and historian, she also has the distinction of being its first Zionist. For she entertained no doubt of the return of the people to Israel, to its ancient homeland. She corresponded with Rabbi Gershom M. Seixas of Shearith Israel about Jewish beginnings in America and noted with satisfaction that "the United States is, perhaps, the only place where the Jews have not suffered persecution . . ."[5] Hannah Adams was touched with the greatness that is America. She was the forerunner of other Christian women whose broad sympathy, understanding and insight impelled them to approach the Jews in their community holding out the hand of friendship and fellowship.

5

Along the seaboard in South and North America, from the beginning of the sixteenth century, individual Jews were found. Gradually, as families made the momentous westward crossing, provisions were made for group religious life. By 1776 there were organized Jewish communities in New York and in Rhode Island, in Pennsylvania and South Carolina. The names these congregations bore were symbolic and meaningful:

Shearith Israel—The Remnant of Israel. (New York and Montreal)

Jeshuat Israel—Salvation of Israel (Newport, R.I.)

Mikveh Israel—Hope of Israel (Philadelphia and Savannah, Ga.)

Beth Elohim—House of God (Charleston, South Carolina)

They came from many lands, these early founders. They spoke many languages. They practiced and cherished the *Minhag* (custom) which they had known in Europe—Sephardi, Ashkenazi. Spanish, Portuguese, Dutch, English,

German, Yiddish were the languages that could be heard
in their homes. In the synagogue, Hebrew was the sacred
universal tongue and the Sephardic ritual largely prevailed. From the very first, Ashkenazim made their presence felt in congregational life. Jews were united in an
awareness of their responsibilities. The needy and destitute, the aged and the poor were a communal obligation.
That women shared in carrying out of these charitable
and communal enterprises was obvious.

Sometimes a poignant letter describes timeless anguish.
In the year 1796, a bereaved husband, Jacob Mordecai,
wrote of his loss: "While I deplore the stroke that has
bereft me of life's greatest comfort, and know death to be
the irrevocable law of our nature, and that man . . . must
submit to part with the life that was given him . . . I find
there is no reasoning down our feelings when the heart
is corroded by affliction."[6] Bereavement speaks a universal
language.

The roles that women filled, their essential importance
in the economy of pioneering life, their acceptance of the
many burdens which the vicissitudes of life required of
them, the stretching of homes to include the traveler and
the orphan, the meeting of the countless demands which
membership in an organized community exacted from
them—far surpassed what is required of women today.
Then the place of the American Jewess was determined
and bounded by the life that her father, husband, brother
carved out for his family. Its affluence or privation, its
fortune or misfortune, in private life, in public affairs,
was determined by the skill and genius of the men in
her life. Hers was the reflected light. Such recognition as
was granted Jews in American life, making their position
here by far more favorable than they had hitherto known
in Europe, was due in part to the vision and philosophy
of the Founding Fathers of this country. In part also to

the persistent and never-ending pressures which individuals and groups exerted. "Here, the Jew was not in an alien world, a world he never made and was only with reluctance allowed to live in; he was in a land of which he was one of the builders, and he took pride in what he had helped to build."[7]

Many are the official documents which attest to the favorable moral climate in the United States. George Washington in language both sincere and graceful acknowledged the congratulatory "Addresses" of the Congregations of Newport, Philadelphia, New York, Charleston, Richmond, and Savannah. "The citizens of the United States of America," wrote its first President, "have a right to applaud themselves for having given to mankind examples of an enlarged and liberal policy—a policy worthy of imitation. All possess alike liberty of conscience and immunities of citizenship." President Jefferson wrote that "I shall see with sincere satisfaction the progress of those sentiments which tend to restore to man all his natural rights . . ."[8] Such sentiments were reaffirmed by President John Adams, Madison, and others.

Much may be written about those early days of acculturation, of establishing of old folk ways and mores in a new setting, of creative adaptation of Judaism to the free and expanding moral climate of America. One might dwell at great length on the confrontation of Sephardic customs with those of the Ashkenazim. One may draw generalizations about the class distinctions between the practitioners of Minhag Sephardi and Minhag Ashkenazi —only to have them immediately demolished by facts patiently researched by many a dedicated scholar. Distinctions there were, but they were not as marked in practice as had once been assumed. The growing literature on the early history of Jews in America is full of new insights and new data. More and more we find that

Jewish history in America can be understood only against the larger frame of reference of all of American history, of its inexorable march from frontier to frontier, of its dramatic encounter with the vast and bountiful land, of its ever-continuing lure of new and expanding horizons, of the gradual evolution of a native philosophy in which Christian and Jew shared. The age of discovery, of exploration, of new settlement was a dynamic time, a time of change and of stretching of physical and mental boundaries. Jews, like others, changed with the times. From New York to New Biloxi we find them—solitary sojourners, footweary hawkers, proud vintners, busy merchants and land speculators, teachers and doctors, craftsmen and entrepeneurs and scholars—the apt and the inept, each after his own fashion.

The earliest years were years of enormous accomplishment by isolated individuals and their anonymous consorts. They were years of adjusting to the host culture and of seeking out one's co-religionists to share in the observance of the faith they cherished through the long centuries—cherished in the open places and in hidden crypts. They were years of re-creating of synagogue worship and synagogue association; years of self-discovery, of God-seeking; years of affirmation after the drought of total rejection, which had been forced upon them by the Holy Office and the Inquisition. Above all, Jews were now embarked on a period of acknowledged kinship with other communities which they or their ancestors had known. We note that the London Sephardi community was a child of the Amsterdam community, and the Bevis Marks community of London claimed Shearith Israel of New York as "to some extent a foster-child."[9] We further note: "The Sephardi Community of Newport . . . was founded in 1658, and in 1763 it constructed the present synagogue building . . . and . . . Bevis Marks was one of those that responded."[10] Similarly Bevis Marks congregation in London helped the Jews of Charles Town (later Charleston) as well as the Jews of Savannah in the acquisition of a cemetery "and it may properly be considered an offshoot of Bevis Marks."[11]

The historian of Bevis Marks congregation believes that the London congregation was to the newly created synagogues in the colonies "when not that of father and son, one of father and adopted son . . ." Whatever the relationship, warm contact was maintained. Aaron Lopez of Newport had a correspondent in Poland. Haym Salomon, a native of Lissa, Poland, received and wrote letters to many Jews in many lands. And the first articulate woman in America, a resident of Charleston, was celebrated on both sides of the Atlantic. So we come to Penina Moïse.

Charleston is like a green thumb thrust into the Atlantic Ocean, with the Ashley River on one side and the Cooper on the other flowing sluggishly on to the inevitable sea. Its natural harbor is one of the finest in the land. Moss-hung trees spread their ancient branches. There is a stillness hovering over the city, an historic mood recalling to the visitor today all the ancient glories and the eloquent voices and the soft moonlit nights and the social graces and amenities of a long-vanished age. The spell that is compounded of old memories and old and long-silenced inhabitants has never quite left.

"The history of the Jews of Charleston is a long and honorable one," writes Thomas J. Tobias, a descendant of one of the first Jewish families to settle there. ". . . These pioneer Jews worshipped at first in each others' homes until they were sufficiently numerous to organize a congregation. In 1749, *Kahal Kadosh Beth Elohim* (Holy Congregation House of God) was founded . . ."[12] John

Locke had written in 1699, in his *Fundamental Constitutions,* "If we allow the Jews to have private houses and dwellings amongst us, why should we not allow them to have synagogues?" From the first the synagogue of Charleston loomed large in the lives of its Jews. No other person gave voice to the honor of belonging to Beth Elohim nor sang the privilege of being a member of the congregation in Charleston and of the "Great Congregation" of Jews everywhere, with the fervor and the passion of Penina Moïse.

Penina Moïse was born in Charleston in 1797, on April 23. Her father, Abraham, was an Alsatian Jew who had fled from Santo Domingo to Charleston. Her father died when Penina was barely twelve, and with his death her formal schooling ended.[13] From then on she was self-taught. She had a hunger for books, a passion for reading, an inexhaustible memory.

Blow after blow struck at Penina. Grinding poverty and cruel afflictions befell her dear ones, making them her responsibility. Her mother became paralyzed. Her brother Isaac was an invalid. The last twenty-five years of her life Penina was totally blind. Yet her spirit was indomitable. Her personality was magnetic. Her interests were wide. She memorized some of the works of English classical writers and was also familiar with the writings of Charlotte Brontë and George Eliot. A Christian friend who knew her well and admired her, Charlotte Adams, wrote in *The Critic:*

> There died in Charleston in 1881, at the age of eighty-three, a Jewish poetess . . . Penina Moïse, who for many years was the literary pivot of Hebrew Charleston, and whose influence extended far beyond the circle of her coreligionists. Blind, poor, getting her living in her old age by keeping a little school, she yet created a literary salon, to which the best minds of

Charleston flocked . . . The melodious Hebrew name born by this remarkable woman seemed to define her position in the Hebrew colony of Charleston. Was not the Peninah of Scripture the sister of pious Hannah and the aunt of the prophet Samuel? And was it not fit that her namesake should be regarded as a "Mother in Israel"? Living her chastened life apart from the gay world, in a rarified, impersonal atmosphere, Penina was, in the finest sense, the mother of her people. To her the girl babies were brought before their names were called aloud in the synagogue . . . her advice was asked upon all important occasions.[14]

Her influence radiated beyond the Jewish circles of her city and her state. Her poems and prose were found in the Charleston *Courier,* Boston *Daily Times, Godey's Lady's Book,* the *Charleston Book,* and the *Occident.* Some of her hymns were known and published in England. But it was to her own congregation that she brought her gifts most freely. The hymnal she wrote for Beth Elohim went through four editions and was widely used— usually without credits—by many other synagogues. She succeeded the founder of the congregation's Sunday school as its superintendent. Sally Lopez had established and headed the school from 1838. There was then only one religious school which had preceded it, the one founded by Rebecca Gratz in Philadelphia.

She was remembered by her pupils long after her death. In 1911 the Charleston Council of Jewish Women published a volume of her poems. The Preface read: "This little volume is compiled by the undersigned members of the Charleston Section of the Council of Jewish Women, who were personally acquainted with the beloved and revered authoress, either as relatives, pupils, or children of dear friends. It has been a work of love . . ." Among the six who signed the preface was Eleanor L. Halsey.[15]

When in 1833, the Charleston Synagogue was burned in
a fire which swept that part of the city it was a cruel loss
to the congregation. Later the beautiful synagogue on
Hassell Street was erected. The new building had an
organ and a choir and Penina Moïse provided the hymns
of dedication.

In 1854 yellow fever mowed down many Charlestonians.
Penina, wrote those who knew her, was "like a second
Florence Nightingale" nursing its victims "without regard to sect or station." She was a lover of nature, had a
"feeling of nearness to God," yet was endowed with a keen
sense of humor which made her popular because of her
"social banter, pun and brilliant epigram which made
her presence a light wherever she was . . ."

During the Civil War, Penina with her widowed sister
Rachel and her niece Jacqueline moved to Sumter, South
Carolina. Penina was then totally blind. There "The
Trio," as they called themselves, opened a little school
in the two bedrooms they rented. Their supplies con-
sisted of "an old wardrobe and a piece of chalk." Returning to Charleston after the war, The Trio opened a girl's
school in a little whitewashed house on Coming Street.
Penina, wearing dark glasses, sat in a high-backed rocking
chair, plucking at a piece of black cloth and unraveling
its strands. (Was this symbolic of a life of mourning?) [16]
Sometimes she played the piano "sweetly and correctly."
She had a whole group of volunteer readers, friends who
came in and took turns reading aloud from the authors
she loved. On High Holy Days a regular schedule was
worked out and volunteers would leave the synagogue at
five minutes before the hour to read the prayers to her
until the next reader came. Because this blind woman,
sensitive and responsive to the beauty and the pervasive
strength of her religion expressed what her contemporaries
felt and could not put into words and because her life

was synagogue-oriented, we examine some of her poems in which she speaks not only for herself but for her co-religionists and for her contemporaries for nearly a century.

Her poetical subjects ranged far and wide. In a note to the editor of the Charleston *Courier* she wrote: "It is my peculiar felicity to be gifted with a sixth sense, that not only concentrates the powers of the other five, but expands its perceptions to sights and sound invisible and inaudible to common organs." This perceptive quality enabled her to write "Reflections on the Death of an Infant"—"It is a fearful thing to love what Death may touch." In "A Thought" this aphorism: "One cannot think of one's own existence, without thinking of the author of it." Of the end of life and its brevity there are many poems. She seemed poised always on the threshhold of eternity, as in

> Pilgrim! Thy house in order set!
> Thy soul for sudden change prepare,
> Ere thou, to cancel nature's debt,
> Art forced into an unknown sphere.

That note of the nearness of death appears again and again.

> The fugitive will strike his wings,
> Impatient as a bird may be
> Of splendor in captivity;
> Yet ever to mankind repeating,
> "On to Eternity ye're fleeting!"

When the Jews of Damascus were persecuted and assaulted her thoughts turned to Palestine and to ancient valor:

Why slumbers now, on Palestine, the spirit of the past?
When thy holy hills re-echoed to the silver clarion blast,
That summoned to the battlefield the tribes of the elect

Whose tents like snowy pyramids, thy sacred borders
   specked.

In a poem titled "The Rejection of the Jew Bill by
the House of Lords," Penina wrote:

> Truth flashes warning of that nation's fall,
> Which in the revel of prosperity
> Profanes the cup—nor heeds the captives cry.
> It cannot be—Britannia must explode
> The dark deformity from Freedom's code.
>
> It shall not be! With prescient exultation,
> My joyous harp rings out Emancipation!

One wonders whether in Israel today the "prescient
harp" of the blind singer of Charleston is recalled.

In the *Southern Patriot* of February 23, 1820, when
Penina was just twenty-three years old, her sense of "pre-
science" inspired her to write lines which are reminiscent
of a poem of Emma Lazarus a generation later:

To Persecuted Foreigners

> Fly from the soil whose desolating creed,
> Outraging faith, makes human victims bleed,
> Welcome! Where every Muse has reared a shrine,
> The respect of wild Freedom to define.
>
> If thou art one of that oppressed race,
> Whose name's a proverb, and whose lot's disgrace,
> Brave the Atlantic—Hope's broad anchor weigh,
> A Western Sun will guild your future day.

To synagogue-oriented women who find solace in prayer,
in contemplation of God, in meditation and dedication to
mitzvoth (good deeds) Penina speaks with a relevancy of
spirit which deserves to be known and cherished and re-

called. Here is a gentle evocation of the Sabbath mood:

> Source of mercy, truth and grace!
>   Humbly we this Sabbath-day,
> In Thy holy dwelling-place,
>   Grateful adoration pay.

In another hymn she celebrates the feeling of Sabbath repose known to countless generations of Jews:

> In harmony with Heaven's peace,
>   Sabbath's deep repose descends,
> From toil the weary to release,
>   The sordid draw from worldly ends.
> Lord! let devotion fill our hearts,
> Ere time's serenest day departs.

She sees the role of women as an active one, in which they are enlisted in a moral crusade of self-fulfillment. Again and again she invokes the "daughters of Israel to keep the faith."

Here was the articulate voice of a Jewish woman voicing sentiments which bring her close to Jewish women everywhere, expressing an inner longing for closeness to God, for self-perfection, for preservation of an ancient way of life, an attitude which her ancestors had known and reverenced and which she acknowledged and practiced with humility and grace.

We need not review the romantic legends which clustered about her both during her lifetime and posthumously. Her life was lived with dignity in the midst of constant trials, of blindness accepted with grace, of pain and severe illness borne without complaint, of total submission to "the author of her being," of a firm conviction that in the presence of God "there is fullness of joy" and that immortality awaited one at journey's end.

In her last poem, having nothing to leave but love and

gratitude to those who had upheld her, she sums up both
life's anguish and life's ultimate promise. "Old, blind and
poor, Penina Moïse, in her 83rd year, addressed her last
poem to all her 'dear relatives and friends in acknowledg-
ment of their unremitting kindness,'" it was in effect a
last will and testament:

> Long past the allotted term of mortal years,
> My soul, a captive in the vale of tears,
> Flutters its wings to shake the dust away,
> Contracted in its narrow cage of clay;
> Conscious the hour of freedom is at hand,
> When it will soar to Faith's own fatherland.
>
> Praise to my young associates who delight
> To be as 'twere to me a second sight,
> Through which alone I may again behold,
> Flowers and gems of intellectual mold,
> Whose gentle ministry, with soothing power,
> Brightens my spirit in its cloudiest hour,
> Till e'en through darkened vision it perceives
> The silver interlining Mercy weaves.

This is the lyric spell Penina weaves. These are the
heard melodies she leaves behind. There are also in her
life and works the sweet unheard melodies which span
the generations uniting her with our times and time still
to come.

In 1951 a Jewish woman writer visiting Charleston
wrote: "On Coming Street—the old cemetery. Thither I
went to pay my respects to Penina Moïse. It is a small and
crowded plot of ground where imposing tombstones and
tablets stand beside crumbling, mouldy markers. I
wanted to stand quietly beside the grave of a dauntless,
valiant Jewess—to salute her in my heart—to bow my
head before the last resting place of one who lived her

days in the eternal night of blindness. A simple stone, green with age, with the simplest of inscriptions:

PENINA MOÏSE. DIED IN HER 83RD YEAR.

And nothing more . . ."

That was in Charleston, South Carolina.

In Philadelphia, Rebecca Gratz. . . . She was the daughter of Michael Gratz, the granddaughter of Joseph Simon, an enterprising landowner and Indian trader. Her mother, Miriam Simon Gratz, was a representative woman of the colonial period, a true mother in Israel. Michael and Miriam Gratz were the parents of twelve children. Of those who grew to maturity, Rebecca has left the liveliest record of her life and times. The years of her life from 1781 to 1869 spanned a most significant period in American history. She was born and died in Philadelphia. She found in her family, in her native city, in her times, enough to challenge and to amuse her. Drama there was aplenty—vicarious and not involving her directly. Her days were fully occupied. The demands upon her were unceasing. Her letters—and they were prolific—dealt largely with the affairs of others. Of her own romantic involvement we have only indirect evidence, for she never referred to it. It is known that she had either in her late teens or early twenties formed a close friendship with a young lawyer, Samuel Ewing, whose father was Provost of the University of Pennsylvania. In 1802 he was her escort at a City Dancing Assembly. They had much in common but their religion, and that to both of them was a gulf they could not bridge. It is said that Ewing, who married in 1810, made no secret of his erstwhile love for Rebecca, confiding it to his future wife. When he died after fifteen years of marriage at the age of thirty-nine, Rebecca stood quietly beside his coffin, "placed three white roses on his breast, put a miniature of herself next to his heart, and left as proudly and silently as she had come in."[17]

Rebecca looked the heroine. The portraits which were painted in her lifetime showed a delicacy of face and a sensitivity of character which must have delighted the several artists to whom we owe so much. The portrait of Rebecca Gratz by Malbone might well be titled "Portrait of the Eternal Jewess." It captures the brooding, the sadness, the withdrawal and renunciation which were the alternatives to intermarriage and obliteration of Jewish identity.[18]

For two reasons Rebecca Gratz absorbs us. First she was one of the first of the articulate Jewish women in the New World. Deeply devout, synagogue-oriented, committed unalterably to the faith of her fathers, she spoke through her letters for herself and for her times. Penina Moïse wrought hymns by way of sublimation. Rebecca wrote letters. She tied the many distant members of her family to herself with a selfless devotion and a total absorption in them and their crises which gave her a vicarious share in their lives, in their triumphs and sorrows. She was committed to her kin, to the unfortunate in her community, to the lonely and the thwarted and the rejected. She identified herself with those who had been deprived by providence of the normal joys and fulfillments to which a woman could look, who channel their normal needs into service for others.

Intermarriage was no abstract problem in the day of her lifetime. "When a woman married out of the faith," we read in Wolf and Whiteman's *History of the Jews of Philadelphia*, ". . . she and her children were lost to Judaism . . . Sensational instances of intermarriage, where one of the partners embraced Christianity, upset the

Jewish community very much. If New York society had been distressed by Dr. Nicholas Schuyler's choice of a Jewish bride, Shinah Simon, her father Joseph Simon and his friends were no less heartbroken by her action."[19] When her grandfather, Joseph Simon was dying at the age of 92, Rebecca Gratz was his devoted and untiring nurse. On his deathbed, Joseph asked Rebecca how he could possibly compensate her for her devotion. She pleaded with him to "forgive Aunt Shinah." Shinah Simon Schuyler was sent for and there was a tender deathbed reconciliation, with Joseph Simon blessing his daughter and dying in her arms. The year was 1804. It was on George Washington's Birthday two years before that Rebecca had proudly and radiantly entered the City Dancing Assembly on the arm of Samuel Ewing.

Years later, Rebecca was to write to a friend that ". . . it is impossible to reconcile a matrimonial engagement between persons of so different a creed, without requiring one or the other to yield. . . ." When Rebecca's youngest brother Benjamin married a Christian, Rebecca and her family were at first plunged into grief. Maria Gist, daughter of Colonel Nathaniel Gist of the Revolutionary War, and a granddaughter of Colonel Christopher Gist who was an intimate friend of George Washington, was "a woman of rare charm and culture." Later, a deep and abiding friendship developed between Rebecca and Maria.[20] Maria was perceptive enough to have saved Rebecca's letters to her and to them we owe our knowledge of Rebecca as a brilliant commentator on her times and a loyal participant in the joys and sorrows of those near and dear to her.

We trace her life from early beauty and affluence and happy rounds through renunciation and good works and financial reverses. We see her young and flawless face change from radiance to that final last and pathetic photograph of a shrunken and very faded old woman from whose appearance time had erased all beauty.

The facts of her life, as the facts of any life, can be briefly stated. Rebecca was one of twelve children born to Michael and Miriam Gratz. She grew up in what was the current equivalent of the affluent society. She was one of ten children who survived the rigors of infancy and there must have been great love and little sibling rivalry in that home. For the strong sense of kinship that survived and the family loyalty that flourished was lifelong. To that large family circle many friends were drawn. Jews as well as Christians were intimates of that household. Members of Judge Ogden Hoffman's family, in whose office Washington Irving studied law, were very close to Rebecca. Washington Irving frequently enjoyed the hospitality of the Gratz home and introduced others into the hospitable circle. When Thomas Sully, the famous artist, planned to visit Philadelphia, Washington Irving wrote to Rebecca: "I think I can render him no favor for which he ought to be more grateful, than in introducing him to the notice of yourself and your connections." Another close friend was Mary Elizabeth Fenno of Baltimore whose correspondence Rebecca invited. In one of her letters to Miss Fenno, Rebecca shows a rare bit of humor. In a letter dated November 23, 1802, Rebecca writes: "Miss Pemberton whose death you lament with so much sensibility is much better. . ." It is a sentence that an English contemporary could have written, although Rebecca Gratz makes no mention of having encountered the work of Jane Austen, who lived between 1775 and 1817. She was, however, well acquainted with another English woman writer, Grace Aguilar, a dedicated English Jewess whose gentle involvement with the history of the Jewish people enriched her times, uniting Jewish women in a trans-Atlantic universe of discourse.

It is impossible to describe adequately without enlarging Rebecca's biography beyond the allotted space, the countless activities in which her spirit sought fulfillment. In service to her family, to her synagogue, to the larger community, she seemed inexhaustible. "Devotedly attached to her family, she was the home-maker for her unmarried brothers and for the orphaned children of her sister, Rachel Moses. She took the mother's place . . ."[21] One of her nieces wrote of her: ". . . nothing could be lovelier than her every day life, which commenced every morning with prayers and thanks to the Creator . . ." "This piety," writes Dr. Philipson, "was the keynote of her life, both private and public." In her twenty-first year she became secretary of a philanthropic organization, the Female Association for the Relief of Women and Children in Reduced Circumstances. She helped organize the Philadelphia Orphan Society in 1815 and from 1819 on served for forty years as its secretary. The other officers described her work in terms of highest praise adding that "to her dignity, grace and noble personal qualities the managers have always yielded the tribute of their warm admiration and personal regard." One of her most important contributions to her own synagogue—and to many others that were influenced by her—was the founding of the Hebrew Sunday School Society in 1838.

Morais has pointed out that the Hebrew Sunday School of Philadelphia was "the oldest institution of its kind in America," and that Rebecca served "as its Superintendent and First Directress for a period of thirty-two years." She was also active in the work of the Female Hebrew Benevolent Society, the Jewish Foster Home, the Fuel Society, and the Sewing Society. "Gentiles as well as Hebrews were made the recipients of the same kindness. At the Philadelphia Orphan Asylum, the Widows' Asylum, and wherever she labored, the zeal exhibited met with . . . the gratitude of her beneficiaries." Her plans for her many educational projects "induced the writing and compilation of textbooks for instruction in the Jewish faith." Her friend and co-worker, Isaac Leeser, "dedicated his catechism to her, as a mark of esteem and veneration for a Jewess so exemplary . . ."

Her letters cover a staggering number of subjects. Not only to the student of American sociology and history do they offer a wealth of data on every conceivable enterprise involving the great society. But they cover the books that were then in vogue, the plays that were produced, the controversial articles which agitated the contemporary scene. Here are Lord Byron and Fanny Kemble and Bulwer-Lytton and Walter Scott and Charles Dickens and Harriet Martineau and James Fennimore Cooper and Grace Aguilar and Mrs. Gaskell and Maria Edgeworth— to mention but a few well-known to Rebecca and to her contemporaries.

In Grace Aguilar (who died September 16, 1847) Rebecca found a kindred spirit, as did many of Rebecca's contemporaries. She read and discussed Aguilar books in her letters. Here was a descendant of marranos who in the *Vale of Cedars* chose to describe the sorrows and trials of the crypto-Jews of Spain. In the Aguilar two-volume work *The Women of Israel,* she concerned herself with "the female biography of Scripture," a subject also close to Rebecca's heart. Grace like Rebecca a spinster, sought sublimation, insisted that Judaism was "a religion of love." She spoke not only for herself but for all those women who chose the solitary path rather than oblivion. Are not these words the motif of a personal credo:

Let us not, as women of Israel, be content with the mere performance of domestic, social, and individual duties, but vivify and lighten them by the rays of eternal love and immortal hope, which beam upon us from the pages of the Bible. A religion of love is indeed necessary to woman, yet more so than to man. Even in her happiest lot there must be a void in her heart, which everacting piety alone can fill; and to her whose portion is to suffer, whose lot is lonely, o what misery must be hers, unless she can lean upon her God, and draw from His word the blessed conviction that His love, His tenderness, are hers, far beyond the feeble conception of earth . . .

Thus Aguilar! Many a spinster who forswore marriage out of the faith, would echo these sentiments. Rebecca Gratz lived them! Long before Freud, Grace Aguilar was grappling with feminine motivation. "Women, and single women more especially, are more liable to petty failings than men, simply because they have less to engross their minds. . . . Unless taught from earliest years to find and take pleasure in resources *within,* they must look *with out* . . ."[22]

How close these two contemporaries were in spirit is eloquently expressed in a letter which Rebecca wrote on September 15, 1848, in which she mourned the death of an author she admired and had never met:

I see they have just published a new novel 'Home Influence' by Grace Aguilar . . . I wish you would read it, and give me your opinion of its merits, because I see many excellences in it, and found it deeply interesting—I know nothing so touching as the distresses and difficulties of childhood, and am glad to see them treated with consideration and sympathy by matured intellects . . . it is to be lamented the gifted author did not live to complete her design of continuing her subject through another work . . .

In a work published in Philadelphia in 1880, *Eminent Israelites of the Nineteenth Century* by Henry Samuel Morais, he writes of Rebecca just eleven years after her death in much the same vein:

> Truly it has been said, that woman is the crowning work of the Creator . . . There stands the princess of philanthropy, Florence Nightingale; Lady Judith Montefiore and Lady Burdett-Coutts closely follow her footsteps. The lady, to whose character attention is drawn, was not so widely known, but the inestimable services she rendered, in a comparatively narrow sphere, have endeared her to many, especially to her co-religionists . . .[23]

Perhaps nothing shows Rebecca's moral grandeur more clearly than the attitude which was hers when sudden financial reverses brought about "the fall of this house"— the phrase is hers—in a letter of August 6, 1826.[24]

She wrote to her sister-in-law, Maria Gist Gratz: "One misfortune has followed so swiftly on the wings of another . . ." She referred to the bankruptcy of her brothers, Simon and Hyman Gratz. She goes on ". . . I believe the anticipation of all evils is hardest to bear. It is 'the dreadful note of preparation' and the human mind when prepared may sustain the worst that is permitted . . ." She refers to the kindness, "universal sympathy . . . respect and consideration from the whole community . . . indeed we have shed more tears of gratitude than grief and I begin to philosophize on the subject—and examine the question whether poverty be so great an evil, as it is represented to be . . ." From affluence through bankruptcy to a limited and restricted life in a much smaller home, yet her "implicit faith in Scripture" permits her to make all necessary adjustments. "When you come to see us again . . . you shall still find us a cheerful & contented race—and I doubt not just *for vanity* we shall consider a humbler house full as pleasant. *You* always loved the quiet little Library where I am now seated . . . so a snug little parlour will be our Library. . . ." She concludes: ". . . the worst is over and we now look forward to better times—the commercial world has been terribly rent in pieces—but the fragments are not totally lost—they may be gathered in patches—and used more prudently in future and they will still be fit for service." Rabbi Philipson, who edited her letters, adds in a footnote: "After the financial misfortune the family removed from their spacious home on Chestnut St. near Seventh to the smaller house Number 2 Boston Row on Chestnut St. near Twelfth."[25]

When Rebecca Gratz died, August 29, 1869, her last will and testament was characterzied by Philipson as "a noble document."

It reads: "I Rebecca Gratz, of Philadelphia, being in sound health of body and mind, advanced in the vale of years, declare this to be my last will and testament. I commit my spirit to the God who gave it, relying on His mercy and redeeming love, and believing with a fine and perfect faith in the religion of my fathers, 'Hear, O Israel, the Lord our God is one Lord.'"

So from silence and anonymity to stirring prose and poetry their voices go echoing through the generations. Faith is eternal, continuing. The human situation is unchanged. The plots are unalterable. Costumes differ. But the sorrows and triumps, the joys and victories, the defeats and challenges inevitably succeed each other. Who has not tasted happiness? Who has not known bereavement? Are not our days as grass? And "from the rising of the sun unto the going down of the same" the procession of events is an endless and unchanging repetition.

Spinsters were the self-deprived.

There were also the "lost girls" who wore the Christian disguises dictated by conversion and acculturation which usually followed intermarriage. That they experienced anguish and sorrow at the betrayal of faith and separation from kin we have already seen. There were other women who entered the Jewish fold and partook of its glories and hardships with valour and dignity. Of these we note Rebekah Hyneman.

She was born in Philadelphia, September 8, 1812. Her maiden name was Gumpert, and all we know of her antecedents, according to her admiring biographer, Henry Samuel Morais, is that she "was not born in the Sinaic law." Her life, he avers, entitles her "to a place by the side of Israel's illustrious daughters." Like Penina Moïse and Grace Aguilar and Rebecca Gratz and others, some of her writings survive. "Her varied effusions," writes her contemporary in the prevalent style of his day, "breathe devotion to the belief she eagerly embraced in her womanhood; such a devotion, that it alone might commend the character of the authoress to the respect of the Hebrew community . . . she combined a clear intellect with a pure heart, and both were directed to a righteous end." Like Penina she was almost completely self-taught and mastered not only the florid intricacies of the then current English composition but also had considerable knowledge of French and German.[26]

When she was twenty-three Rebekah married Benjamin Hyneman, whose brother was editor of the *Masonic Mirror and Keystone*. She was frail in health and the target of many blows of providence, a female Job. Her husband died after five years of marriage. One of her sons who had enlisted in the Union Army during the Civil War starved to death at Andersonville where he was a prisoner. Her other son died in his youth. Her husband's sister-in-law, Sarah, wife of Leon Hyneman also died. As they were very close, this was another tragic bereavement to Rebekah. "Still the bereaved woman arose above gloom, and turned her mind to the task of communicating to others her godly sentiments." She became a frequent contributor to her brother-in-law's paper. She wrote many essays, a number of short stories, "fugitive pieces of poetry," and translations from foreign authors. "Many of the subjects are Scriptural, and show, in vivid colors, the feelings she entertained for the religion of her choice." She also wrote "some beautiful delineations of the Women of the Bible and the Apocrypha." She wrote a number of "Tales for Children" which were calculated to "elevate" and uplift her juvenile readers.

Like Penina and Rebecca Gratz she attracted many friends and had a salon of sorts. "Mild of disposition and endowed with rare conversational powers, Mrs. Hyneman possessed a large and select circle of friends who sympathized with her in the tribulations she was doomed to bear. She developed an acute and extremely painful illness and was "under intense agony." Fortunately her friends continued loyal. On September 10, 1875, "the spirit of Rebekah Hyneman passed into the abode set apart for the just."

Morais concludes this "sorry" tale: "She was truly a woman whose example may well be imitated by every daughter of the race of Abraham."

Regionalism played a crucial role in determining individual biographies of Jewish men and women in America. Distance from synagogues and religious fellowship, separation from group pressures and group solidarity which upheld one's convictions and one's faith—these were among the factors that predetermined many a life story.

Sheer loneliness and isolation condemned many a young person to find the antidote in acceptance of another way of life. When Benjamin Gratz took the long journey from Philadelphia to Kentucky, it needed no crystal ball to prophesy his mating there. In a scholarly work published by the University of Kentucky Press, Dr. Joseph R. Rosenbloom traces in capsule form the lives of the known Jews from Colonial times through 1800.[27] Modestly the author calls it "an attempt to provide a reference work for historians, a source for sociological and cultural analysis, and a basic tool for the study of American Jewish history." At least one-fifth of the Jewish population, he feels, "remains totally obscure and unknown . . ." Yet here in thumbnail sketches there are enough dramatic narratives to keep the Hollywood mills grinding for generations. Such, for example, is the recorded fragment: "MINIS, Hannah. Born June 13, 1744. Daughter of Abraham Minis, she was married to David Leion on April 17, 1798, and was divorced on August 22, 1799, in the first recorded Jewish divorce. In 1779 she was in Savannah."

In leafing through the lists of colonial Jews, we note the usual threefold patterns: marriage within the fold, intermarriage, celibacy. A Revolutionay War soldier, Abram Mordecai, became an Indian trader and a government agent in Georgia. There is no record of his marriage. Caroline Mordecai, daughter of Jacob Mordecai (probably of the same family as Abram) had a daughter Caroline who was born in 1794 and married Achille Plunkett, a gentile. Another daughter of Jacob's did not marry. Moses, a son of Jacob Mordecai, a native of Raleigh, North Carolina, became a noted attorney of his state. His first wife was Margaret Lane; his second was Ann Willis Lane. Another Moses Mordecai, a German-born merchant of Philadelphia, married Elizabeth Whitlock, "a gentile who was converted and became an observant Jewess." Jacob

Gratz, brother of Rebecca, had an action-packed life and succeeded in befuddling historians: "He had a gentile wife or mistress." There were interracial unions also, as the following entry shows: Nunes, Alexander. Mulatto son of Moses Nunes." There is a record of his being in Georgia in 1787. The first wife of Moses Nunes was a Jewess named Abrahams, his second was a mulatto. Another member of the Nunes clan was Zipporah, who was a native of Portugal and born a Catholic, daughter of a marrano court physician. "She was a very cultured and charitable woman" who emigrated to the New World and was successively married to David Mendez Machado and then to Israel Jacobs.

Endless variety and endless changes in plot are in evidence. One of the shortest biographies on record is the following: "Cohen, Cornelia. On December 19, 1799, she was married to Thomas McIntyre in a Charleston Church." Lost—like a stone cast into a pond! There is no additional information. Adaptation involved more than traditional marriage, the acceptance of celibacy, or concubinage. The moral climate in the new land was a challenge to keen minds, both Christians and Jews. The age of enlightenment culminated in the Declaration of Independence, in the Constitution. The winds of Deism and Transcendentalism were blowing through the land. Jeffersonian liberalism had enthusiastic followers. In the South orthodoxy and conservatism were in the saddle. Always there was cultural interaction in Christian and in Jewish ranks. Soon, evidence of religious revolt against ancient folkways and mores would rend Jewish ranks. The first breach was to take place in the native city of Penina Moïse, in Charleston.

To summarize life in scattered hamlets, in lonely trading outposts, in little enclaves within a few of the larger cities is to indulge in generalizations which may be true for some groups and inaccurate for others. To say that there was endless variety and endless change in a fluid, mobile population moving from seaboard to hinterland would more closely approximate the overall picture. The Jews of early America reflected every change in locale, in mood, in moral climate. There was among them no unanimity. For the Jew of Lodz and the Jew of Lisbon had little "universe of discourse." What did unite them and hold them together was an ancient faith, a history which was in truth a martyrology, an allegiance to the God who had covenanted with them and chosen them for a specific role in human history. And a common memory of a land which had given them the dream of grandeur, a place where patriarch and prophet held a continuing dialogue with God.

In the New World Jews were on a pendulum which oscilated between adherence to tradition and social osmosis which percolated through their ranks making imperceptible but noticeable changes. This is what made both for rigidity in synagogue administration and a simultaneous insistence on admission to every civic and legal right and privilege enjoyed by their neighbors.

Estimates of vital statistics and population studies are always haphazard. It is safe to say that by 1800 there were some three thousand Jews in the United States. There were Sephardim and Ashkenazim among them from the first. The differences between the groups were not as great as had at first been noted. While Sephardim usually sought mates from their own ranks, yet marriage between Jewish groups of different geographic origins was not uncommon. Haym Salomon, Polish immigrant married the daughter of a Sephardic family. The favorite son-in-law of Rabbi Gershom Mendes Seixas was Israel Baer Kursheedt, an immigrant from Germany. A separation of status and social position may be noted between the

native American Jew and his immigrant fellow worshipper. More and more native Jews displayed aspects of
cultural assimilation which reflected the folkways of the
community in which they lived. It was Isaac M. Wise
who noted that "there were Episcopalian Jews in New
York, Quaker Jews in Philadelphia, Huguenot Jews in
Charleston . . . everywhere according to the prevailing
sect." While the influential editor of the *Occident,* Isaac
Leeser, staunch and undeviating champion of Orthodoxy
accused the Reform group of plotting to set up in America
"a new system which is to be acceptable to gentiles."

Life was never dull in Jewish circles or in their contacts with their Christian neighbors. Their initial activities were often unpretentious and modest enough. There
were hawkers and walkers, lowly peddlers who began with
the few commodities they carried on their backs. After
tortuous apprenticeship they graduated to the horse-and-
buggy stage. Gradually hard work and unceasing effort
was rewarded and the little store gave the itinerant a permanent address, a place to sell his wares and a place to
live either back of the store or above it. The isolated
trader and storekeeper became the center of a little community as his relatives and friends and former European
fellow dwellers of the same *shtetl* (village) were drawn
into the same orbit. Gradually a little Jewish community
evolved. They needed a place to worship and a place to
bury the dead. Provision had to be made for the widow
and the orphan and the mendicant. Dowries were to be
provided for young marriageable women without families.
The sick and aged had to be cared for. Schools had to
be established for both secular and religious training. It
took concerted group effort and group discipline to maintain such customs and rites as they practiced.

It took women of all kinds to make this burgeoning
activity possible. The quiet and anonymous ones. The

self-effacing workers. The gifted and magnetic. The articulate and dynamic. Jewish women lived background lives.
Their records were almost totally obliterated until that
final time of reckoning when they were summarized on
tombstones. Change was in the air. There were some
articulate heroines who have left traces of their having
lived, of their having shared in their times, of their having
influenced ever widening areas of activity. There were
the silent shadows who left no record.

More and more as women relate to historic contemporary events, their roles change from spectator to participant. The record of social change in a new environment,
of evolving goals, of new religious practices permits greater emphasis on the role of women. There was one sphere
where they dominated—that was in the home. The home
life of Jews in America was a citadel of Jewish continuity
and survival. Here old folkways were cherished, old lullabies were crooned, old recipes were redolent. Every Jewish
home differed to a greater or smaller degree from its
Christian neighbors. Many writers have testified to the
sense of closeness, to the bonds between parents and
siblings. Whatever compromises were demanded outside
the home, whatever lack of ease and estrangement prevailed on the part of members of an alien culture in an
all-engulfing host culture, whatever hurdles were to be
taken by non-English-speaking immigrants in the heart-
breaking efforts to communicate in the market place, all
of these fell away like sodden garments. In the home dwelt
memory and dignity and an ancient and revered religion.
Every housewife partook of the creation of a sanctuary.

Women presided like good fairies at confinements. They
nursed the sick, visited the old, prepared the dead for
burial. They accepted orphans into their homes and the
bereaved of their kin. Before the general availability of
inns and hostels, the home served as a haven of hospitality

to the known and to the stranger. This was true in spacious homes and in overcrowded tenements. Walls seemed to stretch. The pot of soup was inexhaustible. The very tempo of life underwent a periodic change in rhythm as the Sabbath rescued Jews from the commonplace, as it permitted time for prayer and meditation and rest.

Of course there were many incidents, personality clashes, temperamental outbursts which ruffled the waters at home. Grace Aguilar, whom Rebecca Gratz and other American Jewish women read with interest and admiration, could tell her readers "the Bible does give both sympathy and encouragement, even to the most constitutionally weak . . ." But even the weak may identify with the strong! She writes of Queen Esther, "To the women of every faith, race, and land, then, her history is alike instructive and inexpressibly consoling; but it is in the hearts of her descendants, the women of Israel, she should be most closely enshrined . . . Every woman should take it to her own heart, and remember, with holy joy and thankfulness, that the preservation of her people, which that day recalls, was, under the Eternal, the work of a woman not stronger, not more gifted than herself."[28] There were many Esthers in the land.

Grace Aguilar reached women on both sides of the Atlantic, exhorting them to see themselves as keystones in the world that God built. The role of the Shunammite fascinated her. This woman was in the words of the Bible "a great woman." Nameless she remained, an anonymous doer of good deeds, who befriended Elisha and offered him shelter and food. As for the prophet he saw at once that his hosts "were indeed those with whom a prophet of the Lord might enjoy the delights of social intercourse with innocence and peace." So "the Shunammite and her husband made him a little chamber . . . and set for him there a bed, and a table, and a stool, and a candlestick . . ."

Grace Aguiler extols the Shunammite further: "That she did not at first know Elisha as a prophet, does not enhance the mild benevolence of her character. . . . It is wrong to suppose that benevolence is but synonymous with acts of charity to the poor and needy. . . . It was this rare and beautiful benevolence which the Shunammite so richly possessed."

For the women of her time and her generation in America, Grace Aguilar was the clear voice of conscience. Her credo reveals a soul that had in its loneliness sought and found spiritual strength and sustenance to share with her readers in America through the pages of the *Occident*. "Let us then endeavor to convince the nations of the high privileges we enjoy, in common with our fathers, brothers, and husbands. . . . Let us not, as women of Israel, be content with the mere performance of domestic, social and individual duties, but vivify and lighten them by the rays of eternal and immortal hope, which beam upon us from the pages of the Bible. A religion of love is indeed necessary to woman, yet more than to man. In her happiest lot there must be a void in her heart . . . and to her whose portion is to suffer, whose lot is lonely, O what misery must be hers, unless she can lean upon her God . . ." Here is the cry of the disinherited Jewess, the spinster finding consolation and sublimation in other-wordliness. Her words, available in America, had great relevance to many Jewish women. Her testament is timeless: "We need faith to believe that God is love, and our souls immortal . . . Faith to know that we are individually objects of His love and care, as surely as that every blade of grass and invisible insect are alike the work of His hand . . . It is for all these things we need Faith; that faith which instead of banishing *Reason*, welcomes and rejoices in her . . ."

Grace Aguilar whose eloquence has not diminished,

died September 16, 1847. She had lived but thirty-one years. She spoke for the anonymous women and for those who were known on both sides of the Atlantic.

Unanimity eluded the Jews as it did all other elements of the American population. Religious differences loomed large because of geographic differences of the immigrants. To be sure, in the six congregations which sent greetings to the first President of the United States, the Spanish or Sephardi *minhag* (custom) prevailed. This was true of New York, Newport, Savannah, Philadelphia, Charleston, and Richmond. "During the first four decades of the nineteenth century," writes Moshe Davis, "the Jewish population multiplied fivefold." New immigrants from Germany and central Europe brought new customs. Particularly did the ranks of the Ashkenazim swell and with that population increase came the establishment of newer synagogues where Minhag Ashkenaz prevailed. Penetration of the plains and distance from seaboard authority brought additional changes. . . . There were new frontiers to be conquered—physical and spiritual.

Nowhere is there greater evidence of the changes wrought by new immigrants than in the pages of the *Occident*. Here as in a huge mirror communal activities are reflected. Here we learn much about the American Jewish woman in mid-nineteenth century. Its editor, Isaac Leeser, was a man who has been described as "the spiritual father of Conservative Judaism in America."

At the High Holy Days in 1829, as a twenty-three year old German-born immigrant he became *hazan* of Congregation Mikveh Israel in Philadelphia. He inaugurated a period in American Jewish history which is accurately described as "the Age of Leeser."[29] The congregation to whose post he was elected was founded March 17, 1782. In the first two decades of the nineteenth century it gained

many new members. Still larger migrations from Germany
and Central Europe were to come. The America to which
Isaac Leeser came was a bold, brash, wonderful place, a
land of hope and boundless opportunity. Isaac Leeser
dreamed vast dreams for its Jewish inhabitants. Here they
could lead a dedicated, creative, fruitful life as Americans
and as Jews. It was a time of expanding horizons, physical
and moral. Emerson was pleading that the immigrants
be accepted into full American fellowship: "We must
learn to grasp heroic hands in heroic hands." He wanted
"opportunity—doors wide open—every port open . . ."
Leeser's soul glowed and expanded here. He began an
intensive study of English, reading every book and periodical he could get his hands on. When he accepted the
call to Mikveh Israel he had already done an outstanding
piece of writing, a defense of Jews who had been defamed
in a series of articles in the *London Quarterly Review.*
From then on his record of accomplishment became truly
staggering.

Isaac Leeser was deeply involved in everything that
concerned his fellow Jews. He was the champion of traditional Judaism. He was dynamic, creative, vibrant, both
as author and editor. In 1843, Leeser founded a publication which was his imperishable legacy to the Jews of
America. The *Occident and American Jewish Advocate,*
which he edited for 25 years, survived him by only one
year. Perhaps the demise of the journal was the most eloquent testimonial to the genius of its founder. A contemporary wrote of him: "The present advanced condition
of Hebrews in this land of freedom must be chiefly attributed to his ceaseless exertions for their moral and
spiritual welfare. In fact the history of American Judaism
and that of Isaac Leeser are one and the same." Rebecca
Gratz, who knew Leeser well and worked closely with him,
refers to him frequently. She writes in February, 1834,

when a smallpox epidemic had stricken Philadelphia:
"poor Mr. Leeser is one of its present subjects, his attack
has been unmitigated smallpox, and tho his life and eye-
sight have been spared I am told his countenance will
bear many marks of its ravages—he has always been so
sensitive on the subject of personal disadvantages—that
his former humility will appear like vanity to his present
state—and unless some Desdemona shall arise to see his
visage in his mind—all his future expectations must be
confined to solitary studies." No Desdemona arose and
he remained a solitary soul until his death.

He achieved facultative immortality through his writing, much of which was addressed to women. "It would
be regarded as mean in a wealthy father," he writes, in an
editorial titled "Demand for Education" which appeared
in the *Occident,* "not to give his daughters an ample opportunity, at least, to acquire the science of music, and to
learn French, say for a space of ten years at the smallest
calculation; we will not mention at what an expenditure
of money . . . But how many are there who are willing to
spend as much time and treasure to teach their sons and
daughters the noble science of fearing God, and the ele-
vated language in which our blessed Scriptures are composed?" He wrote a series of impassioned appeals to Jews
not to violate the Sabbath. He asks that a league be formed
where each member would pledge himself to the others
to keep the Sabbath holy.

Women, their reading, their education, their position
in American and in Jewish life found frequent mention
in his pages. The works of Grace Aguilar were published
in the *Occident.*[30] Even her death did not stop publication. Her writing continued to be published posthumously
in the *Occident* as selected by her bereaved mother. A
"Pilgrimage to the Grave of Grace Aguilar," reverently
undertaken by a Mrs. S. C. Hall and published in the

Occident, called her "the golden link between the Christian and the Jew." This was as true in America as in England. Isaac Leeser's obituary simply stated that "there has not arisen a single Jewish female in modern times who has done so much for the illustration and adornment of her faith as Grace Aguilar." Many an American Jewess concurred. Concern with education of children, with the quality of teachers and of teaching, continues to get full coverage in the pages of the *Occident*. Women and their needs occupy much space. Always chivalrous, Leeser points out in general terms the need for silence and decorum in the synagogue and while his inward glance strays toward the woman's gallery, he does not specifically mention the offenders. Hebrew as a language of holiness and beauty is constantly extolled. News of Jews and Jewish needs in Palestine is uppermost. Also news of the scattered brethren in distant places. Not only did he keep his readers abreast of all the good and all the evil which befell his coreligionists, he left to posterity an accurate and undistorted picture of the times in which he lived and of the Jewish community which to a large extent he molded.

How many Jewish women were thus recalled to their ancient faith and folkways we have no way of estimating. How many would have been utterly lost without the gadfly called the *Occident* is anybody's guess. But where can we in our time read of the cornerstone laying of Jewish hospitals and synagogues more than a century ago as his contemporaries did in his day? Where trace the growth and development of the Reform movement which so grieved the editor of the *Occident?* Or the death of Jewish literature be mourned? Or the education of Jewish "pauper" children be espoused? Or the ancient ways of our people be defended and extolled? Who but Leeser would have the courage to attack and expose the ignorance and worldliness of Jewish lay leaders? Few had his courage

and the vision. Here was a valiant Jew—a man for all
time and for all seasons.

Many a Jewish woman came to know and love the
Bible because in 1853 Isaac Leeser had translated the
Bible into English. It was his great oblation. Many an
occupant of the woman's gallery had reason to be grateful
to this indefatigable scholar. A contemporary said of
Leeser, "The present advanced condition of Hebrews in
this land of freedom must be chiefly attributed to his
ceaseless exertions for their moral and spiritual welfare.
In fact the history of American Judaism and that of
Isaac Leeser are one and the same."

Before summarizing the salient historical trends of nine-
teenth-century Jewry in which dynamic changes rent their
community, in which new leaders arose, in which the
lives of ever-increasing numbers of Jews and other new
immigrants were involved, let us consider the impact of
two Jewish women upon the inhabitants of the land.
These two women differed in every possible way, in place
of birth and religious antecedents, in their sense of mission
and dedication, in the way their genius flowered and in
the people they reached. And last but not least, in the
influence which their personalities exerted upon their
Christian contemporaries. Early Jewesses had been quiet
and anonymous, these protagonists were vocal and dynamic.

In a little Polish ghetto town, on January 13, 1810,
Ernestine Louise Potowski was born. She was the daughter of a rabbi. She was an only child and showed an early
aptitude for the study of Hebrew and Torah. In her father, who was an extraordinarily devout man—he fasted
every Monday and Thursday—she found not only a mentor
but a hero-figure whom she revered. Nevertheless she
questioned the ascetic practices which undermined her fa-

ther's health. She questioned the purpose of self-denial as an act that was pleasurable to God. She continued to ask questions, both pertinent and impertinent, for the rest of her life. "She was a rebel at the age of five; at the age of fourteen she was a heretic."[31] She became increasingly difficult at home. The community which her father headed found in her deeds and attitudes a perennial topic of discussion, criticism, and gossip. Her mother died when Ernestine was sixteen. Her dowry was large. Without consulting his daughter but no doubt overwhelmed by his wife's death and the insoluable problems presented by Ernestine, her father arranged for his daughter to be married to a man much older than she. This was a prevailing custom but one which the young rebel found justifiably repugnant. She went to the prospective groom pleading to be released from the distasteful prospect. She was told that if she refused to go through with the marriage, her dowry would automatically be forfeited to the spurned man. She decided to try the case before the Polish High Tribunal at Kalish. Ernestine made history by pleading her own case. The court awarded to her her mother's inheritance. She came home a victor. With her own money she paid her way out of Piotrkow, Poland, never to return. She lived for a while in Germany and visited other lands.

In London, while she studied English, she made her living by teaching Hebrew and German. It was there that this unpredictable Hebrew teacher of twenty-two met the famous and renowned social reformer Robert Owen. He was sixty. It was a congenial meeting of minds of a Jewish rebel and a Christian nonconformist reformer. "The aging reformer found in Ernestine a young and dedicated disciple . . . and Ernestine . . . found in Owenism a social philosophy that gave her both a program and a direction."[32] She also found a jeweler and silversmith, William E. Rose, another Owenite, to whom she was married in a civil ceremony. In 1836 the young couple emigrated to America.

The year was an historic one. A gifted young American philosopher, Ralph Waldo Emerson, had just published a collection of his essays. Transcendentalism was the rallying point of many young intellectuals. Henry David Thoreau was of that dedicated number. William Cullen Bryant ardently espoused the cause of exploited New York tailors. William Lloyd Garrison spearheaded the anti-slavery movement. It was an age of ferment, of protest, of utopian plans. Here was the moral climate in which the Jewish rebel from the Polish ghetto could join hands with a noblewoman from Scotland, Fanny Wright. "It would be difficult to imagine two more dissimilar backgrounds . . . than those of a Scottish noblewoman and a rabbi's daughter from a ghetto in Poland. Yet, as social reformers in America, Frances Wright and Ernestine Rose had more in common with each other than each had with any other woman of her time." Soon both found huge audiences, some as large as two thousand people, sponsored by a group which called itself the "Society for Moral Philanthropists"—a group attacked by journalistic crusaders. Ernestine was described as a handsome young woman, immaculately dressed with "flowing black ringlets framing a handsome face." Invariably she was referred to as a "Polish lady," which she apparently did not bother to contradict. Her eloquence, despite a heavy foreign accent, was unchallenged. She traveled widely and was an indefatigable lecturer. Reporters poked fun at her advanced ideas and garbled English but they did add that she was greeted "amid thunders of applause."

When in May of 1845 she was discovered seated beside her mentor and teacher at a large public meeting in the New York Coliseum, a reporter for the New York *Herald* wrote: "Seated by our side was the venerable Robert

Owen, and the highly accomplished, talented and intellectually beautiful Mrs. Rose."[33] The following year after
lectures in Detroit and Ann Arbor, "the House of Representatives passed a special resolution expressing high
praise for her oratorical skill, eloquence and grace of
delivery." And many years later the women of the State
of Michigan recorded that the woman suffrage movement
in their state began in 1846 "with the advent of Ernestine
L. Rose."[34]

The causes she espoused were many. There could be a
moral here and the germ for many sermons. Was not the
Polish ghetto a spawning ground for countless generations
of reformers who championed many worthy causes? The
vehemence of her rejection of ghetto folkways schooled
her to take on other adversaries. She was a female Don
Quixote tilting at many windmills. She was an embattled
champion defending a thousand lost causes. She was re-
viled and attacked. She was admired and adored. The
great women of America who fought step by step for the
recognition of rights for women were her fellow crusaders.
The Quaker Lucretia Mott made common cause with
her. And Elizabeth Cady Stanton was her friend. Susan
B. Anthony called her "Brave and fearless of all Wom-
en . . ." The antislavery people adored her. One fellow-
worker, a well known abolitionist, Sallie Holley wrote of
her: "Ernestine L. Rose is a charming woman and at
times playful . . . She is far before any woman speaker I
ever heard . . . I cannot give any idea of the power and
beauty of her speech . . ."[35]

In the critical year of 1848 when Europe was seething
with revolution and mass migrations to America swelled
in volume, on Bastille Day, July 14, a call was issued for
a woman's rights convention, in a New York paper published in a small community—Seneca Falls, New York. It
was the first call of its kind, a landmark in social prog-

ress. "Until then Ernestine Rose and a handful of brave women had made speeches about woman's rights; from then on they made history . . ."[36] Three years later, in Worcester, Massachusetts, Ernestine continued her agitation as she was to do again and again: "At marriage (woman) loses her identity. . . . What an inconsistency, that from the moment she enters the compact in which she assumes the high responsibility of wife and mother, she ceases legally to exist and becomes a purely submissive being . . . resistance to wrong is virtue, alike in woman as in man."[37]

She wore seven-league boots to leave behind the age of anonymity. It was a giant step for a Jewish woman to become "Queen of the Platforms." It took the emancipated daughter of a rabbi to take that step.

Ernestine Rose, like all people who enter the public arena, had her share of detractors. She was called an atheist and an infidel by those who took issue with her. She was in truth "far out" in ideological terms for her time and age. The causes she espoused are now part of the law of the land, yet she was then a target for those who represented the pro-slavery and anti-feminist and anti-labor point of view. She fought so many battles on so many battle fronts that historians seem to have lost track of Ernestine as a Jewess, as a daughter of an ultra-orthodox rabbi, as one who had known prejudice and bigotry and anti-Semitism in her native Poland.

She was shocked and unprepared for anti-semitism in "free thought circles." (One need only recall, as she seems not to have been able to do, that one of the most despicable and vicious attacks on Jews in her day was written by Karl Marx!) On October 28, 1863, her former friend, the editor of the Boston *Investigator,* wrote an editorial in a frenzy of hate and venom which she read with astonishment and anger. She immediately wrote a letter to the editor, saying, "I almost smelt brimstone, genuine Christian brimstone . . ." Horace Seaver, her erstwhile friend, had said that ancient Jews "were about the worst people of whom we have any account." He then stigmatized modern Jews and Judaism as "bigoted, narrow, exclusive, and totally unfit for a progressive people like the Americans . . ."[38] An epistolary exchange in the scurrilous paper lasted for ten weeks. Gradually both Ernestine and the detractor became more heated in their denunciation and rebuttal. Ernestine accused Seaver of "as much folly as bigotry." She finally served notice on the enemy that she had had enough "and unless forced by further quibbles, insinuations, new issues and prevarications, I am quite content to let the subject rest, satisfied in having done my duty in defense of justice."

She made friends in distant places. One of her admirers wrote to her that he had named his only daughter Ernestine Rose. The editor of the *Jewish Record* saluted her from the sidelines as having retained her Jewish spirit even though she had forsaken the practice of her religion.

She too died in her eighty-third year, almost the last survivor of a series of wars that ennobled her time. She was deeply mourned by her many friends. When Susan B. Anthony as President of the National American Woman Suffrage Association was asked to prepare a list of women who pioneered in the suffrage movement, Mrs. Anthony wrote ". . . begin with Mary Wollstonecraft as your first Great Champion—then Frances Wright—then Ernestine L. Rose . . ." And Yuri Suhl, Ernestine's chronicler, adds: "An Englishwoman; a Scottish noblewoman; and a Jewish woman from Poland, a child at the ghetto."[39]

6

At no time in American Jewish history was there unanimity of practice and belief. Each man and woman achieved a personal solution, an adaptation, an accommodation to conscience and condition in which he lived. Some lived out their lives within the ambience of the synagogue. Others sought only occasional shelter and comfort there or turned to their ancient folkways to mark the rites of passage which celebrated the cycles of life. There was one group of women in every generation uniquely apart from the mainstream of Jewish life. There were the "lost girls"—and their biographies are singularly alike, lending themselves to a formula of sorts. A "lost girl" is one who, because of circumstances over which she does not always have control, meets and falls in love with a non-Jew. She undergoes deep, traumatic periods of self-examination. She weighs the effect upon her parents and family circle. She braves total or partial alienation and estrangement. She is likely to face rejection and hostility from those who constitute her future mate's family. She is for much of her life thereafter a woman who is written off as if she had never been. Separated from all that made her early life meaningful she spends the rest of her days attempting to achieve an equilibrium of sorts. The death-bed reconciliations which are occasionally described reveal the anguish and loneliness of such an existence. Loss of Jewish identity is usually the price that is paid. There are thousands of such case histories.

In a biographical sketch of a noted German-American, Carl Schurz, his wife who is nameless merits but a part of a sentence.[1] "He married in July 1852 and removed to America, living for a time in Philadelphia." As a case history of a "lost girl" Mrs. Schurz becomes an example of intermarriage at its most serene level, where interfaith clashes are absent, where peace is maintained by non-emphasis on the antecedents of the Jewish partner, where the Christian member of the family continues to maintain cordial and unbroken contact with his wife's family, even after the death of the mate. It also occurs where the marriage partner embraces Judaism, surpassing in piety and observance and loyalty those who were born to the faith. One thinks of Mrs. Martin Buber; of Mrs. Berthold Stokvis of Holland who not only became a devout Jewess but risked her life again and again to save Jewish children from annihilation at the murderous hands of Nazis; of a Mrs. Paul Immerwahr who accompanied her husband into exile, giving up fortune and security in Germany to be a hard-working doctor's wife in Downers Grove, Illinois, accepting poverty and privation with an inner radiance which inspired all who knew her. Such sacrifice must be acknowledged. Nevertheless a perpetual minority, its ranks forever depleted by Inquisitions, pogroms, economic and professional and residence restrictions, seduction and blandishment at the missionary level—that such a minority should be more decimated by the voluntary separation from its source of some of its members, and that their children should be unaware of those ancestors whose pluck and genius flows in their veins—that is a cause for deep and sincere and never-failing regret.

Back to the "lost girl." There is a conspiracy on the part of those who chronicled the life of that dynamic and vigorous liberal who fled authoritarian Germany because he joined the revolutionary movement, to omit or gloss over the antecedents of Mrs. Carl Schurz. Not so her husband, who cherished her all of her life. Carl Schurz was a man who had many talents, unfailing courage (he rescued a former professor from a German prison), and unlimited resourcefulness. An immigrant who lectured on "true Americanism," helped found the Republican Party, became a friend and strong partisan of Abraham Lincoln who rewarded Schurz by naming him minister to Spain in 1861—such a man has permanently carved a niche in American history. He fought in the Civil War, at Bull Run and Gettysburg and Chattanooga. He was elected Senator from Missouri, vigorously opposed President Grant, helped found the Liberal Republican Movement, became an owner and editor-in-chief of the New York *Evening Post* and an editorial contributor to Harper's *Weekly*, served as Secretary of the Interior under Hayes, made countless friends. It is an indelible record. His *Autobiography* is replete with references to his wife, all unfailingly tender and appreciative. Briefly we look at the record of this marriage through his eyes.

Carl Schurz met Margarethe Meyer in Hampstead, London. She was introduced to Carl as a "daughter of a well-to-do Jewish manufacturer of Hamburg." She had just completed her formal schooling and had come to England to visit her sister, who was married to an ex-priest who had fled Germany and was leading the impoverished life of other revolutionary emigrés. Carl Schurz and

Johannes Ronge were both irreconcilable revolutionaries. Mrs. Ronge was Margarethe's sister. Carl describes his first glimpse of Margarethe in his Autobiography:

"Now something happened that infused into my apparently gloomy situation a radiance of sunshine and opened to my life unlooked-for prospects." There is an exquisite photograph which bears out his description: "A girl about eighteen years entered, of fine stature, a curly head, something childlike in her beautiful features and large dark, truthful eyes. This was my introduction to my future wife."[2]

Margarethe Meyer apparently did not find the course of her love unimpeded by family objections. For "although she had always been sheltered and protected from annoyance, she did not lack courage, and she was sufficiently in love to be willing to disregard the wishes of her family."

Their first meeting took place in February of 1852. They were married in the Parish Church of Marylebone in London, July 6 of the same year. Young Mrs. Schurz was described by an acquaintance as "an imposing, elegant woman with large brown eyes and an open countenance." Happy she must have been, yet very lonesome too! Could her subsequent years of semi-invalidism have had something to do with her enforced separation from kinsmen? Shortly after they were married, they spent 28 days in crossing the Atlantic on their way to America. "With the buoyant hopefulness of young hearts, we saluted the new world," Carl recorded. In New York "my wife and I longed for the face of a friend." Carl's closest and most cherished friend in New York, an intimacy that was to continue as long as they both lived, was Dr. Abraham Jacobi. Like Carl Schurz, Abraham Jacobi had been a revolutionary in Germany and had been imprisoned. He emigrated to New York and became a pediatrician of eminence and renown. He invented the laryngoscope and pioneered in the establishing of pediatrics as a separate discipline which he taught in various medical schools in New York from 1860 to 1892. He is credited with having established the first free children's clinic. Jew and Christian became friends. Carl had an easy relationship with Jews which he never lost. He modestly attributes some of their most intimate family friendships to "the beauty, grace and ingenious conversation of my wife . . ."

Margarethe "never quite overcame her longing for her parents . . ."[3] Carl was understanding. They visited her parents' home near Kiel, with their children. He always maintained cordial relations with her brother and one of the most delightful surprises occurred when he took Margarethe's brother to the White House to lunch with President Lincoln. As in every life, pleasures and triumphs alternated with grief. "It was a period when Schurz was saddened by a succession of domestic calamities. His beloved Margarethe . . . died on March 12, 1876, from illness following the birth of her son, Herbert. Mrs. Schurz had been a semi-invalid from lung trouble for some years and had frequently taken the cure in sanitariums. She was, moreover, in her fourty-fourth year, and the strain of childbirth was too much for her exhausted physique."[4]

Eight days after Margarethe's death, Carl wrote to Henry Cabot Lodge, "The beauty of life is gone, but I may still make an effort to make myself useful." He turned more and more to "his intimate friend of long standing, Dr. Abraham Jacobi . . ." For Carl, Margarethe's death was a devastating blow. He wrote: "The loss of the wife of one's youth is unlike any other bereavement. It is the loss of the best part of one's life."

Many were the "lost girls," the anonymous ones, the forgotten ones. Each generation saw intermarriage increase and individuals melt away. Yet sometimes they

were dramatically catapulted into public notice. Such an
unwilling heroine was one whose tombstone does not
recall her married name. In the Jewish cemetery in Richmond, Virginia, is a simple slab which reads:

> Rebecca Davis
> Born October 30, 1840
> Died July 27, 1915

"The central character in an international drama is a
heroine whose biography is so brief and whose personality
is so shadowy that she is almost an anonymous figure."[5]

She was involved in an incident in American diplomatic
history known as the "Keiley incident." It was precipitated
by intermarriage. We know everything about the hero,
little about the heroine except that she was Jewish. Her
biography is one of almost total self-effacement. There
is no photograph; she leaves no letters. Of her husband
we know much. We have his photograph and there are
many references and historical data describing this handsome, accomplished hero. He was a well-known journalist
and the founder and editor of two newspapers, the Nor-
folk *Virginian* and the Petersburg *Index and News*. He
served in the Civil War. He entered politics and was
elected mayor of Richmond. He met and became a friend
of a number of Jews in the course of his many careers.
In the city of Petersburg where he founded one of his
newspapers, he met and married Rebecca, daughter of
George Davis.

President Cleveland appointed Keiley in 1885 as Minister Plenipotentiary to Austria-Hungary. The State Department sent the usual notification from Secretary Bayard bespeaking the usual courtesies. "The shocking reply
from Count Kalnoky rejected the appointment"—reads
the record—"as here, too, like in Rome, *prevail scruples
against this choice* . . . The position of a foreign envoy

wedded to a Jewess by civil marriage would be untenable and even impossible in Vienna." A Richmond historian recalls that Keiley had been previously appointed United States Minister to Italy and had been given a farewell banquet at Singer Hall, only to be notified that he was *persona non grata* to Italy and to King Victor Emmanuel. The reasons given—that Keiley had spoken at a meeting which had been held in Richmond at St. Peter's Cathedral "to protest against his occupying the domain of the Pope . . ."

When Secretary Bayard received the unexpected and shocking communication from Kalnoky, Anthony M. Keiley was already on the high seas (presumably with Rebecca) and was unaware of what was ahead. Secretary Bayard's reply makes one proud of the earlier tradition of the State Department. He wrote on May 18, 1885, that "It is not within the power of the President nor of the Congress, nor of any judicial tribunal of the United States, to take or even hear testimony, or in any mode to inquire into or decide upon the religious belief of any official, and the proposition to allow this to be done by any foreign Government is necessarily and *a fortiori* in-admissable.

"To suffer an infraction of this essential principle would lead to a disfranchisement of our citizens because of their religious belief . . . Religious liberty is the chief corner-stone of the American system of government, and pro-visions for its security are imbedded in the written charter and interwoven in the moral fabric of its laws . . ." In language dignified and forthright, consistent with Ameri-can tradition, he further amplified this doctrine that was inaugurated by the founders of this nation and cherished by succeeding generations of Americans.

The ensuing diplomatic double talk in which the Austrians engaged was unacceptable both to Bayard and President Cleveland. European papers got hold of the story. It became a *cause célèbre.*

Bayard, in impassioned prose that is vibrant and clear, continued to uphold his country's tradition. He stated in no uncertain terms that his nation was affronted and indignant: "It is a cause of astonishment that in an era of advanced civilization in which musty prejudice and illiberal discrimination among religious sects and races of mankind are giving such gratifying proofs of their rapid extinction, when throughout the wide world the death of the venerable and philanthropic Montefiore is so genuinely mourned, when the council of highest rank and most exclusive privilege of the British Empire is glad to enroll in its peerage a member of the noted house of Rothschild, that from so enlightened a government as that of Austria-Hungary should proceed the declaration that 'proximate Semitic descent' will be sufficient to proscribe individuals of admittedly blameless and virtuous personality from appearing at that court clothed in the representative character of a friendly power."[6]

Anthony M. Keiley was justifiably indignant. He returned to the United States, submitted his resignation to President Cleveland, refused all compensation both for his travel expenses and for the four months of waiting in Europe. Keiley considered the matter "a gross insult to the American people . . ." He went on ". . . in the official regard of Austria, Hebrew blood brands us with a leprosy . . ." President Cleveland, Secretary Bayard and Anthony M. Keiley saw eye to eye on this. For two years the United States had no minister in Austria. In 1886 President Cleveland appointed Keiley to the "International Court of First Instance" at Cairo, Egypt. He met with a fatal accident in Paris, January 24, 1905. His wife survived him by a decade.

"Anthony M. Keiley cast a long shadow. His wife was buried with her kin in Richmond. She is like a candle that once gave a light briefly, and then sputtered out . . ."[7]

In 1898, Mark Twain attended a lecture in Vienna. He heard Dr. Karl Lueger, Mayor of Vienna, talk about "the Jewish question." As he listened, Mark Twain decided that he must state his own views. So there in the city that had so callously rejected Rebecca and her husband, the seed was planted for his essay "Concerning the Jews." Who in his time could better speak for America than Samuel Langhorne Clemens?

7

Emma Lazarus stood at the apex. For if the broad base of the pyramid be represented by the anonymous women and the gradual ascent from anonymity be marked by narrowing as the pyramid rose in height, then there is no one among American Jewish women of the nineteenth century who has outdistanced her. Within her person she united a lyric gift, a responsive soul, a spiritual identification with her kinsmen of the past and of her lifetime, a deep and abiding faith in God and an undeviating loyalty to Judaism. Within her all-too-brief lifetime much had happened to Jews in America and the world over.

She was born in 1849, the year that Isaac Leeser founded the Hebrew Education Society. Her life ended in 1887 when the Jewish Theological Seminary of America was a year old. The year before her birth witnessed the historic assembly of women at Seneca Falls,

New York. The "Declaration of Sentiments" in which women voiced their just claims for recognition as individuals had been published. Emerson and other transcendentalists were needling the American conscience—also Thoreau, who had recently emerged from his self-imposed spiritual exile at Walden. Geographic frontiers were changing as the population spread ever westward. People were restless. It was a time of horizontal mobility and the emergence of regionalism. Jews like their neighbors differed from each other not only in point of their geographic origins from which their families had come in Europe, but also because of the peculiar flavor of their own congregations in various parts of the United States.

Emma Lazarus was a passionate pilgrim in a moment of history charged with drama. She was peculiarly destined, peculiarly endowed. She made a glowing contribution to the literary scene of her times. Yet she is remembered mostly for a fourteen-line poem etched in bronze at the foot of the Statue of Liberty. Here it is:

The New Colossus

Not like the brazen giant of Greek fame,
With conquering limbs astride from land to land;
Here at our sea-washed, sunset gates shall stand
A mighty woman with a torch, whose flame
Is the imprisoned lightning, and her name
Mother of Exiles. From her beacon-hand
Glows world-wide welcome; her mild eyes command
The air-bridged harbor that twin cities frame.

"Keep, ancient lands, your storied pomp!" cries she
With silent lips. "Give me your tired, your poor,
Your huddled masses yearning to breathe free,
The wretched refuse of your teeming shore.
Send these, the homeless, tempest-tost to me.
I lift my lamp beside the golden door!"

If this sonnet has become the theme song of millions of transplanted immigrants seeking refuge in a land of hope, then Emma's name is secure. Then she is an immortal and her fame is imperishable.

Emma Lazarus was named for the heroine of a novel by Jane Austen. Yet a more dissimilar biography one cannot imagine. Emma Woodhouse, "handsome, clever, and rich, with a comfortable home and happy disposition, seemed to unite some of the best blessings of existence . . . With very little to distress or vex her." Emma Lazarus was comely but thought herself exceedingly plain. She too was born into easy and comfortable surroundings. She lacked a happy disposition. She was frail and tired easily. She had everything in the world to vex and distress her because she bore upon her soul and person the stigmata which a sensitive Jewess responding to the sorrows of a persecuted people must perforce register.

Henrietta Szold wrote of Emma Lazarus that she needed a great theme "to make her a poet of the people . . . Such a theme was provided by the immigration of Russian Jews to America . . ." The greatest American Jewess of the twentieth century wrote about her counterpart of the nineteenth: "Doubtless she is the most distinguished literary figure produced by American Jewry, and possibly the most eminent poet among Jews since Heine and Judah Leib Gordon."

Hers was a strange life with many unresolved plot turns. Certainly many "blessings of existence" were vouchsafed her—and many more denied. She was an enigma to her contemporaries and so she remains to this day. Like other noted Jewish women she found no mate. Biographical legends of romance and apocryphal fairy tales abound. But her passion for personal privacy (like that of Jane Austen) prevailed. Freudian explanations, glib and facile, will not do in Emma's case. So a large portion of her life's story remains undisclosed. We do have some facts. We have her written words. We have a magnificent biographical sketch by her very gifted sister Josephine.

We also have an intimate pen portrait by Philip Cowen, founder and editor of the *American Hebrew*. He met many men and women of prominence. He considered Emma Lazarus as "pre-eminent." She stood "in the forefront of those Americans who endeavored to help the Russian Jew . . ." In the pages of the *American Hebrew* she found a forum where her prose and poetry could be heard. Her first poems were published there in 1882. Cowen calls her series of articles titled an Epistle to the Hebrews "her most fruitful work."[1] Emma was greatly influenced by Herzl's *Judenstaat*. That was "almost a generation before it was made the Zionists' creed . . ." writes Cowen. Her articles were later reprinted by the Zionist Organization.

On May 9, 1883, Emma Lazarus addressed a communication to the *American Hebrew* in which she told of having received a letter from Laurence Oliphant in Haifa describing the almost total destitution of some three to four hundred Jewish families who were being helped by the Christian Missionary Society there. Emma astutely pointed out that converted Jews "are probably not only the most expensive of all marketable commodities but also are most worthless after they are purchased . . ." She pleads that we "raise our own hands to rescue these wretched creatures . . ." Her interests had a wide range. Perhaps the greatest and most difficult triumph of her adult years was the zeal with which she studied Hebrew. Dr. Gustav Gottheil had found for her a gifted and inspired Hebrew teacher, Louis Schnabel. She worked hard at it. Her sense of victory and achievement may be noted

in a gay note to Cowen in which she submitted her first
translation from the Hebrew, "I have translated this from
the original Hebrew, and so am very proud of it as my
first effort." The poem was titled "Consolation." She apparently found many sources of consolation in her activities in behalf of her deprived coreligionists and in the
many other friends she made among those who shared
her interests. Her friends were of all faiths. In the *Cambridge History of American Literature* she is compared
with Julia Ward Howe, author of *The Battle Hymn of
the Republic,* as being "of equal intellectual rarity." We
read on:

> Nor was the regard wherein Emma Lazarus (1849-
> 87) was held by such men as Emerson, Gilder, Stedman,
> Channing, Eggleston, Dana, and Godkin due alone to
> those poems and essays which did more than the writ-
> ings of any other American author to instil among
> Christians a sympathy for that people for whom Emma
> Lazarus was so brave an exponent. Quite apart from
> her poems and articles on Jewish themes, there can
> be no question that, if one excepts Margaret Fuller,
> there was no woman among our authors more ardent
> than Emma Lazarus in her interminable search for
> aesthetic culture, no woman whose conversation . . .
> was more "deeply interesting and intensely instructive."[2]

Particularly singled out was an essay of hers considered
timely on "Russian Christianity versus American Judaism." "To this trio of noble women—Margaret Fuller,
Julia Ward Howe, Emma Lazarus" the editors added a
fourth, Harriet Beecher Stowe. It was a goodly company.

Small wonder that at the time of Emma's death John
Greenleaf Whittier wrote, "Since Miriam sang of deliverance and triumph by the Red Sea, the Semitic race
has had no braver singer . . ." Jews will mourn her, he

added, but so will "the sympathizing voice of Christian daughters." The lives she touched, the friends she made in her short lifetime in her ivory tower, continue to astonish those who turn to the record. A slender volume of her letters in the Columbia University Library is a feast for name-droppers.[3] In his Preface written in August, 1937, Professor Rusk notes that there is "a renascence of interest in this almost forgotten writer." These letters addressed to Emma show her many concerns, her eager need for intellectual companionship. She was "mentally famished" until she made these contacts through her work, wrote a friend who knew her well.[4] Her correspondents praised her, made suggestions to her about her work, criticized her. Yet throughout these letters there runs a constant thread of warm involvement with her work and her person. So Henry George could say to her: "The history of your people is so interesting to me, that I can well understand the enthusiasm that the study of their antiquities must arouse in you. But don't let it narrow your view . . ."[5]

Turgenev wrote that he had read one of her books "with the liveliest interest" and that he felt "very proud of the approbation you give to my works . . ." John Burroughs and Emma differed about Carlyle (who was no friend of the Jews). Wrote Burroughs "We differ so radically about him that we should probably never come together." Yet he could conclude another letter to his friend by saying "Yes, Whitman is Hebraic; so is Carlyle, so are all the more vital literary forces of our century, I think."[6]

Emma could feast at many Olympian tables. Perhaps her greatness lay in the fact that she chose to share the crumbs which fell to the lot of her impoverished coreligionists. Indeed the yellowed pages of the *American Hebrew* may be mined for many treasures which explain

Emma Lazarus. In a poem titled "The Choice" there is
a moment of passionate self-revelation:

> I saw in a dream the spirits unbegot . . .
> Two paths are offered . . .
> "Choose now for all the ages" . . .
>   Then I saw
> The unveiled spirit, grown divinely bright,
> Choose the grim path. He turned, I knew full well
> The pale, great martyr-forehead shadow-curled,
> The glowing eyes that had renounced the world,
> Disgraced, despised, immortal Israel.[7]

Emma's preoccupation with the past had long before
been noticed by Emerson. He urged a commitment and
involvement in the present: ". . . the sole advice I have
to offer is a pounding on the old string, namely, that
though you can throw yourself so heartily into the old
world of Memory, the high success must ever be to penetrate unto & and show the celestial element in the despised Present, & detect the deity that still challenges you
under all the gross & vulgar masks."[8] Now the present
moved in with all its crushing burden. When Grant became President of the United States in 1869 (the year
in which Emerson wrote the above letter) the news from
Rumania was devastatingly bleak. Jews had been expelled
from Russian Bessarabia. Simon Wolf called on his friend
in the White House urging that this country protest this
persecution. Fortunately, our State Department was headed
by a man of courage and idealism—Hamilton Fish. "The
people of this country universally abhor persecution,"
he wrote. President Grant appointed Benjamin Franklin
Peixotto, a former law clerk in the office of Stephen A.
Douglas and political editor of the Cleveland *Plain Dealer*
and one-time president of the Supreme Lodge of the
B'nai B'rith, to look after Jewish interests there. Peixotto

made significant strides in enlisting men of influence to curb the rampant savagery. But it was a virulent infection that spread.

It was partly due to Peixotto's insistence that three International Jewish Conferences were held in Europe. At the Congress of Berlin of 1878 the Jewish question was on the agenda. But barbarity and persecution took no holiday in Rumania and moral indignation alone was not enough to lesson present horror. The Secretary of State under President Hayes, Mr. W. M. Evarts, received a report from our legation in Vienna in 1878 stating that "It would be to the honor of the United States Government if it could initiate a plan by which at once the condition of American Hebrews resident or travelling in Roumania, and the conditions of natives of the same race, would be ameliorated and their equality before the law at least partially assured."

Now followed Russian pogroms of April and May, 1881. Anti-Semitic decrees compounded the felonies. What was there left for the survivors but to take to the road again? There followed an exodus from Russia in which refugees from persecution, some 62,000 during the years 1881-1884, stripped of possessions, ragged and tattered, poured in a steady stream into American ports.[9] It was then that Emma Lazarus, long under the spell of George Eliot, whose *Daniel Deronda* had fired her imagination, urged that as a practical solution of their overwhelming burdens and sorrows, Jews be helped to go to Palestine. In the United States she foresaw either new ghettos or apostasy. In Palestine, rebuilding and renewal. For she saw no middle way between ethnic isolation or assimilation. She made powerful enemies as well as ardent disciples. She was accused of "illusive hopes," "mistaken zeal." She was "an ardent champion of the eleventh hour," at a time when Rabbi Isaac M. Wise urged the Jews not to disturb "the rubbish of 2,000 years in Palestine."[10]

The immigrant tide to America swelled. Destitute they were and under-nourished and frightened and unwashed. They aroused sympathy or contempt. The urban areas they took over, crowded and unsanitary, caused editorials to be written in which the conditions in which the immigrants were wallowing obscured the human beings who suffered them. The averted eye and nostril was the rule. The moving miracle of the reaction of a gently bred young American woman, accustomed to luxury and surrounded by friends of all faiths and conditions whose names were among the elite of this nation—that such a young woman should see and feel the verities, should espouse their cause, should dream of a regeneration of these victims and of all Israel—that stands out as a blazing and imperishable fact. Hers was a lonely voice triumphantly vindicated by later events. She belonged to those of prophetic vision who could look far ahead. Such a gift was also vouchsafed to Sir William Osler, who wrote in a letter dated May 1, 1884, of a time when a new Moses would arise and preach a Semitic exodus from Germany. Had not Disraeli written: "A race that persists in celebrating their vintage, although they have no fruits to gather, will regain their vineyards." An American poet, Joaquin Miller, sang his "Songs of the Hebrew Children," and the beloved Mark Twain wrote an imperishable prose poem titled "Concerning the Jews," and Julia Ward Howe repeatedly cried out her wrath. Eloquent voices all—but the most stirring call came from the indomitable Emma Lazarus.

Her sister could write of "a life so hidden and a personality so withdrawn as that of Emma Lazarus." The record she left is one of passionate involvement. "Of dramatic episode or climax in her life there is none; outwardly all was placid and serene," her sibling could write.

Yet there was drama in her household situation, ideological conflict among the sisters, a deep and absorbing loyalty and identification with her father.[11]

On February 27, 1885, John Burroughs wrote to Emma: "I am very sorry to hear that you was under the shadow of such care & anxiety about your father . . . The thought of losing ones parents makes the heart cower & tremble as before an awful abyss . . . I have seen this dreadful calamity approaching me like an eclipse . . ."[12] Nearly a month later he wrote: ". . . I am not going to invade your sacred sorrow with any expression of condolence . . . What you tell me of your father & your relation to him, is very beautiful: it realizes ones ideal of what such a relation should be . . . I hope your health keeps good, & that you have some congenial work in which you can absorb yourself. There is no gift to mortals like a congenial task."[13]

Reticent as is the biographical sketch which her sister Josephine wrote about Emma, that and the loving evocation of her by Philip Cowen, editor of the *American Hebrew,* remain as the most revealing portraits of this almost shadowy figure whose truncated life has not to this day been adequately assessed. She was one of seven children. There was a brother, Eliezer Frank. There were three older sisters, Sara, Mary, and Josephine, and after Emma came Agnes and Annie. That there were deep subterranean currents of conflict in her home we can surmise. She was her father's favorite and completely returned his love. They had pride in each other. Her mother remains in the shadows, a stranger to posterity.

H. E. Jacob, in his biography of Emma Lazarus, refers to Emma's mother as Hettie. Henrietta Szold who was a scholar with a passion for accuracy refers to her as Esther Nathan Lazarus, a member of an honorable and well-known family, which made signal contributions to American Jewish life.[14] In her teens Emma showed her great poetic gift by translating poems of Victor Hugo, Schiller, and Heinrich Heine. William Cullen Bryant praised her Civil War poems. And then she met Ralph Waldo Emerson! There flowered in Emma's soul a harvest of gratitude for his benign guidance and warm friendship. He opened many doors to her, to ideas, to people. He gave her confidence in herself and in her claims on other writers. His recognition brought her untold joy. His omission of her work in an anthology of his brought her deep personal anguish. Yet she needed Emerson. Who can estimate his influence on Emma's thought and life?

Soon recognition came from many quarters. Emma was a celebrity. She was writing. She was translating. She was recognized and acknowledged from her teens. Still it was not enough. Writes Henrietta Szold: "What was needed to make her a poet of the people as well as of the literary guild was a great theme, the establishment of instant communication between some stirring reality and her still hidden and irresolute subjectivity." This came with the devastating news from Russia. "Hitherto her life had held no Jewish inspiration." For although affiliated with the Spanish and Portuguese Synagogue Shearith Israel, "her family had hitherto not participated in the activities of the Synagogue or of the Jewish Community." This estrangement from Jewish contacts left indelible traces on the lives of her two youngest sisters. Philip Cowen writes: "A sister, Annie Humphreys Johnston, living in Rome . . . has refused, in response to a suggestion to reprint her 'Collected Poems' to grant permission to include any items of a Jewish character, she being an ardent Catholic."

With her sister Josephine, Emma had a close rapport which survived her death. Josephine, who in herself is worthy of further study, had a facile pen. Her biographical sketch of Emma which appeared in *The Century Magazine* is a restrained and tender study of a beloved sister. Later she wrote on two other women who were luminaries of their day, Louisa May Alcott and Margaret Fuller. Her collected essays on Jewish subjects appeared in a book titled *The Spirit of Judaism*. She urged a greater self-knowledge for Jews; greater contact with Christian neighbors to advance mutual esteem; a larger and more liberal understanding of Jews and Judaism. She identified herself with the Zionist cause and wrote several pro-Zionist articles. Fascinated by the personality of Madame Dreyfus, as anyone must be who has read her tender and valiant letters to her husband, Josephine wrote a book titled *Madame Dreyfus*. In many ways her understanding of Emma's nature and goals, dreams and yearning, came closest to her famous sister.

When the first break in the family circle occurred with the death of their mother, writes Josephine, without giving us the date of that event, but marking its aftermath by a visit to the Emerson home in August of 1876, Emma kept a record or a journal with "every event and incident" noted. Here is not only a detailed picture of the Emersons at home but a description of Concord, and of the Emerson circle. Here she met Bronson Alcott and William Ellery Channing, who "took a liking to me," records Emma. She goes on: "The bond of our sympathy was my admiration for Thoreau, whose memory he actually worships . . ." And when she came home Emma again turned to Heine. For Heine was a man who spoke directly to her. "Charmed by the magic of his verse, the iridescent play of his fancy, and the sudden cry of the heart piercing through it all, she is as yet unaware or only vaguely conscious of the real bond between them: the sympathy in the blood, the deep, tragic, Judaic passion of eighteen

hundred years that was smouldering in her own heart
was soon to break out and change the whole current of
her thought and feeling."[15]

Like a delicate instrument attuned to record distant
earthquakes, Emma reacted to distant atrocities to which
her fellow Jews were subjected. Like many Jews generations later, who in the comfort and ease of democratic
nations had forgotten that in many parts of the world to
be Jewish was to be forever insecure, and who were seared
by the bestial excesses of the Nazis, who learned that
rescue would apply to thousands and death and annihilation to six million—Emma was to be wrung and emotionally depleted, tortured and sapped by events "in the
distant province of Russia . . . then on the banks of the
Volga, and finally in Moscow itself . . . And not alone in
despotic Russia, but in Germany, the seat of modern
philosophic thought and culture, the rage of Anti-Semitism broke out and spread with fatal ease and potency."[16]
Americans were stunned and unbelieving. Christians as
well as Jews. In January of 1881 the *London Times* published from eyewitness accounts and official sources and
documents the blood-curdling arithmetic of the Russian
pogroms. At an indignation meeting held in New York's
Chickering Hall on February 4, Mr. Evarts spoke for
"civilized Christendom": "It is not that it is the oppression of Jews by Russia," he said, "it is that it is the
oppression of men and women, and we are men and
women."

In Emma's heart "slumbering and unguessed echoes"
were aroused. There was no turning back. Her frail self,
her sheltered and protected inner being was pierced. This
was to be her major preoccupation until early death came.
Her identification with Jews was complete. Many were
"the literary fruits" of this hour of truth. Contact with
Russian Jewish refugees led her to the Bible, to Jewish

history, to the study of Hebrew. Her sister writes: "All this time she had been seeking heroic ideals in alien stock, soulless and far removed . . . Hitherto Judaism had been a dead letter to her . . ." It was a dead letter no longer. In "The Banner of the Jew" she rose to new heights. She was a prophet exhorting her people in language as majestic, as exalted, as ever the Prophets uttered:

> Wake, Israel, wake! Recall today
> The glorious Maccabean rage . . .
> Oh, deem not dead that martial fire,
> Say not the mystic flame is spent!
> With Moses' law and David's lyre,
> Your ancient strength remains unbent.
> Let but an Ezra rise anew,
> To lift the *Banner of the Jew!*
> A rag, a mock at first—erelong,
> When men have bled and women wept,
> To guard its precious folds from wrong,
> Even they who shrank, even they who slept,
> Shall leap to bless it and to save,
> Strike! For the brave revere the brave!

Emma from now on neither "shrank nor slept."

Like other seekers after a solution, like a few who came before and many who came after her, Emma Lazarus found the answer to persecution, to martyrdom, to degradation, to humiliation, to exile. Her answer: "a restored and independent nationality and repatriation in Palestine." In February, 1883, she wrote in *The Century,* quoting from George Eliot's *Daniel Deronda* who is determined "on restoring a political existence to my people . . ." And Emma's comment: "I am fully persuaded that all suggested solutions other than this are but temporary palliatives . . ."

This was her handwriting upon the wall of history. Israel's existence today is in part the fulfillment of her

dream and of her prophetic vision. And so the anonymous
Jewish woman, the dim shadow whose name is all but
lost in early American annals has at last in the person of
Emma Lazarus found an articulate and moving heroine
whose voice reverberates through the corridors of time.

For the Jewish woman life has always been twofold.
First it reflected as in a pool the conditions of life about
her. Its hazards and discomforts, its pleasures and in-
dulgences. She is in the mainstream of all the social and
political currents, of war and peace, of hardship and
abundance. Yet she also leads an insular existence. For
each Jewish home in the wilderness or lonely trading
post or mushrooming township was an island complete
unto itself. It was a life within a life.

Much of what we know about life of pioneers, pilgrims,
hawkers and walkers, entrepeneurs, real estate operators,
sutlers and speculators, merchants and farmers, teachers
and civil servants comes to us from the general pool of
knowledge. Always the Jewish historical narrative must
unfold against the backdrop of the larger events of the
times. Once that is established we turn to the minute
books of congregations, to the business records and household inventories, to the diaries and letters, to the journals
meant for only one pair of eyes. Finally we open the
printed pages of books and magazines and leaflets which
have been recently discovered, edited and made available
to the historian. To find the main thread of our narrative,
to bring a sense of order into the tumbling stream of
facts, to isolate the peculiarly Jewish experience and to
focus on the Jewish saga in America, we ask ourselves
three questions: What had they sought? What had they
brought? What had they wrought?

The answer to the first question is short. Jews sought
sanctuary. They looked for escape from pogroms, from

the Inquisition, from Edicts of Expulsion, from enforced baptism, from false accusation, from mobs on wild blood-thirsty rampage, from proscriptive laws and pales of settlement and ghetto living and unbearable tax burdens and deprivation of rights to pursue farming and crafts and trades. They wanted security of life and limb. They wanted personal dignity. They wanted freedom to commune with God according to their ancient practice, to cherish their folkways and mores and to maintain their kinship with their ancestors and patriarchs, holding them dear, acknowledging their teachings as sacred. They wanted to build homes and synagogues. They wanted to serve as soldiers and watchmen, they wanted to acknowledge with love and loyalty the government that gave them shelter, to be sharing citizens of the land they inherited.

What had they brought? They brought a tradition steeped in moral grandeur. They brought a love of the Bible and of their sacred commentaries. They brought the Ten Commandments. They brought an allegiance to their Maker that had withstood centuries of persecution. They brought the dreams that they had nurtured in a thousand crypts and the hopes they had intoned at countless cradles. They brought folk tales and anecdotes and humor and a love of an ancient land that had once been the birthplace of grandeur and that had faded and withered in their absence. But would some day be green again.

What had they wrought? That is our story. It is a tale of adaptation and acculturation and of many loyalties. To God and country and neighbor. To the past and to the demanding present and to the dim and distant and unrealized future. It is a tale of sharing the gifts of others, their freedom and privileges. Of offering freely the gifts of self-discovery and the experience and the knowledge so dearly bought. It is a process of learning and teaching. Of helping build a nation where many cultures can flourish and the individual is free to explore the vast outer universe and the inner caverns of his own being.

The events of history encompass every one. It is only in the individual reaction to the challenge of these events that differences are found. Men and women crossed the Atlantic, spilled over the seacoast, penetrated the hinterland, established homes and congregations, scrabbled to earn their daily bread, met their immediate needs and cared for the stranger and the needy. Their lives were at times totally unrecorded. At other times etched into the fabric of history. It is these lives we would re-create. We let the articulate ones speak for the silent.

The letters left by our protagonists range from highly literate and perceptive comments on life and politics and communal conditions to poorly spelled and totally trivial complaints about life and family connections, myopic scrawls reflecting only the troubled soul who penned them; ". . . go ware i will i meat with troubel," wrote Hette Hays. Yet Fanny Sheftall, whose husband, Mordecai, was listed by the British in Georgia as "Chairman of the Rebel Parochial Committee," was able to look out with energy for the interests of their family while her husband and her son were imprisoned by the British and to write vivid letters to them. Another Georgia family, the Minis family, was known not only for its sons in the Georgia Line, but for its women who were "great whigs." Mrs. Minis brought food to the Sheftalls when they were captured. After the British seized Savannah, Mrs. Minis and her daughter were first ordered to keep to the house and then banished from the town.

Not all Jews were patriots. Rebecca Franks was the daughter of David Franks whose career was checkered and eventful, including a period when he was "conveyed to the new gaol" for his Tory sympathies and who could not travel without a manservant for himself and two servants for his daughter. Rebecca continued her rounds of parties, flirtations, balls, appointments with hairdressers at a time when hardship stalked her land. A time of contrasts. Philadelphia, so near Valley Forge, presents a glittering picture of carefree and thoughtless social trivia. Nearby, men had reached the depths of misery and privation.

"You can have no idea the life of continued amusement I live in," wrote Rebecca Franks in 1778. "I can scarce have a moment to myself . . . I spent Tuesday at Sir Wm. Howe's where we had a concert and Dance . . . I've been but 3 evenings alone since we mov'd to town. I begin now to be almost tired . . ." Exiled with her father to New York, she took up residence in Flatbush. She wrote a bitter and disillusioned letter in 1781 bemoaning the lack of elegance and the few opportunities for the kind of gayety she had known in Philadelphia. She found New York women dull, unable to carry on an intelligent conversation, limited to cards for entertainment, "Here . . . in New York . . . all's dead calm 'till the cards are introduced, when you see pleasure dancing in the eyes of all matrons and they seem to gain new life." So she whiled away the tedium until she married Sir Henry Johnson of the British Army. Rebecca became another "lost girl." Rebecca and her husband moved to England and took up their residence in Bath. Jane Austen's novels best describe the stately procession of empty days and inane nights of such people endowed only with conspicuous leisure and total detachment from real involvement with life.

But it was involvement and not detachment that characterized the majority of American women in the days of the Revolution and in the critical decades that followed. Women formed clubs to speed up production of supplies, wore drab homespun garments, shared privation and hardships, took over farm tasks for absent men. One British writer in South Carolina complained that "the females seem to bid us defiance."[17] A British officer stated that if the men were all destroyed "we should have enough to do to conquer the women."

The threshhold of the nineteenth century found Americans reveling in the new climate of freedom, "exalting their rights, and undermining special privileges."[18] Washington bade farewell to his countrymen. John Adams was elected President and Thomas Jefferson Vice-President. Relations with France became strained. Between 1798 and 1800 the two countries were in a state of undeclared war. European refugees were eyed with suspicion. Alien and Sedition Acts appeared on our statute books, introducing an atmosphere of suspicion and hostility and the new nation was sharply divided ideologically. Republicans especially in Kentucky and Virginia attacked these Acts as both despotic and unconstitutional. In the last days of the eighteenth century, December 14, 1799, George Washington died at Mt. Vernon. An era had ended.

Jewish women busy with household tasks and synagogue activities were too small in number and too lacking in special spheres of influence to be noticed except as they made friends through their neighbors and through their relatives by marriage, Jewish and non-Jewish. Occasional glimpses come to us from the letters and diaries of Christians of the special events and the peculiar ceremonies which they observed among the Jews. No less a person than Dr. Benjamin Rush is our chronicler for a description of an eighteenth-century Jewish wedding which took place in Philadelphia in June of 1787.[19] Dr. Benjamin Rush, Philadelphia patriot and physician had as his patient, Mrs. Jonas Phillip. When Mr. and Mrs. Jonas Phillip extended to the doctor an invitation to be present at the wedding of their daughter Rachel to Michael Levy of Virginia, he accepted with alacrity. Dr. Rush wrote

his wife on June 27, 1787: ". . . As soon as this canopy
was fixed, the bride accompanied with her mother, sister,
and a long train of female relations, came downstairs.
Her face was covered with a veil . . . She was handsome
at all times, but the occasion and her dress rendered her
in a peculiar manner a most lovely and affecting object.
I gazed with delight upon her. Innocence, modesty, fear,
respect and devotion appeared all at once in her countenance . . ." There followed a detailed description of
the traditional prayers in Hebrew, the partaking of the
wine and the breaking of the glass "designed to teach
them the brittleness and uncertainty of human life . . ."

Dr. Rush then had to attend professionally the bride's
mother who had fainted under the impact of the celebration and who, on recovering, ". . . as the Doctor left,
pressed upon him a piece of cake for Mrs. Rush, an old
New York friend of the bride's mother, the former Rebecca Machado." On a later occasion, the good doctor attended and described a circumcision ceremony. "There
were above 30 persons, all Jews except myself . . ."[20]

Of such bits and pieces is our tapestry woven.

In *Memoirs of American Jews* edited by Dr. Marcus
one may find many poignant fragments in which the
vicissitudes of life, romantic and personal, are interwoven
with biographies of early pioneers. One immigrant from
Westphalia to London, and then to America, ran afoul
of an amorous widow, a Mrs. Moses (who might have
come straight from the pages of *Pickwick Papers*), "whose
overweening affection for him caused him to relinquish
his situation, where he had been foreman and factotum.
His poor mistress . . . in despair followed him to Ports-
mouth (where he was detained by contrary winds) in the
vain hope of persuading him to return and relinquish his
project of embarking for America." He was a resolute
young man and emigrated to America and became a clerk

in the office of the Gratz Brothers.[21] Another episode describes the state of mind of "mothers with marriageable daughters, the sisters with marriageable sisters . . ." Matchmakers on the prowl. The letters of Rebecca Gratz are filled with many vicarious romantic items as came her way and they concerned both Jewish and non-Jewish acquaintances. She writes to her brother Ben: "There are no new engagements spoken of in the beau monde . . . This is a long idle talk to send so far but, My dear Ben, you must excuse its stupidity, as my object is to keep up the interest of Philadelphia trifles in your recollection."[22]

Whatever their circumstances, whatever their condition in life, whatever their geographic location, women have left traces of their daily concerns, their dreams and ambitions, their goals, their plots and counterplots and involvements, in letters, in autobiographical fragments, in diaries. There is infinite variety here. There is also much repetition.

A fragment dealing with life on a Virginia farm throws some light on an early Jewish schoolmaster, Jacob Mordecai, and some of his female descendants. The furnishings of another age and time are here from trundle beds to children's toys to cherry orchards to long hours spent at practicing the piano. The diary of a South Carolinian deals in depth with the relationship of mothers and sons and the guilt feelings felt by the younger generation at the inability to fulfill the demands of the older. "Mother writes me of the misery that Raphael has brought on his mother by . . . keeping his store open on Saturdays. Now, this I would not have done . . ." writes Joseph Lyons.[23]

The Anglo-Jewish periodicals of this period may also be profitably mined for the narrative of the Jewish women of their time. They mirror the strange and unfamiliar as well as the usual problems. The advertisements testify to the prevalence of many ailments real or imaginary and the perennial search for cures. Pills and pill boxes are popular items. Elixirs, ointments, hair restorers, salves vie with each other in making extravagant promises to restore, renew, revive. All-Healing Ointment. March's Superior Pain Reliever. Hutching's Dyspepsia Bitters. Bush's Celebrated Renovating Aromatic Cordial. Cures for hypochondriacs! Watches and life insurance, fur coats and musical instruments, furniture and imported laces are offered for sale. So are courses in musical instruction and foreign languages. Boarding and day schools vie for pupils. The Misses Palache conducted from 1841 a "Boarding and Day School for Young Ladies of the JEWISH FAITH." English, French and German teachers were on the faculty of the Reverend Dr. Max Lilienthal's "Hebrew Commercial and Classical Boarding School." A variety of subjects was included for children. Unending supplies of medicinal aids for ailing adults. A Dr. Tobias claims a record of 10,000 cures for his Venetian Ointment. "A Balsam so curative that it has Death and Doctors Baffled" is not to be ignored. And if all else fails, phrenologists are available to read and analyze cranial bumps and give patients a deeper understanding of their potential talents.

Eloquent of medical and other problems is a letter written by Rebecca Gratz from Philadelphia to Mrs. Ogden Hoffman of New York, in 1817.[24] Rebecca describes the illness of a visitor, John Myers, who came to them "with the remains of a fever on him, which so affected his nerves as to alarm us . . . Dr. Chapman attended him and recommended his going home, and if the symptoms did not soon disappear to put himself under a course of Mercury . . ." She next discusses intermarriage, a subject brought up in a novel they had both read, and Rebecca sums up her point of view with these words: "I believe it is impossible to reconcile a matrimonial engagement between persons of so different a creed, without requiring one or the other to yield . . . I have known many Jews marry Christian women, whose wives have become strict conformists to the rites of our religion—and Jewesses married to Christians who have entered the church, as in the instance of my Aunt Schuyler . . . but the parties lived very unhappily . . ."[25]

How much therapy the women of the early nineteenth century lacked in terms of what is available to them now may be seen from a few of the following facts. The first ovariotomy performed anywhere in the world was performed in Danville, Kentucky, in 1809. Three years later the great and brilliant Dr. Benjamin Rush wrote a book on the *Diseases of the Mind,* a pioneer study of mental healing, "foreshadowing modern psychoanalysis." The dedicated humanitarian Dorothea L. Dix pricked the conscience of her day by urging better care for the insane, and in Pennsylvania and Massachusetts and New York in 1817 and 1818 asylums were opened.[26] Oliver Wendell Holmes wrote a paper on contagiousness of "puerperal fever" which menaced the lives of many women.

Medical education was stimulated by the opening of 27 new medical schools in the United States during the years 1810-1840. But still it was to many European trained physicians that the practice of medicine owed much in the early period. Pediatrics, a science so dear to mothers, was introduced in the United States by Abraham Jacobi, whose career and friendship with the Carl Schurz family has already been described. In a thirty-year period, a pharmocopoeia and a textbook on pathology were published; chloroform and other forms of anesthesia were first used, and a woman got her M.D. degree (Elizabeth Blackwell) ; the first Women's Medical College was established in 1850, and five years later the first Women's Hospital. These were giant steps of progress. But how sad to reflect that many died for want of the simplest medicines and most elementary therapeutic measures. "Women had been doctors and surgeons since the dawn of human history," wrote Charles and Mary Beard, "but licenses were now being required for the practice of the healing arts."[27] There were acute shortages of medical personnel and medicines.

The resounding phrases about liberty and freedom which we now cherish were evolved in an atmosphere of both free and bound labor. That there were some indentured servants among Jews is an historical fact. That much still remains to be unearthed is also true. There were "indigent wretches" among some early Jewish immigrants who "beg their passage, and are set on shore without sixpence in their pockets," reads one contemporary source.[28] In addition to indentured servants, there were spinsters sheltered beneath many a roof who were little more than household drudges. There were youngsters who served as apprentices in order to learn a trade. There were labor combinations before there was organized trade unionism. First of all there were groups of master workers whose purpose was to perpetuate monopoly. Then there were "Combinations of white servants to redress grievances by strikes or insurrections."[29] Fishermen struck off the coast of Maine in 1636. Carpenters struck in Georgia in 1746 and tailors in New York in 1768; printers in Philadelphia in 1786. A tradition of labor protest and redress was being established.

Among the various combinations of skilled laborers there were none in early history involving women except as there were groups which advocated the amelioration of debtor laws and we know that there were women debtors. There are documents testifying to the insolvency of many a widow and orphan.

In 1840 Rebecca Gratz could write with deep compas-

sion of the vicissitudes of Queen Mariamne—"you know
the history of Herod's wife is tragical enough to make the
truth more romantic than any fiction"—yet a most careful
reading of Rebecca's writings fails to show her equal
concern for the female slave or the indentured servant
whom she saw every day. She seemed immune, as many of
her contemporaries were not (the Grimké sisters, Ernestine Rose), to some of the sorrows on her doorstep. Still
her letters are full of the daily effort to help orphans,
deprived children, abandoned wives, those who suffered
a sudden reversal in fortune. Corruption she deplores and
crime and acts of arson and "all sorts of wicked things—
this city of 'brotherly love' has become a den of thieves—
there have been prison insurrections . . . citizens patrol
the streets from early in the evening till sunrise, but have
not yet succeeded in detecting the gang . . ."[30] In the next
paragraph she singles out David Seixas as having "distinguished himself among the benefactors of mankind."
He had established a school for "indigent Deaf & Dumb
children."

Unnoticed by Rebecca was the first recorded strike of
women workers. Female weavers of Pawtucket, Rhode
Island, struck in 1824. And four years later in the city
Rebecca knew and loved and lived in, the first United
States Workers' Party was organized in May of 1828, to
be followed by branches in New York and Boston. Frances
Wright who was a "pioneer agitator in U.S. for women's
rights"[31] counted Ernestine Rose as a valiant associate.
Ernestine seems to have had few if any Jewish followers.
Women's rights always lagged behind those of men. By
the outbreak of the Civil War, the ten-hour law which
was fairly standard among skilled male workers did not
extend to the women who worked in the mills of Salem
and Lowell.

Ernestine Rose, described to her audiences as "a child

of Israel"—"a daughter of the downtrodden and persecuted Jews," invariably championed the cause of working women. Speaking in Syracuse, New York, in the fall of 1852, she said: "woman is a slave from the cradle to the grave. Father, guardian, husband—master still. One conveys her like a piece of property, over to the other . . . In claiming our rights, we claim the rights of humanity . . ." From her first days in America Ernestine tried to secure a Married Woman's Property Act. Her first petition was signed by five petitioners. She continued her efforts "with increased number of signatures" until 1848 when it was enacted into law by the New York State Legislature.[32]

Jewish women may have been somewhat timid about following avowed rebels. But Jewish women's societies dedicated to "causes" proliferated. Scholars list many such organizations prior to 1875. These ranged from synagogue auxiliaries, such as the Ladies' Army Relief Society of Shearith Israel and the Ladies' Relief Association of Shaaray Tefila of New York, to the Jewish Ladies Penny Society and several Ladies' Hebrew Benevolent Societies. Individual Jewesses belonged to a number of nonsectarian civic enterprises and general philanthropic clubs as well as to music and library circles. But as agitators they did not contribute significant leaders until after the mass migrations of the 1880's. Ernestine Rose always excepted.

A very interesting summary of the conditions and accomplishments of "Jews in 1860" appeared in the *New York Journal of Commerce,* on October 17, 1860.[33] It noted the ushering in of the Jewish year 5621. Errors and clichés abound. Beethoven is listed as a Jew. The Shylock canard is aired. The writer claims for New York some forty thousand Jews "of whom the majority are rather indigent." "They are largely unlettered," and "the minds of such students may be cultivated, but they are not enlightened." Attention is called to the seventeen synagogues then extant in New York and to a hospital which is generously supported. Jewish festivals are mentioned. "What a world of emotion the celebration of these revered ceremonies must excite! . . . Is it after all very wonderful that men who can trace their lineage to such an origin, should cling with tenacious vigor to their rites and refuse to blend with others of the race? Is it strange that they wish to preserve pure in their veins, the blood of Moses, of David, of Solomon and the Prophets?"

Though largely absent from the militant ranks of feminists, Jewish women did not live in intellectual vacuums. They read. They attended lectures and the theatre. They met and entertained celebrities in their homes. On December 27, 1834, we find a charming letter from Rebecca Gratz describing a visit which Harriet Martineau (1802-1876), brilliant English author, had paid to her native city. She had spent about a month in Philadelphia where she was "entertained at 'great mens' tables'—gone the round of fashionable routs—received the suffrage of philosophers & poets—been admitted to all public institutions—from the academy of science to the grim penitentiary— . . . quite unassuming & willing to talk of her own works with candour and in all respects such a woman as one rarely meets, and cannot fail to admire . . ." Rebecca adds that she hopes that Miss Martineau will not write critically about America, which is exactly what she did. For Harriet Martineau gave wholehearted allegiance to the Abolition party and her *Society in America* published in 1837 "gave great offense."[34] Three years before publication of this work Rebecca had written: "you may imagine how much gratified I was to find their author so accessible and warm hearted—if she turns upon us the point of a 'satiric pen' when she leaves the country I shall never again trust to my judgment in descrying the reality of candour from its courtly counterfeit." Here Rebecca was obviously recalling another visitor to America, Mrs. Frances Trollope, whose *Domestic Manners of the Americans,* published in 1832, hurt Americans to the raw. Soon Charles Dickens was to join that great fraternity of critics after he had been lionized and adored in every corner of the land. Rebecca is appalled that there are some Christians who avoided Miss Martineau because she is a Unitarian. This permits her to add a bit of her own religious philosophy: ". . . all who lift their souls on high in Adoration—may walk the earth in charity with one another . . ." Jews excluded in many parts of the world from legal rights which others took for granted must recall gratefully that Harriet Martineau was pleased and stated it on her return from her American visit, that the Jews of the United States enjoyed a superior status as compared to their kinsmen in England and elsewhere. She wrote in 1834: "The disgrace of the exclusion of the Jews is so deep that, as soon as their lordships in the Upper House become fully conscious of it, they will be in a prodigious hurry to get rid of it." Welcome as are these contemporary glimpses, they are still too scarce. Much remains to be discovered about early conditions in mills and factories, in shops and stores where Jews were employed. Notices in Anglo-Jewish papers advertising for help are available but fourteen-year-old boys and girls did not keep diaries or write letters, and the memoirs that survive are those that were recalled in ease and tranquility, mellowed by age, with the poignant experiences erased by time and pride.

In the decade before the Civil War, many seamstresses were employed in their homes and numerous jobs were farmed out to women by subcontractors. Usually these home factories were staffed by immigrants in areas of first settlement. Conditions under which these women worked, took care of their children and their aged and sick, beggar description. Here and there protests erupted. In Roches-

ter, New York, following a two-year agricultural recession
with many crop failures, the approximately two thousand
workers employed by the clothing industry were very hard
hit. The Jews in the community formed the Hebrew
Benevolent Society to cope with the desperate economic
conditions and acute hardship among recent arrivals. "The
economic unrest was the cause of a series of strikes not
only in Rochester but across the country . . . While
strikes were successful elsewhere, most Rochester stop-
pages failed."[35] Conditions continued to deteriorate until
the panic of 1857. In Rochester attempts were made to
stimulate new industries. "Actually it was the clothing
industry which infused vitality into the economic scene
and almost singlehandedly saved the situation."[36] Dr.
Rosenberg quotes from an early source: "The sewing
machine is already doing more than the water power can
do hereafter."

Surveying the American scene more than a century
later one is struck by the impression that these waves of
immigrants crossed the Atlantic like schools of fish, each
breed separate from the other. Mortality rates on the
Atlantic crossing played no favorites. Ships were terribly
overcrowded, conditions deplorable, leading to Federal
laws in 1819, 1847, 1848, and 1855 aimed at protecting
immigrants from noxious conditions. These laws were
impotent. Immigrants were undeterred by the hazards.
During the years 1827 to 1838, the causes for migration
were listed as follows:[37] (1) cold winter 1829-1830; (2)
restrictive legislation against German Jews; (3) economic
and political distress in Ireland.

By 1848, "Jewish emigration from Bohemia had ceased
to be merely the concern of scattered individuals motivated by personal reasons."[38] Many of these immigrants
were drawn from the laboring classes. "Labor disturb-
ances" in Europe were usually attributed to Jewish work-

ers. That "Jewry and the pressure it exercised upon the
working class were alone and solely responsible" was only
one of the many oversimplifications one may find for the
unrest and flight of Jewish workers to America.[39] These
migrations were unprecedented in numbers. The high
peak of immigration reached in 1851 was 221,253. The
overall number reached in the post-Civil War period was
in 1883, when the number rose to 81,486.[40]

In that historic year, the *American Hebrew* noted the
crisis brought on by the vast numbers of immigrant Jews
in New York and other cities. In the general press, also,
this inundation is given considerable coverage. They
came singly or in family groups. They were rejected or
accepted, pitied or scoffed at, gaped at, deplored, resented,
exploited. Prosperous Jews resented them—and yet helped
—after a fashion.

Women too had "arrived." They were being noticed
and described. Reporters, travelers and others were taking
note of the Jewish woman in America. The native-born,
the foreign-born, were in the news.

A Jewish traveler from Europe, I. J. Benjamin, wrote
a two-volume book, *Three Years in America, 1859-1862,*
which contains some very astute, if somewhat one-sided
observations on the American Jewess. Notable is the chapter "About the Upbringing of Jewish Women in America."[41] It bears comparison with conditions in the twentieth century.

Israel ben Joseph Benjamin (1818-1864) was a native
of Rumania who in tribute to Benjamin of Tudela, noted
traveler of the twelfth century, called himself Benjamin
the Second. He was a seeker after the remnants of the Ten
Lost Tribes of Israel and an astute contemporary observer
of the life of Jews in the Western Hemisphere, in Asia
and Africa and the near East. He finds that in the United
States Jewish boys "after a fashion" do receive a Jewish

education, many of them attending a Hebrew school or
receiving private instruction at home. But "I must say
with the deepest regret that the study of the Holy Scriptures . . . is much neglected among the daughters of
Israel."[42] The results are deplorable, he goes on. The duties devolving upon the Jewish woman are vital and
exacting and yet "half of the American Jewesses are at
present unable to undertake and fulfil worthily the place
in life for which they are intended . . ." The first five
years of a little girl's life are spent under the mother's
tutelage. But once the child goes to school, she associates
with children of other religions and backgrounds . . . "but
as for Judaism, the child experiences nothing and knows
nothing." When at fifteen, the little Jewish girl graduates
to a higher than elementary school, she has "lost" ten
years of her life in acquiring "nonessential" information
while being deprived of "the roots of her being." "What
she has learned is of no use to her and of no profit," says
this exacting and zealous reporter.

These ten "wasted" years often mark great economic
prosperity on the part of the parents. "Accordingly, they
provide her . . . with a music-teacher, a singing-teacher,
a drawing teacher, and a governess to continue the practice of French . . . and . . . they assign a teacher to give
her Hebrew lessons . . . She will find the last teacher . . . a
bore. She will find Hebrew too dull and also too difficult;
she will weep over her lessons so that her yielding parents . . . will give the teacher notice—he whom they should
have engaged first and dismissed last."

Benjamin calls this type of Jewish education "completely inadequate"—and well he may. But magnanimously
he insists that he blames neither the girl nor her parents
but rather all the members of the Jewish community.
Jewish children quickly assimilate American ways and
speak to their parents in English only. "They become

part and parcel of the American way of life . . ." So the women of America "deteriorate." The cause of this "deterioration" may be found in two factors. Americans worship Mammon first and second "the female sex." He deplores the great influence of women in America. The new feminism is abhorrent to him. There are too many shotgun marriages. There are too many broken marriages. While such evils are less prevalent in Jewish circles, nevertheless they do exist. "American women have dignity and refined features, and . . . of all women in the world know best how to dress. Their conversation is very cheerful, they are always lively. . . . Many do not even wish to have children because they are afraid of losing their beauty." He has been asked by a New York physician whether an Oriental drug used as a contraceptive "is still in existence." The doctor was sure that he could make a million dollars a year with such a drug. Benjamin promised to look into it. Women love to eat, especially sweets, and so dentists prosper in America. Many women marry for money. "The women know nothing of love—the salt of marriage—for if a man has only money enough to serve their love of luxury, he is good enough for a husband . . . If his money vanishes, naturally so does her loyalty and love." He attributed the fact that American women are so spoiled, to their scarcity in the days of early settlement when a man considered himself lucky to find a wife at all.

He notes that most American women are chaste before marriage, that they practice charity, and "give thought to the higher pleasures of life." Yet American women are superstitious and gullible. They flock to spiritualist lectures. He tells of a lady who, dominated by spirits, preached to large audiences on "America and its Destiny" from notes dictated by "the spirits"—"and people came streaming from all sides to listen to the revelations of the spirit that ruled the lady . . . Therefore any absurdity or madness, if only mad enough creates a stir in this country . . ." He concludes with this ringing plea: "Teach the Jew fully about the essence and history of Judaism and he will at once distinguish what to accept as part of Judaism and what to reject . . ."[43]

Dimly remembered or vividly recalled are some of the other extant narratives. An example is Julia B. Heller's little book titled *Some of Her Writings* and published posthumously by her grandchildren. It may serve as an example of events recalled in the tranquillity of a secure old age. "Oh! how we all abhorred the War. How happy we were when it ended. We denied ourselves luxuries . . . Prices soared . . ." Thus Julia Heller recalls her childhood impressions of the fratricidal Civil War. "The unhappy affair of Lincoln's death is brought back to my mind very vividly; it is my saddest recollection. The only time I ever saw my father in tears was when Abraham Lincoln was assassinated . . ."[44] There is a great gulf, a deep chasm, between the emotion dimly recalled and the trauma actually experienced. Emily Seasongood of Cincinnati relives the days following the Emancipation Proclamation with an unenviable detachment: "The slaves were all set free, and there were trying times, as most of the Southern people were so dependent upon them and were unable to do things for themselves. Many young ladies were helpless . . ." A strangely imperceptive, insensitive reaction! It was in every sense "a little world" in which she had her being.[45] These late recollections lack emotion and depth and understanding. The hair shirt of a long distant past no longer pricks the aged participant. So much for remembrance of things past.

By contrast journals, letters and jottings which are recorded as they are currently experienced have that ring of truth and passion and conviction which is totally void

of counterfeit. The record left by Emma Mordecai has
an authentic ring. Here is a spinster in her fifties, daughter of a North Carolina schoolmaster, who was "a loyal
Jewess who, in her devotion to the faith, followed in the
footsteps of her father, who had on occasion served as
rabbi of the Richmond congregation . . ."[46] Emma Mordecai had a sense of history. She writes on December 15,
1864: "From this date up to April, 1865, the leaves of
this journal have been destroyed by mice or roaches and
converted into paper crumbs. I will fill in the interval by
copies of letters which I think worth preserving as pictures, vividly representing the experiences of the War . . .[47]
Her diary pulsates with authentic emotion. "Oh! how I
have thought of you and all our beloved ones in N. Carolina. Our agony was great, but yours must surpass it.
We have been most mercifully preserved thus far from
injury. Our faith has not been strong enough to preserve
us from terror and dread of every conceivable outrage and
injury and insult, but the result so far has proved that our
trust in God's mercy should have been more firm and
consoling . . . Every sound, every footstep, has sent trem-
bling to the limbs of us three helpless and unprotected females and made our hearts stand still . . ."[48] When their
desperately needed horse was stolen this intrepid woman
walked from their farm to Richmond to complain to
authorities.

Emma Mordecai's narrative continues: "The walk . . .
to the Capitol seemed interminable, and Richmond could
no longer be recognized . . . I had to pass through what
might be called a *nasty* crowd . . . but I met with no rude-
ness, and was, myself, studiously polite and dignified . . ."
Later she was "grossly insulted by the negro picket on the
Camp Lee Road . . ." She describes the desolation and
devastation, the heavy spirits, the perpetual anxiety. "We
must still wait on God in cheerful hope." So the journal

proceeds, step by dismal step, describing the collapse of the old order, the daily challenge of new conditions, new attitudes. "The events of the last two days have arisen from the moving of Sherman's Army from Richmond to Washington . . . May 13 . . . I must here record two anecdotes told me by an eye and *ear* witness, illustrative of the new *disorder* of things." One of them dealt with an emancipated negro who was heard to mutter: "Dis what you call freedom? No wuk to do, and got to feed and clothe yourself." The indescribable postwar hardships are chronicled with a sense of tact and detachment which does great credit to the narrator. The poverty and illness and deaths of dear ones is recorded with restraint. "Jacob Mordecai's place six or eight miles north of Raleigh—*ruined.*" Her brother Sam is dead. "For himself he had little left to make life desirable . . . The tattered sheet containing this sad record is the last I can find of those containing my diary . . ."[49]

Eugenia Levy Phillips, described by Marcus as a "defiant rebel," lacks the forbearance, sufferance and imperturbability of Emma Mordecai. Eugenia was the daughter of Jacob C. Levy, a respected citizen of Charleston, South Carolina. Himself a literate and well-educated man (and very handsome man), he made sure that his daughter had every educational advantage. She married at sixteen, and moved with her husband, Colonel Phillips, first to Mobile and then to Washington. She was the mother of nine children and, despite the hardship endured during the war, lived to be eighty-one years old.

Eugenia was an outspoken enemy of the Union forces and ran afoul of the splenetic Union General Butler in New Orleans. She was banished to an ill-starred exile on an island in the Gulf of Mexico. She was later imprisoned in Washington. Her journal dealing with her imprisonment and later exile to Ship Island pulls no punches, describing conditions when "revolution and civil war show the way to anarchy and riot." She spent her twenty-fifth wedding anniversary imprisoned and feels that "memory will be pleasantly engaged in recalling the pleasures of the past. Few women have lived more in the sunshine of life . . . Did the wildest imaginings ever vision forth present realities? . . . We have almost become accustomed to our prison life and feel decidedly *tamed down* to a state of monotonous forbearance. Poor girls! It is truly hard for them to realize that the gaiety of youth must give way to the contemplation of the wisest way of enduring such an imprisonment. But I am getting prosy and uttering mere moral platitudes."[50]

Such jottings and journals are invaluable in reconstructing the past. Some recreate a general picture, applicable to all women, all rebels, all prisoners. Others are specifically faith-oriented giving both doubts and misgivings as well as affirmations of blazing faith expressed by the Psalmist "O look to Him and be radiant!" The articulate Jewess heeding the words of Zephaniah finds comfort in adversity in the Biblical exhortation:

> Sing aloud, O daughter of Zion;
>   shout, O Israel!
> Rejoice and exult with all your heart,
>   O daughter of Jerusalem.

Geography plays its part as well as faith. What determines a protagonist's feelings is not only the thread by which he is tied to the past. It is the setting where he finds himself that subtly and inexorably shapes social usage, opinion, partisanship, involvement. What would Eugenia, daughter of Jacob C. Levy, have felt had she been born in Boston, or Brooklyn, or Bratislava? What windmills would she have chosen to attack? What causes would she have espoused? Who would be her enemy then?

Her friend? Would a girl who worked in the mills of Massachusetts lament the loss of personal servants? Would a woman working in the dark surroundings of a New York shop run by an erstwhile rabbi and present hoop-skirt manufacturer see the world in "the sunshine of memory"? Economics was a crucial determinant. But what of the European antecedents of immigrants? How did the European background color life—even when forever left behind after a flight of terror?

The data that have survived are largely those kept by families of education and with room for storing papers. A certain permanency of address is involved. For the mobile are obviously limited as to what they can move and carry. Keeping a diary was the accepted thing to do in certain circles in Charleston, in Cincinnati, in New York. Getting and answering long letters implied leisure which usually meant that servants were available and routine household tasks were done by others. The detailed accounts of social activities, of meeting with others in pursuit of philanthropy or pleasure, the references to books read and celebrities met describe a very small segment of the Jewish population of this era. The amenities were not as universally known or practiced by the rank and file as the records which have been saved would imply.

One finds numerous advertisements of Jewish secondary schools for young ladies, but the numbers of pupils involved were not large. Jewish women were also educated in schools with Christians, in both public and Christian denominational schools. "We have records of Jewish women teachers in public schools from New York to San Francisco . . . And numbers took to writing."[51] Some Jewesses served as heads of orphanages in institutions like the Jewish Widows' and Orphans' Home in New Orleans. Others taught in Sunday schools and tutored children in many subjects. There were always student vacancies in

"Select Schools for Young Ladies of the Hebrew Faith" such as those administered by Mrs. H. Simon or the Palache sisters. And Jews also were successful in establishing nonsectarian schools like the Warrenton (N.C.) Female Seminary.[52]

Although Jewish women were held up to criticism for their neglect of traditional observances in *kashruth* and in the keeping of the Sabbath (with some justice), they were also praised for their whole-hearted involvement in synagogue affairs, for their attendance at services, for their synagogue-oriented charities. Isaac Mayer Wise, who was always gallant in his attitude toward women, in sermons and in his writings includes frequent panegyrics in which their intelligence and religious ardor is praised. Rabbi Wise referred to women as "priestesses of the house" and to him many reforms in temple observance may be traced, such as the seating of women members in family pews. Other rabbis in scattered communities endorsed in glowing terms the loyal cadre of women who helped furnish and beautify many a synagogue. From carpets to chandeliers to candlesticks to Torah mantles, their gifts were gratefully acknowledged. "Let not our readers smile," wrote one scribe in 1861,[53] "at our mentioning the ladies in connection with the Synagogue. We should indeed fare badly were it not for their influence. They are the main pillars of the Synagogue . . ." The congregational balls and celebrations were festive and gay—even during the war years. They were fund-raising affairs and gaiety prevailed in a time of acutely tragic news, with the bereaved in mourning, still the women were "always foremost in every noble and generous undertaking." Every synagogue and temple had its organized women's auxiliary. In addition to serving the religious needs of the community, there were spontaneously organized Benevolent Societies of women designed to meet acute needs of the indigent and the bereaved. "Jewish women responded as devotedly as did their neighbors to the spoken and unspoken needs of the time. In Columbus, Georgia, fourteen-year-old Isabel Adeline Moses became the youngest member of the Soldiers Aid Society and spent long hours in the Columbus Hospital nursing the wounded . . . Mrs. Rosanna Osterman of Galveston, Texas, contributed large stores of food to the overcrowded hospital in that city and spent an incredible number of hours at the bedsides of convalescing soldiers."[54]

Women met in synagogue vestry rooms or in private homes directing their major activities to helping the war effort. In the North and in the South, from Charleston to Syracuse, in every part of the country there was a welling up of a compassionate desire to alleviate wherever possible the suffering of wounded soldiers and their deprived families. The rolling of bandages, the sewing of garments, the collecting of funds, the preparation of booths and items to be sold as part of the activities of the Sanitary Fairs went on apace. In Philadelphia under the inspiring leadership of the Reverend Sabato Morais of Mikveh Israel Congregation, the women organized and obtained 250 contributing members within the first month —at fifty cents a year. In one year they sent ten crates of supplies which ranged from "23 bundles of lint and linen" to several hundred shirts of which only eleven were old, to 144 pounds of smoking tobacco, sixty-three pair of woolen socks and a whole assortment of writing supplies, cereals, cocoa, rice, ear warmers, slippers, and "12 cakes of fancy soap." In Pittsburgh, on December 9, 1863, at a Sanitary Commission Fair, the Hebrew Ladies' Soldiers' Aid Society participated and a Professor Josiah Cohen spoke in praise of the Jewish tradition of charity. Isaac Mayer Wise was one of the guests and commented with generous praise on the character of the occasion.[55] All sorts of earning funds were earmarked for war relief purposes. At the Sanitary Fairs needlework was sold and many hours of Female Hebrew Benevolent Associations sewing bees were accounted for. "At the Purim balls which were held in many cities to celebrate the Feast of Esther, refreshments were frequently sold for the benefit of the Sanitary Commission.[56] In Philadelphia there was a Jewish women's group called "Alert!" In Phoenix, the women called themselves "Independent Ladies"—their purpose to raise money for war relief. One New York private school run by Dr. Ridskopf, most of whose pupils were Jewish, even gave a performance of music and declamations at Niblo's Saloon in order to swell the funds of the Sanitary Commission. Jewish women insisted that they were serving as Americans and not as nationals of another group. One Jewish periodical protested against descriptions of participants in these activities as "pretty Jewesses." Why does not one read references to "demure Quakeresses" or "smiling Presbyterians?" he asked.[57]

Nor was this all. Several wards of the Jews' Hospital in New York were reassigned for military casualties. The facilities provided in addition to medical care included food and clothing, books, fruit, and the inevitable therapeutic chicken soup. "The patients were rarely without visitors; young ladies of the community sat at their bedsides and read to them; the rabbis made regular visitations, and Christian clergymen were invited to pray and converse with non-Jewish patients; wealthy women called for ambulatory cases in their carriages and took them riding through Central Park."[58]

The needs of Jewish soldiers and their families were pressing. In 1861, Rebecca Gratz as Secretary of the Philadelphia Female Benevolent Association pointed out the many needs of families where the husband's and father's absence from home created cruel hardships. A year later she reported on a soldier's mother who was "literally starving to death" and then told of a child whose father was a soldier and whose mother had died leaving the baby as a ward in the Jewish Foster Home.[59]

The Hebrew Relief Association in Cincinnati in 1862 supported eight orphans and seventeen widows. The Jews of Knoxville established the Hebrew Benevolent Association for the burial of Jewish soldiers. Jewish women shared in the raising of funds for the creation of memorials and monuments to the Jewish war dead. The Jews of Syracuse and of Chicago established their own Jewish companies. In Chicago, ninety-six men joined. This was a remarkable performance for a relatively fledgling community. Chicago itself was incorporated as a community in March, 1837. Eight years later there were just enough Jews to form a *minyan,* a group of ten men. In a small room over a store, Yom Kippur services were held. The first congregation was organized November 3, 1847. All 15 members who organized Kehillath Anshe Mayriv were German Jews. Several of the new arrivals had brought their families with them. When, in 1861, Lincoln called for volunteers, the Jews of Chicago responded so quickly as to prompt the Chicago *Tribune* to report that "the rapidity with which the company was enlisted has not its equal in the history of recruiting." The diaries and papers which have survived dealing with the men and women of the Chicago Jewish community throb with their awareness of the significance of the war and its ultimate goals. These men of immigrant antecedents yielded nothing to their native neighbors in patriotism, in sharing in the hazards and privations of war. They were simple businessmen with a long way to go in establishing themselves on a secure financial footing. Their wives too were heroines, each after her own fashion.[60]

Out of the sewing circles and the Ladies' Hebrew

Benevolent Associations and the kindred groups, organized philanthropy was to develop. These groups served
not only to meet immediate critical communal needs.
They developed a continuing concern for the deprived
and the underprivileged, for the orphan and the widow
and the aged, for the insecure immigrant unable to communicate, for the dowerless girl of marriageable age looking for a husband. While these good women were busy
helping others they were in countless ways growing as
human beings. Emergence from the home into the larger
world gave them an opportunity for leadership, for
spiritual growth, for personal fulfillment. This was shown
in the enlarged endeavors during their lifetime and in
continuing concern after death. The will of Rosanna
Dyer Osterman, in 1866, left money to build synagogues
to her own city of Galveston and also to Houston. A part
of the bequest was to help the cause of Jewish education
in those cities. Other bequests in Rosanna's will went to
three Jewish hospitals—in New York, New Orleans, and
Cincinnati; to Jewish schools in Philadelphia, Cincinnati,
and New York; to the New Orleans Hebrew Foreign
Mission Society; and to the North American Relief Society. This concern was typical of others, both of individuals and groups of women. Fifty Cincinnati "Hebrew
Ladies" helped establish an orphange for children of
Ohio, Indiana, Missouri. In Philadelphia the Ladies' Hebrew Relief Sewing Association stressed "having kind
remembrances for those brave ones who have sacrificed all
for their country's honor," by making renewed efforts to
have large supplies of "lint and bandages manufactured
for the sick and wounded . . ."[61]

Loyal as they were to the native areas that nurtured
them, identified as they were with the host culture that
surrounded them, they could also change with the impact
of changed conditions, with new and enlarged experiences.

A native South Carolinian, Septima Levy Collis, whose
husband worked with leaders of the Northern armies,
explained her changed sentiments by saying that she had
"gone with my state, mine being the state of matrimony."
She went on to add, "I had learned to love Mr. Lincoln
. . . I had seen him weep, had heard him laugh, had been
gladdened by his wit and saddened by his pathos. I had
looked to him as one inspired."[62]

In society news and in reports of cultural and musical
events Jewish women figured frequently. In Baltimore
a Jewish choral group was referred to as "an ornament"
to Hebrew Society. In Cleveland, twenty young Jewish
women and twenty male vocalists sang at a "Sacred Concert"—and the appearance of the young women was
described as reflecting the "dark-eyed beauty of the
Orient." One reporter covering a Purim ball was so
eloquent on the subject of their appearance that "he
couldn't detect a homely face."[63] So much admiration for
these female protagonists led to increasing intermarriage.
At first it would seem that more women were marrying
out of the faith. Eventually the trend in intermarriage was
reversed.

In the Jewish and non-Jewish press, the middle-class
daughter of a prosperous merchant was singled out for
those activities which today are encompassed by such
groups as the National Council of Jewish Women, Hadassah and ORT and other organizations affiliated with
synagogues and temples. They worked hard, but there was
also time for "conspicuous leisure and conspicuous consumption." In 1862 a Jewish editor could exhort his
women readers to make only those activities be central to
her life which prepared her for marriage. Too much
dawdling over novels, too much make-up, failure to take
a daily walk decrease the chances for matrimony.[64] Again
and again, moralizing editorials and uplifting fiction held

up Biblical and historical heroines as people to be emulated. Placating a husband, practicing all the wiles of femininity in holding his affections, directing all activities to the harmonious administration of household and children, using the soft answer to turn away his wrath—these it was pointed out, should be the ultimate feminine goals. Correct outward demeanor was stressed. The emphasis on inner self-discovery was largely absent. This lack of insight into the ultimate significance of the role of woman was to lead eventually to a moral revolution.

Theories as to the prevalence of intermarriage range from guesswork to speculation. Data are scarce, statistics inadequate.

It was one thing to educate young girls in all the housewifely arts, to give them a smattering of religious education, to involve them in synagogue activities, to condition them to value a life of ease and abundance. It was quite another matter to provide suitable young men of some education and culture, capable of earning a good living, as eligible suitors. Often the barriers were insurmountable. Jews who came from Germany and those who came from Poland were strangers to each other. There was more to divide than to unite the young people. "One of the most serious problems with which they had to contend," writes Korn, "was the uniqueness of the American experience. . . . The systems of organization which they had known in Europe, the literature they had studied, the uses of authority to which they were accustomed . . . none of these would serve here."[65] "Mixed marriage was the condition which most penetratingly weakened the congregation in its earlier days," write the scholarly chroniclers of Congregation Shearith Israel, David and Tamar de Sola Pool.[66] "The records show that a Jewish girl marrying a Christian usually abandoned Judaism."[67] For almost two hundred years "there was no rabbinic

authority or *beth din* (rabbinic court) available in the
New York community to train and accept prospective
converts." Applicants into the fold were usually rejected.
When in 1835 a Mrs. Maisa Valentine decided to become
a Jew she was informed that the trustees of the congregation were prohibited from taking part "in the ceremonies
necessary to be performed. . . ." Sometimes Christian applicants for conversion were more successful with other
congregations. However considering the facts as now
available one must admit that the losses through intermarriage to this small Jewish minority were immeasurable.

The *shtetl* (East European village) wove its own spell
of memory, the West European community another. The
denizen of one was divided from his fellow Jew of another land. Each had his own "cake of custom." "The
Jews in Eastern Europe lived more in time than in space.
It was as if their soul was always on the way, as if the
secret of their heart had no affinity with things. . . . The
charm came from the inner richness of their being—from
the polarity of reason and feeling, of joy and sorrow, from
the mixture of intellectualism and mysticism which is
often bewildering to analytical observers." So writes the
poet-philosopher Abraham Joshua Heschel of "the inner
world" of the Jew in East Europe, in *The Earth Is the
Lord's.* [68] Guido Kisch paints quite a different picture for
Jews living among the Czechs.[69] "The Jew, living in a
bourgeois atmosphere and owing the recognition of his
human dignity in his non-Jewish surroundings to the
philosophy of Enlightenment, showed a great suscepti-
bility and a fine adaptability to the ideology of the awakening Czech cultural nationalism. After the walls of the
spiritual ghetto had fallen, he found himself in a position
to look for his cultural orientation among the peoples
amid whom he was living."[70] It is obvious that the Jews
of Eastern Europe and those in the West were miles apart.

And the daughters of one culture did not always look with favor upon those of another.

It is these forces—the ones that divided and the ones that united the Jewish community that we would now consider.

The pages of the *American Hebrew* as one turns them today are yellowed with age and fragile to the touch. Fragments of faded paper confetti and clouds of dust flutter like moths as one opens the volumes. The calendar of another time takes over. What, one asks, were the occupations and thoughts and interests of the men and especially of the women of that time?

Let us take a year of the great migration, May 1, 1883, to May of 1884. On May 18, "a proud day," a goodly number of spectators turned out to see the cornerstone laying of the new Orphan Asylum. There was a moving oration by Carl Schurz, a speaker much in demand by Jewish audiences. "Among the many great thoughts enunciated by the Hon. Carl Schurz, there was none more beautiful than the one suggesting to the lady members to select each at least one orphan who shall look upon her as its particular friend and patron to whom it may freely unbosom its troubles. . . ." It was important, Schurz pleaded, that orphans "should feel like other children."

It was the time of the year when the Hebrew Free Schools were visited by rabbis, when annual examinations were held, prizes awarded. The Touro Institute of Newport, Rhode Island, was advertising its summer sessions. It was designed as a sort of study camp for children. "Songs of a Semite" by Emma Lazarus was advertised in the pages of the *American Hebrew*. Poetry vied with patent medicine. The usual ailments and their cures were paraded. Dyspepsia was a popular ailment. "Dr." Clark Johnson's "Indian Blood Syrup" was described as "the

Best Remedy Known to Man" and presumably to women readers as well.

Hebrew Free Schools in New York and elsewhere were described. Hebrew books were advertised by H. Sakolski of 53 Division Street. News from Palestine was ever present. The Rosh Pinah Colony near Safed was described as prospering. There were troubles everywhere. "Dr. Samuel Hirsch of Philadelphia has again besmirched his rabbinical garb . . . by uniting in holy wedlock a Jewess with a Gentile. . . ." A book by Isaac M. Wise, titled *Judaism and Christianity,* was advertised. The editor sometimes appeals for worthy causes, sometimes chides his readers, sometimes expresses his gratification at their response. An appeal for financial help for a "consumptive young Jewess" brought in contributions of six dollars, for which generosity the editor gives thanks!

Later that year as more and more immigrants poured into New York, the editor, Philip Cowen, scolded his readers for the averted eye and the deaf ear toward these refugees: "What the late George Eliot termed the 'vulgarity of exclusiveness' might almost be applied to the comparative indifference and inattention with which well-to-do Jews have in the past contemplated the wretched lot of their brethren who live in the crowded quarters of New York. [71] This editorial was written on Columbus Day! There were many other human crusades. The editor was critical of Jewish journalism in New York. "The poorest Christian weekly excels them in amount of original study." Although there was little reference to women's activities, children's needs were uppermost in Cowen's mind. "Cannot our synagogues be built," he asks, "that the quarters of the religious school need not be situated in the dingiest, darkest and dampest part of the building?" His compassion for the bereaved was boundless. "Don't crowd the mourners, give them time to weep." The death of Judah P. Benjamin was announced in a story from London. A Philadelphia woman, Mary M. Cohen, sends in a poem honoring Sir Moses Montefiore "Entering His Hundredth Year." And on the ninth of November, 5644, (1884) the editor notes with considerable regret the disbanding of the Young Ladies' Charitable Union which furnished shoes and garments to the poor. Eulogies of Carl Schurz on the passing of noted men in the Jewish community are usually printed in full. Emma Lazarus is always warmly welcomed in the pages of *American Hebrew,* as well as to its offices as a caller. "Like many writers, Miss Lazarus liked the atmosphere of the printing office . . . she came to see me at odd times, especially on Sunday afternoons when I was likely to be in and have comparative leisure." Cowen goes on: "Miss Lazarus took a delightful personal interest in the paper. . . . We welcomed her suggestions and were glad to have her criticism."[72]

8

Isolated facts about women turn up. They are in the mainstream of life, involved in all its vicissitudes. Scholars and journalists write or edit books about the Jew in America. The President of the University of Illinois, Edmund J. James, undertook to edit a book titled *The Immigrant Jew in America*.[1] He was a man of vision and unlimited tolerance. There were others.[2] The study edited by James was sponsored by the National Liberal Immigration League of 150 Nassau Street, New York. Among his collaborators were Henrietta Szold, Charlotte Kimball Patton and Charles S. Bernheimer. It was for its time an ambitious project. The editor realized it: "No survey of this subject which approaches this investigation in compass has heretofore been attempted." James stresses "the accuracy of reporting, irrespective of possible effect." The mirror held up to the Russian Jew is accurate.[3] "The conclusions reached by the investigators fully sustain the just appreciations of the character of the Jewish race and its certain advance in this country." At the University of

Illinois, President James had surrounded himself with notable Jewish scholars—Jacob Zeitlin, David Blondheim, Simon Litman whose wife, the eminent Ray Frank Litman became an inspiration to Jewish students on the campus.

The timing of the book is very interesting. James refers to the Two Hundred and Fiftieth Anniversary of the Settlement of Jews in the United States—a work which contained "Addresses delivered at Carnegie Hall, New York, on Thanksgiving Day MCMV (1905) ." He quotes from President Eliot of Harvard: "For the whole civilized world this race has been the source of all the highest conceptions of God, man and nature."[4] Perhaps one simple statement from one of America's most respected journalists, Dr. Lyman Abbott, editor of *The Outlook* served as the keynote of the celebration: "In my judgment, the American people owe more to the ancient Hebrews than to any other ancient people."[5] The celebration and the book served to turn the spotlight on the living protagonists, the shabby, driven, insecure, exploited Jews whose very appearance offended and whose presence was resented by the descendants of earlier immigrants, both Jews and Christians. Stratification within Jewish ranks was as marked as the gulfs which separated some Jewish groups from the host society.

As the twentieth century opened, the earlier immigrants and their descendants were looking to the celebration of two and a half centuries in America. The recent arrivals, while frantically seeking a foothold and a bare subsistence in America, were sending passage money or steamship tickets bought on the installment plan to the women and children they had left behind. In 1880, there were 275,000 Jews in America. Twenty years later, in 1900, there were 1,100,000.[6] As the numbers increased so did the problems multiply. It is a strange historical anomaly that the migration of the two generations before the Jewish catastrophe which began in 1933 was a life-saving operation. Only extermination awaited the descendants of those who remained. "The move from Europe to the Western Hemisphere saved millions of Jewish lives," writes Lestschinsky.[7] His statistical studies give the following figures for immigration to the United States:

1840–1870	150,000
1871–1890	250,000
1891–1925	2,200,000
1926–1955	400,000

Whatever the importance and the contributions of the earlier Jewish immigrants to American life, they were to be outnumbered by the East European Jews. Gradually their ascent from the slums to the suburbs, their group and organizational and congregational activities spurred these new immigrants and their descendants to help rescue some of the victims and survivors and to help in the establishing of a place of refuge in Israel. East European Jews played the midwife role in the birth of a new nation, Israel.

With increasing numbers the Jews of America developed separationist tendencies based on European geographic origins or economic stability. The old bromides about the exclusiveness of the Sephardim and their repugnance for Ashkenazim will have to be revised. For Ashkenazim were not as shunned by Spanish and Portugese Jews as were the East European Jews by their immediate German Jewish predecessors. To the credit of German Jews it must be stated that they had a genius for organized philanthropy and that many institutions which alleviated acute suffering were the result of their foresight and planning. When the B'nai B'rith was organized in 1843 it was for the purpose of "alleviating the wants of the poor and needy." "Inculcating the purest principles of philanthropy" was their stated aim.

Women counted in this campaign of philanthrophy. In Philadelphia, Rebecca Gratz was Secretary of the Female Association for the Relief of Women and Children in Reduced Circumstances. New York had an association as polysyllabic—the Society for the Education of Poor Children and Relief of Indigent Poor of the Jewish Persuasion.[8] But "charitable females" were restrained from visiting the poor because of the appalling conditions under which they lived.[9] There was acute poverty even before the floodtide from Europe. The Congregation Shearith Israel had its Female Hebrew Benevolent Society with a fifty-year history by 1870.[10] In the year of its founding, Mrs. Richa Levy wrote to ask for recognition of the group by the congregation of a philanthropic enterprise "established by the Ladies of our congregation for the relief of indigent females. . . ." Always there were "ladies" and "females" in Jewish life. "The eager young women who were doing the work of the Association were glad to invite men to give occasional lectures. Mr. Joseph L. Joseph gave two lectures on Mariamne, the beautiful wife of Herod." The women reserved to themselves the teaching of children. Fund-raising was another aspect of their work which was jealously guarded. Sewing was popular. A "Ladies Hebra" provided shrouds for the dead and garments for the sick and dying. In 1878, on the eve of the great migration, the women of Shearith Israel organized The Ladies Aid Society which carried on its work through 1896. The year 1896 saw the establishment of the Sisterhood. Five women's groups were merged for the purpose of extending relief to the residents of the Lower East Side. "The district was teeming with tens of thousands of immigrants, mostly from the Pale of Settlement in oppressive Czarist Russia."[11] The Sisterhood also established Settlement Houses in which they operated a kindergarten and day nursery, taught English and housekeeping, ran an employment agency and trained candidates for citizenship.

It was at this new immigrant group that Edmund J. James and Hutchins Hapgood and their associates took an appraising look. We see these newcomers through the eyes of their Christian contemporaries, detached observers, free of emotion and sentimentality, largely free of prejudice, as impersonal as the eye of a camera.

What Hapgood called "the spirit of the ghetto," Harry Golden defines as "an intellectual vitality we do not feel today, precisely the special quality which has since made the Jew in America the subject of a vast literature."[12] In 1902 Hutchins Hapgood delighted in the atmosphere of the crowded ghetto of New York. He says: "I was led to spend much time in certain poor resorts of Yiddish New York not through motives either philanthropic or sociological, but simply by virtue of the charm I felt in men and things there." The things Hapgood sought and found were not the superficial aspects of the people who jostled each other in the littered streets and alleys. He saw the scholar's face, the mystic's eyes, the innate manhood of those stripped of present dignity. He saw "submerged scholars" and "prophets without honor." His eloquent description of Moses Reicherson, "probably the finest Hebrew grammarian in New York," who earned five dollars a week as head of a little Hebrew school and lived with his wife "in their miserable little apartment on East 106th Street," is a moving pen portrait of a Vilna-born scholar who had brought his great fund of learning to America, who spent his spare time writing for a Chicago Hebrew journal called *Regeneration,* which stressed the twin causes of the revival of the Hebrew language and the rehabilitation of its proponents. Hapgood compares this "beautiful old teacher" with the father of three children who has become embittered, overwhelmed and lost in his struggle to feed his family. To this vanquished man America is a materialistic jungle and its Jewish leaders totally inept and incapable. Hapgood identifies with the despised Russian and Polish Jew whom the German Jew looked down upon from his secure Olympian heights. The submerged, the ragged protagonist, emerges as the hero.

It is interesting to read Hapgood's description of the Jewish woman and to recall what Benjamin had described some two generations earlier in his *Three Years in America*. Hapgood's chapter titled "The Old and New Woman" is a subtle study in depth and contrast. The marked contrast between the immigrant woman and her native American opposite is based in part on "simplicity of mood as opposed to capriciousness." The American woman has "subtle charm." The immigrants are poor, many have had to work in sweatshops. They are "under-nourished and lack the physical well-being and consequent temperamental buoyancy which are comforting qualities of the well-bred American woman." They compensate for this lack of outward grace by a strong sense of duty, by loyalty to principle and to causes and to their leaders. There are two distinct groups among the immigrant women—the unlettered homemaker whose only language is Yiddish and whose only skill is that of keeper of the home. The second group is composed of intellectuals and from its ranks and from the climate of social ferment in which they existed came women like Lillian Wald, Rose Pastor Stokes, Rose Schneiderman.[13]

At the bottom of the social ladder was the stocky, pudgy, bewigged woman who resembled a carelessly stuffed sack. Illiterate she was and hard to communicate with. But piety permeated her being. Family loyalty was her undeviating creed. Love for her own and compassion for others ruled her. She gave of herself freely and asked

nothing in return. Her dreams and hopes were vicarious
—for her children and for her husband. The rabbi and her
husband were her authorities and the Jewish way of life,
its rites, its ebb and flow, her circumference. Says Hapgood: "She is drab and plain in appearance, with a thick
waist, a wig, and as far as possible for a woman, a contempt for ornament." She is also a magician transforming
her dingy quarters into sparkling cleanliness for the coming of the Sabbath. An aromatic cloud hovers over her
stove where she achieves culinary miracles. The Sabbath
candlelight flickers through her arthritic fingers changing
her into a priestess as she intones the hallowed words
which usher in the Sabbath. The experience once felt is
unforgettable.

It is an ancient custom dating back to the mystics of
Safed from the middle of the sixteenth century. "The
vision of the mother thus praying for her loved ones ac-
companies the loyal Jew or Jewess throughout life," wrote
Dr. Joseph H. Hertz, the late Chief Rabbi of the late
British Empire.[14] Exaltation was the Sabbath mood.
Raskin, a Yiddish poet, states it lyrically:

> From memory's spring flows a vision tonight,
> My mother is kindling and blessing the light;
>
> My mother is praying and screening her face,
> Too bashful to gaze at the Sabbath light's grace.
>
> And some hidden feeling I cannot control
> A Sabbath light kindles deep, deep in my soul.[15]

That was the Jewish housewife. There were others.
The unmarried spinster whose life was unfulfilled, whose
days were spent in the fog of factories and whose evenings crowded with attending uplifting lectures and night
school classes. Causes were her concern and social better-

ment her goals. As economic conditions improved and the acculturation process began its transformation, subtle changes occur in the wife of a peddler or small businessman who becomes a more successful provider. She plunges headlong and ill-equipped into fractured English. She discards wig and shapeless garment and buys modish clothes. She joins a society of charitably oriented neighbors. She nudges her husband into looking around for a better address. She enjoys the universal Jewish woman's avocation of matchmaking.

"As we ascend the scale of education in the ghetto," writes Hapgood, describing the Jewish intellectual woman, "we find women who derive their culture and ideas from a double source—from Socialism and from advanced Russian ideals of literature and life. They have lost faith completely in the Orthodox religion, have substituted no other, know Russian better than Yiddish, read Tolstoy, Turgenev, and Chekhov, and often put into practice the most radical theories of the new woman . . . There are successful female dentists, physicians, writers, and even lawyers by the score in East Broadway who have attained financial independence through industry and intelligence."[16]

The New York ghetto may be a larger laboratory but similar conditions are found in other American cities. In a study by Seymour Jacob Pomrenze titled "Aspects of Chicago Russian-Jewish Life, 1893-1915" and based on Chicago Yiddish and Anglo-Jewish periodicals, the same conditions are noted.[17] Sweatshops in Chicago were so bad that they were investigated by a Congressional Committee on April 4, 1892. Among its findings the Committee reported: ". . . tenement work is of a medium and low-grade ready-made goods . . . The households in which it is made include many of the most wretched in which human beings exist among us . . . The conditions of filth and squalor are such as in large proportion of cases to make even inspection impossible *except by one hardened to the process.*[18] Hester Street or Maxwell Street had the same common denominator. This was the bottom of the social pyramid. Beatrice Webb's American Diary which she kept in 1898 when she and her husband visited New York and Chicago, among other cities, permitted her to describe the apex of the pyramid. The two Webbs met a number of Jewish college professors who impressed them favorably with their "Jewish intelligence" while holding in contempt both Irish and Jewish politicians.[19]

The cloud of poverty, the perpetual fog of deprivation were also recognized by Edmund J. James. Yet again and again he refers to the strange and inexplicable "vitality" of the Jewish masses. He as well as other observers noted that "Beyond any other nationality, too, the Jew in America cares for his own poor and needy."[20] His collaborators (whose individual contributions are unsigned) give a factual and graphic report of the background of the East European Jew and of his experience as an uprooted immigrant seeking sanctuary in the United States. The story is old and familiar. It has been described repeatedly. Many autobiographies have recaptured the sorrows and the privations, the tragedies and the horror of those early days. There is neither space nor time to recall it. Descriptions vary with the beholder.

Jewish women were cultured, sensitive, educated, compassionate. They were graceful and full of charm. They were ornaments of society and enriched the circles in which they moved. They were gently reared in private and finishing schools and were specialists in a "paper flower culture," an art which they learned along with embroidery and painting and French and music. They were also ragged and dumpy, illiterate and uncouth, driven to exhaustion by poverty, sweatshop labor and

malnutrition. Their homes sparkled with cleanliness on
the Sabbath and Holy Days. Their homes also reeked with
disorder and clutter at other times. They were patient
and long-suffering. They were angry and bitter and mal-
adjusted and without hope.

There were among them women of simple faith and
selfless dedication to family. Their walls stretched to
accommodate the sick and aged. Generations tolerated
each other. The old had something to say to the young.
The youth who listened often became the gifted poet or
the enchanting storyteller, the painter of nostalgic scenes,
or composer of traditional melodies. There were agnostics
and defiant and rampant unbelievers among them seeking
to erase God who had chosen them for strange ends. There
were daughters of grandeur and children of despair.

Social distance created a vast and impassable gulf between the entrenched and prosperous earlier immigrants—
largely German—and the insecure and impoverished East
European Jews. In the periodicals of the time, the Jew
emerges as a split personality. The *Sentinel* of Chicago
was largely intended for the secure and well-to-do reader.
Yet from its very first issue it could not keep out the
bulletins of disaster from Russia, nor the cries of the
beleaguered Jews in Poland. Interwoven in its printed
pages is the record of the stately procession and the dance
of death. There is praise for the Jewish poet and artist.
There is reluctant reporting of the speeches of soap-box
orators like Emma Goldman. Both the entrenched and
the windmill tilters are noticed.

The area of first residence is beyond the pale to prosperous German Jews across the river in Chicago. Only
an occasional man or woman of valor bridges the gap.[21]
When an indignant new immigrant to Chicago complained to the "Briefkasten" in Chicago's Yiddish paper,
the *Courier,* of the terrible condition in which he found

himself, he was told unceremoniously and brutally "Go
back to Russia if you don't like it here."[22] Closed minds
were everywhere. The *Courier* described Chicago as the
New Jerusalem, the "second city" being more democratic,
more American than New York. It was a place where
opportunity flourished, where women more readily found
employment, even as teachers in the public schools. Soon
it would in every way surpass New York. Jewish Charitable institutions proliferated in Chicago. Some were organized and staffed by German Jews. Others by East
Europeans. By 1904 there were some two hundred Jewish
congregations, lodges, loan societies, clubs and philanthropic institutions in Chicago, many of them duplicating
each other's work.[23] It was the *shtetl* (the village) transplanted to America. And some of its strengths and some
of its weakness were obvious to the observer. In the *Promised Land* of Mary Antin and the "benighted land" of
Emma Goldman. In the ivory tower of Emma Lazarus
writing an essay on "Renan and the Jews" in 1884.[24] In
Henrietta Szold teaching a class of Russian Jews in Baltimore. In Lillian Wald who pioneered in the field of
public health, school nursing and in the establishing of
playgrounds and whose name is dear to countless denizens
of the Henry Street neighborhood because she founded
and headed the Henry Street Settlement House. In Rus-
sian-born, American journalist Sophie Irene Loeb, who
wrote for the New York *Evening World,* descriptions of
caverns of poverty and the dark, dank, dismal wretchedness of the poor who inhabited the jungles of privation.
The silent anonymous poor had their eloquent spokes-
women. The still small voices of sorrow and deprivation
were magnified and heard throughout the land.

"The needy shall not always be forgotten," reads a
Psalm of David, "and the hope of the poor shall not

perish forever." Dedicated Jewish women put these words to life.

Much has been written of Jewish religious life in America. Subtle and overt influences played upon the Jewish groups as they did on others. It was Isaac Mayer Wise who pointed out that in areas where the Episcopalians predominated, or the Methodists, or Huguenots, Jewish religious life took on the flavor of the dominant group in its outward observances, in the building of synagogues in the prevailing architecture, in congregational enterprises and communal involvement. This was an unconscious practice differing from the conscious contacts with missionary groups whose blandishment and persuasion Jews had no difficulty in resisting. The practice of neighborliness, the general gregariousness to which we are all heir, the pull toward joining communal and nonsectarian groups—music clubs, choral groups, library societies, civic improvement associations, sanitary fairs— all worked to bring individuals of separate groups together There are many forms of contact. The in-group however is the greater magnet. Approval is more readily bestowed to one's own kind. To Greeks all strangers were "barbarians." To Jews, strangers were "goyim," Gentiles. Jewish men and women wove their own looms of custom. Yet they also partook of the larger patterns of the host society.

A new chapter was opening up for the American Jewess. It was a native American Jew who inaugurated the Reform Movement in America. He was born in Charleston, South Carolina in 1788. Isaac Harby in his brief lifetime combined several careers. He was editor, author, playwright, schoolmaster, and one of the founders of the Reformed Society of Israelites in 1824. This was but four years before his death when, a broken-hearted widower, he moved to New York to recover from his bereavement. He died in 1828. He was proud of his American roots and of the contributions members of his and his wife's family had made to the Revolutionary War and since then. His brother, Levi Myers Harby, fought in the War of 1812. He had many friends and admirers. Penina Moïse spoke of Isaac Harby's "mental radiance." His granddaughter, Leah Cohen Harby, must have partaken of that glow for she also made her reputation as an author.

Isaac Harby's writings and speeches are eloquent of his spirituality, mysticism, prophetic vision and devotion to Judaism. He fused within himself his Jewish and American heritage. He wrote to Thomas Jefferson in 1826 stating that, "With patience and industry, we hope in a few years, to be able to establish a mode of worship, simple and sensible; suited to the liberality of this age, improving to the Israelite, and acceptable to the Deity." Both men and women were attracted to the new program. They wanted "such alterations in the customs and ceremonies of the Jewish religion as would comport with the present enlightened state of the world." The Society continued until 1833. In its brief existence it had opened the door to other reformers. In his brief lifetime, Isaac Harby had pointed the way both to reform and to division in the ranks. It was to be a titanic struggle. It is still being waged. In this struggle women were to become deeply involved.

What had Harby sought to accomplish? That services be largely conducted in English so that they could be understood by the congregation. Also to "discontinue the observance of such ceremonies as partake strongly of bigotry." Sermons were to be preached in English so that the younger generation could be taught the beauty of the tenets of Judaism and be inspired by its moral teachings.

Soon newer arrivals to these shores would in one form or another espouse some of these reforms and even the older synagogues would be subtly influenced. "The issue," says Moshe Davis, "was one of content, not merely form . . . in time three approaches to Jewish religious life arose . . . each troubled by the weakening of Judaism in America: Reform, the Historical School and Orthodoxy."[25]

Simply stated, the Reform movement tried to attune Judaism to the new environment, to the expansive spirit of the nineteenth century. "Minhag America"—American usage and custom—was to supersede traditional rites and prayers. With the coming of religious leaders from Germany, the two Reform streams, native and immigrant, merged. According to one historian, "Jews too were encouraged to drift away from their religious moorings by the example of other Americans—particularly in the growing urban centers, where religion was the weakest and where Jews settled most thickly."[26] There were two Titans whose personalities and ideologies clashed—Isaac Leeser and Isaac Mayer Wise. Each had a sense of respect and esteem for the contribution of the Jewish woman despite the ideological differences that divided them.

For the Jews of America, Isaac Leeser had a dream— that in its open spaces, in its vast green mansions they could lead a dedicated, creative, fruitful, American-Jewish existence. This dream became his life work.

Leeser's labors were staggering. He introduced English sermons. He translated books and wrote his own books. He was indefatigable in providing the Jews of America with spiritual sustenance, with aids to learning and to understanding their faith. Providence denied him a family, so he founded, with others, many religious institutions. In 1843 he began a publication, the *Occident,* which was to become his imperishable legacy to the Jews of America. His monumental achievement came in 1853.

More than a century ago, this lonely, frail, valiant Jew translated the Hebrew Bible into English. Now his co-religionists could read the Bible without error and christological distortion. This, write Margolis and Marx, was "his crowning literary effort." His own generation acclaimed him. It was "the production by which he is best known, and which would have sufficed to give him immortality . . ."

That was Isaac Leeser. He was not a solitary worker in the Jewish vineyard. In 1859 a dearly beloved rabbi and teacher in Chicago, Bernhard Felsenthal, wrote, "We say the Bible is not the *source* of Judaism, but we consider it a product of Judaism, and we concede, without reservation, its most splendid and holiest product. But Judaism is older than the Bible . . . *For the kernel of Judaism is natural religion in the soul of man* . . . Every Israelite has the right and the duty to himself to search the sources of religious truth . . . the human spirit is not penetrated from without, *rather from within outward shines the light of divine truth.*"[27] Felsenthal was a contributor to Dr. Wise's *Israelite* and to a paper, *Sinai,* founded by Dr. David Einhorn of Baltimore. Throughout the land many voices were being lifted urging the reinterpretation of Orthodoxy in terms of the new enlightenment, in subtle deference to a land where religious freedom was a part of the national heritage.

Among those clamoring for radical change, Isaac Mayer Wise was the rallying point. Isaac Mayer Wise was born in Bohemia in 1819 and died in Cincinnati at the dawn of the twentieth century. Of him a noted contemporary scholar, Rabbi Solomon B. Freehof, has said: "Not everything that he taught is acceptable today, and he himself changed his mind about many of his earlier ideas. But his basic standpoint of a Judaism united and progressive, and of America, the land of liberty, as the natural habitat of a dynamic and creative Judaism, becomes more understandable and seems more real when we appreciate the character and the ethics of this man who may be called its American father."[28] Like Isaac Leeser he was hard-working. On coming to America and assuming his first pulpit in Albany, New York, he aroused a storm of opposition when he attempted to introduce changes in the Orthodox form of service. The congregation was rent. Some followed Wise. Others adhered rigidly to time-honored custom. When he assumed the rabbinate of the Orthodox Congregation Bene Yesherun in Cincinnati he continued to change the form of services until his temple became one of the leading Reform temples in the land. *Minhag America* was published in 1857. This was a prayerbook containing the changes in services which Wise advocated. He also founded two weeklies—the Anglo-Jewish *Israelite* and a German-language paper titled *Die Deborah*. He toured the country seeking to enlist adherents of the Reform Movement and summoned several rabbinical conferences. He also planned to establish—and succeeded in 1873—the Union of American Hebrew Congregations. He founded and became the first President of the Hebrew Union College in Cincinnati. In 1889 Wise was instrumental in organizing the Central Conference of American Rabbis.

The spiritual heirs of Isaac M. Wise are still facing many of his problems. "The result has been an alienation from the mainstream of Jewish life—a situation with which the leaders of the Reform movement are grappling today, though not with pronounced success. Despite enormous material progress, spiritually the movement has remained sterile. The cathedral-like Reform synagogues which have sprouted all over the land are, alas, devoid of worshippers, except on the High Holy Days. And the Reform laity is not distinguished for learning, or piety, or religious devotion."[29]

To one who would chronicle the place of the Jewish

woman in American life, Rabbi Wise endears himself in
countless ways. His gallantry toward women makes him
unique. He is a dedicated and avowed feminist. "He liked
women and probably found it interesting to observe them
. . . we find him commenting on how a woman should
grow old gracefully . . . It seemed to him that this depended on character more than upon cosmetics . . ." To
him "Beauty (was) a Duty." He admired "the physical
symmetry of youth . . . but (also) the spirit and loveliness
of maturity and age." Wise was "vivid, lovable, sometimes
mercurial . . ."[30] His latest biographer, J. G. Heller, does
not consider Wise "a great creative scholar . . ." He was
"too much a man of action, too deeply involved in issues
and current problems to detach himself from the main
stream and spend the needed time in quiet meditation
and contemplation and study."

Wise longed to unite Jews. He knew the meaning and
direction of their past and present. He hoped to shape
their future. He had "an impassioned longing to bring
back the wanderers among his people to awareness of
their noble heritage."[31] Perhaps that was one of the reasons he worked so readily with the Jewish women he encountered in his campaigns. He was as poor as "a church
mouse," writes Heller. To establish his periodical, the
Deborah, he borrowed a thousand dollars from an anonymous woman known only as "Mrs. B." He eventually
repaid the loan.[32] He wanted to retain and involve the
Jewish woman in the fold. Orthodoxy, he insisted, had
failed to do so. Wise asked "How it happened that of all
the Jews who emigrated to these shores between 1620
and 1829, there were not two hundred families left that
belonged to congregations, while the majority had dis-
appeared among the masses, traces of them being clearly
recognizable in hundreds of Christian families."[33]

Wise was imbued with a deep sense of "consciousness

of kind." But East European Jews were definitely not his kind. Heller states categorically that Wise "did not like these newcomers . . . He found them quite distastefully foreign and quite incurably orthodox." Yiddish, Wise called a "jargon." He was obviously unmoved by its beauty and charm. Its semantics eluded him. He knew little of its content as literature, of its psychological insights, of its linguistic shorthand in adage and slogan. He felt nothing of the humor and pathos, the wisdom and incisiveness of a language that had the ability to deflate and inspire, the therapy to console and assuage. Of this enchanting language one of its writers had said:

In all the attics and cellars from Warsaw to New York
    you lay your head,
You come like an old mother, wearing an old apron, into
    the home of your daughters,
And they are ashamed of you, and your grandchildren
    greet you with scoffing laughter . . ."[34]

Yiddish was repugnant to Wise and so were the people who spoke it. He was charged with "sneering at it, as though it were utterly without strength or virtue as a language, as though it were no more than a badge of shame, a symptom of the corroding effects of persecution."[35] Zionism was also in total disrepute, for was it not a "Russian-Polish hobby?"

But where women were concerned he was their doughty champion. "Throughout his career Isaac M. Wise argued and worked for the improvement of the status of women in Judaism. *This he regarded as one of the primary tasks of Reform.* . . . Among the specific ventures which he considered essential for Judaism in the United States was an academy for women."[36] In 1858 he stated ". . . it is highly necessary that we should have a female academy, where the daughters of Israel would . . . have the benefit of a

thorough and enlightened religious instruction." And
again advocating the inclusion of women as trustees and
members of temple school boards, "We are ready to appear
before any congregation in behalf of any woman wishing
to become a member thereof and plead her cause."[37] He
"believed in the ordination of women as rabbis, something
that has not yet been done by any seminary." He wrote
in 1890: "There are . . . in this country Jewesses who are
both able and willing to occupy the pulpit." Two years
later he reported that "a Miss Frank of Oakland, Calif.,"
had preached on the Pacific Coast, occupying pulpits in
Washington and California. He added: "In the Hebrew
Union College, among the different female students, we
had one who heartily wished to prepare herself for the
pulpit. We discouraged her, because it appeared to us,
she had not the requisite oratorical capacities . . . We
can only encourage Miss Ray Frank or any other gifted
lady who takes the theological course, to assist the cause
of emancipating woman in the synagogue and congregation."[38]

Isaac Mayer Wise "was consistently in favor of the ex-
tension of the suffrage to women." He refused to employ
the word "obey" in the marriage ceremony. He affirmed
that the Ten Commandments did not differentiate between men and women. He preached and practiced equality.

The dialogue between Isaac Leeser and Isaac Wise rose
and fell—nostalgia and memory and ancient usage were
challenged by Reform. They were poles apart.

The problems were not new. Emancipation and enlightenment were responsible for change. The Jew no
longer lived in an encapsulated world. Contact with the
larger community was an insistent challenge that had to
be met daily. Enforced isolation had kept Jewish communal identity separate and intact. "With the nineteenth

century, all pressure was relaxed. The Jew might remain loyal to his past, but the Gentile world no longer insisted that he do so . . . Just as the total effect of the world's pressure had been to drive Jews to cohesion . . . so they reacted to the relaxation of the pressure in almost the same manner . . . Sooner or later, it was inevitable that the Jew should awake to the fact of his intellectual medievalism. The awakening, unfortunately, was a rude one."[39] As the world changed, so perforce did the Jew. It was a question of how far and how much. The crux of the matter was in the degree of adaptation, in the extent of separation from ancient folkways and mores. In his haste to adapt to social change would the Jew consider the past as a dead hand, or a sustaining one? Would erosion be accelerated by reform? Would reform and acceptance of new customs stop intermarriage and escapism? Would inner strength and adherence to custom preserve, maintain and uphold the Jew?

The voice of Isaac Mayer Wise was not a solitary one. There was a chorus of supporters. In America it had begun with a dozen members of Beth Elohim of Charleston, South Carolina. By year's end it had won fifty adherents, about one-sixth of the total membership of the congregation. The ten Articles of Faith stated in forthright terms their adherence to faith in God and belief in immortality; they accepted the Ten Commandments, stressed ethical conduct and urged the love of God as the acme of man's spiritual life. The group had a turbulent history in Charleston. Strife and acrimony marked the emergence of Reform there and elsewhere. By mid-century the arrival of many immigrants from Germany created a more viable Reform movement in New York and Baltimore and Chicago and other large cities. It was to Wise they turned for the preparation of a new ritual. So *Minhag America* was adopted. In 1854 with Wise's removal to Cincinnati

a new chapter in American Jewish religious history was
begun. It was exactly two centuries after the arrival of a
handful of Jews to New Amsterdam. Within a generation
(July 1873) the Union of American Hebrew Congregations was established and the Hebrew Union College with
Wise as its President began its existence two years later.
There were two full time instructors, of whom Wise was
one, and seventeen students. In 1883 the first four rabbis
were graduated. Unfortunately the occasion was marked
by a graduation dinner which has gone down in history
as "the trefa banquet" in which forbidden food was
blatantly served to many men whose observance of *kashruth* had never been violated. Led by Sabato Morais, a
number of dignitaries left the room convinced that
Judaism in America had come to a complete parting of
the ways with the proponents of Reform.[40]

In 1885 at a Reform conference in Pittsburgh, the
umbilical cord with historic Judaism was further severed
by a Declaration of Principles which departed from the
Mosaic code, described parts of the Bible as "primitive"
and rejected dietary laws. Sabato Morais then issued a
clarion call for the creation of an institution of higher
learning to serve as a training center for future rabbis
loyal to traditional and historic Judaism. The opposition
to Reform did not lack for leaders or a constructive plat-
form of its own. Isaac Leeser, Sabato Morais, Alexander
Kohut, and men of their caliber and scholarship spearheaded the movement.

It was in many ways a crusade in search of specific answers. For it was known and acknowledged by the Conservative element that "Judaism historically was both
mobile and static, that it must in measure adjust to the
spirit of the time and in measure resist it . . ."[41] And the
times had changed with the population in America. Jewish
mobility, the eternal response to pogroms and persecution,

had vastly increased the Jewish population in the Western hemisphere. "From 1881 to 1939 some 5,000,000 left their native lands in Eastern Europe . . . in the United States and other overseas countries the ratio of the Jewish population to world Jewry increased enormously—from 3.5 per cent in 1880 to 33.4 per cent in 1939."[42] Social and linguistic and psychological changes accompanied this vast migration. Arthur Ruppin points out that in Slavic countries the bulk of the population was Yiddish-speaking. In Poland, in 1931, eighty per cent of the Jewish population spoke Yiddish and only eleven per cent spoke Polish. In West European countries where the winds of freedom, humanism and enlightenment had dispelled the medieval fog, the Jews spoke the language of their country of residence.[43] If the Jews of Russia and Poland were rejected by their host country, the Jews in turn rejected Russian and Polish and other Slavic languages as a means of communication. In the United States, English became the mother tongue of second and third generation Jews, while the immigrants lived their threshhold lives steeped in the Yiddish they had brought with them, a language rich in content, flowering and abundant in metaphor, sparked with humor and grace, polished by generations of wits and philosophers. These were the people of whom Herzl had written that "they possess the inner wholesomeness which the majority of European Jews have lost . . ."[44] They came bearing their lavish gifts to America. Of this group and its contribution to America, Maurice Samuel has aptly written: "The Jewishness of American Jewry derives from that of Russian and Polish Jewry, with the Russian predominating. What we have in America today in the way of Jewish life came to us with the enormous streams of immigrants that set in with the 1880's."[45]

Numerically strong, economically impoverished, spiritually resourceful, these were the men and women and

children who moved Emma Lazarus to her greatest creative response, who enlisted the energies and support of
Henrietta Szold, earning her respect and admiration in
her English classes for immigrants, who drew the compassionate Lillian Wald as with a magnet to serve them
in the teeming streets around Hester Street. Their needs
of every kind were as overwhelming in the New World
as they had been in the Old. Often appeals on their behalf
fell on deaf ears causing an aroused Chicago rabbi to
plead their cause in ringing words that describe their isolation even from their own co-religionists. Dr. Liebmann
Adler wrote: "Brothers and Sisters: Are these poor ones
less to be pitied, are they less poor, are they less Israelites
because Poland or Russia is the land in which they first
saw the light, or rather the darkness of this world?"[46]

His colleague, Rabbi Bernhard Felsenthal, was no less
impassioned when he cried out, "O help them! save them!
Do not delay!"[47]

Yet the gulf, wide and impassable, still separated the
Jews of German origin from those of Russia and Poland.
With the introduction of Reform practices and *Minhag
America* these differences became more marked and more
discordant. It was at this historic moment that the Jewish
Theological Seminary was born and the Conservative
movement in America came into being. It was a time of
high hopes. "The growing number of men and women
who have accepted the philosophy of Conservative Judaism . . . believe that this movement has the future of
American Judaism in its hands," writes Robert Gordis in
Conservative Judaism: An American Philosophy.[48] This
is only one of a number of scholarly voices which have
reassessed and reinterpreted the historic role of the Conservative Movement in the United States. Here one is
confronted by "the poverty of riches" and the cry of Em-

erson is constantly recalled: "If I only knew what to omit!"

It is to Zechariah Frankel that one first turns. Rabbi Frankel (1801-1875) was President of the Jewish Theological Seminary of Breslau. It was his thesis repeatedly stated that Judaism was never static or arrested in its ideological development. Traditional Judaism was a *continuum* evolving and growing through the centuries. True, it implied reverence for the past and for the traditional values that had been cherished for centuries. Such changes as were acceptable grew out of ancient practices. Hebrew was essential to this stream of evolution. Recognition of historic roots of Judaism was no less vital.

Solomon Schechter stands high in the hierarchy of architects of the Conservative movement. He brought his unique talents and his intellectual vitality to the Conservative orientation. He stressed the universality of Judaism which he described as "catholic Israel." He developed and expounded the idea of religious nationalism. Many books have been written about the institution which he headed and the men and women with whom he was surrounded and the inspiration which went out of the Jewish Theological Seminary seeding the nation from coast to coast and moving into Canada, each one describing not only the individual leaders but the tradition and culture and way of life which gave them birth.

At first the dynamic leadership of the Conservative movement had been largely in the hands of European scholars who had immigrated to the United States. But the reorganization of the Jewish Theological Seminary and much of its visionary program now came from a native of America, Cyrus Adler. It was he who suggested the name of the renowned Solomon Schechter, then Reader of Rabbinics at Cambridge University and the dis-

coverer of the Cairo Genizah, as head of the Jewish Theological Seminary of America. Later, it was Adler who
succeeded Schechter upon his death.

"The Conservative group was cast in the role of me-
diator and interpreter between the Orthodox and the
Reform conceptions of Judaism," states Agus.[49] Ancient
symbolism, historic ritualism were stressed. A policy of
welcome was extended to all scholars and philosophers
who reinterpreted Judaism without departing from its
cherished heritage. Under its hospitable roof, the Recon-
structionist movement as formulated by Mordecai M.
Kaplan would be welcomed. Abraham J. Heschel, contemporary torch-bearer for neo-mysticism, could find himself at home there. Here were the "Keepers of the Roots"
—the phrase is Martin Buber's. Professor Israel Fried-
lander, who brought the creative insight of Ahad Ha'am
to America, was on the faculty. Also Louis Ginzberg,
called in 1945 "probably the greatest living Jewish scholar
in the world,"[50] was an honored member of its faculty.
Among its noted alumni were men like Joseph H. Hertz,
late Chief Rabbi of England, Solomon Goldman, and the
present head of the Jewish Theological Seminary, Louis
Finkelstein, like Cyrus Adler a native of this country.

Among the men given an honorary degree by Harvard
University in 1912 were Henry James the novelist, Josiah
Royce the philosopher, and Solomon Schechter, rabbi and
head of the Jewish Theological Seminary of America.
President Lowell of Harvard University saluted Dr.
Schechter as "expounder of his people's ancient law, dis-
coverer of lost records; tireless in amassing and generous
in sharing his vast stores of knowledge." This was the man
who was called to fill the vacancy created by the death of
Dr. Sabato Morais. There were few material inducements.
"But what moved Dr. Schechter most to leave England
was the fact that nearly all his disciples at the University

of Cambridge were non-Jews," wrote Cyrus Adler. Dr. Schechter felt that America offered him a larger field of service to his fellow Jews. "I am prepared," he wrote to Adler, "to give the Seminary all my faculties and energies, even my very life."[51]

He had traveled a long way from Rumania since 1848. Spiritually he had spanned many centuries. For his background was one of Hasidic pietism. He was an apt student in both *cheder* and *yeshiva* in Rumania and continued his studies in Vienna and Berlin where his personality and brilliance won him the approbation of teachers and fellow students. His life and sphere of service changed radically when he was invited by Claude Montefiore to come to England. He was asked to be a Reader in Rabbinics at Cambridge University in 1890. He and his brilliant young wife became the center of a dynamic group of scholars and writers. Life was overflowing with the blessings of work, of love, of stimulating companionship. Soon with his discovery of the Genizah (depository for old sacred books) in Cairo, Egypt, came still greater opportunities to apply his vast scholarship to the past. He was acclaimed by the learned the world over.

So Solomon Schechter became President of the Jewish Theological Seminary. And the Seminary became a great center of Jewish learning. The lives he touched became enriched, enlarged. One of his students and disciples—for they all became that—Rabbi Herman H. Rubenovitz, wrote of his "master": "Dr. Schechter was an ardent, warm-hearted, benevolent human being . . . His attitude toward his student body was that of father and friend."[52] Much of the warmth that was so freely dispensed depended on the hospitality of the scholar's home where his wife was the presiding genius. She was destined to make an indelible contribution to Jewish women in America.

In every Seminary biography, in each appraisal of accomplishment and influence, there is implicit the influence of the home and the homemaker, for within that frame of reference life takes on added dimensions, new meanings, wider boundaries. Descriptions abound of the Schechter table always bountifully spread, of scholars and students and colleagues perpetually entertained and warmed at their family hearth. To be such a wife is the most demanding role. There were others like Mrs. Schechter. Often the loving biographies which these women write to recall and to immortalize their husbands in all their scholarly glory reveal the fact that the grieving widow was herself a heroine of no mean proportions, serving as helpmate and inspiration in a manner both self-effacing and humble.

Here is a case history, one of many. The author of *Out of Endless Yearnings* does not use her full name on the title page: only C. Davidson. The photographs with which her book is illustrated (and she was a beautiful woman) are merely identified as "The girl he decided to marry." Or with her children "Gladdie, Jessica, and their Mother." She invariably stood on the rung below her husband, Israel Davidson, an eminent scholar and a member of the faculty of the Seminary, where he taught medieval Hebrew literature and under whose hospitable roof he prepared his four-volume *Thesaurus of Medieval Hebrew Poetry*. His wife is totally self-effacing, completely without any claims to personal merit. She was a native of New York, well educated and well brought up in a benign Victorian atmosphere. She seems to have known no childhood deprivation or insecurity. Her husband was a refugee from Russia who fled that country and underwent the usual hardships and privations of an immigrant youth who must make his own way in the world. Yet Carrie Davidson writes of "the feeling of deference that I could not shake off, for I was continually cognizant of the fact that I was in the presence of a superior person." This was in the early days of his courtship, largely an epistolary affair. Israel Davidson wooed Carrie with poetry and fairy tales and legends and his dreams. His ardor was ubiquitous. He even wooed her with a love letter written by an erstwhile Jew, Paul of Tarsus. "Love suffereth long and is kind . . ." The passage is from Corinthians. Davidson did not identify it. Writes Carrie: "He probably refrained from telling me the source for reasons best known to himself."[53]

Their first home on 152nd Street in New York had "the aspect of the home of a scholar." It was to have been "our joint library," she adds. "For I had also experienced the pleasure of collecting books, but little did I then realize that my day for accumulating books was over, and that my own small collection would gradually be crowded out to make way for the rapidly increasing library of the scholar." She speaks self-effacingly for her group, wives of rabbis and scholars, in discussing the discipline imposed on women whose days are a record of vicarious achievement. "Gradually, I began to learn my mission in life—to free the scholar from petty intrusions . . . There are not too many who are willing to undergo the sacrifice that such a life entails," she adds naïvely. For it is of the scholar's sacrifice she writes and not her own.

It seems, according to Carrie Davidson, that the scholar "must have an understanding helpmate . . . He will be in the clouds while she is planning to make both ends meet . . . But rest assured . . . it is all very worthwhile. If you love the scholar, you love his work; and nothing else matters."[54] Carrie had many problems of adjustment. "Class distinctions had not yet become quite as obliterated as now . . . The place from whence your ancestors came was what created the barrier." She had never spoken

Yiddish until her marriage, her parents having been
Alsatians. She conquered both status barrier and the language barrier gracefully. Of her husband she writes, he
"was my only child for three years." When their eldest
daughter was born, it was Mrs. Schechter who decided
that her nickname was perfectly appropriate—for "We
looked up to Mrs. Schechter as to a mother and took her
advice"—and the child was called "Gladdie." It is a
tender story Carrie weaves, a narrative of selfless dedication, of a life spent in service to others. Without being
aware of it, she has proved herself to be a modest, gifted,
enchanting woman, a person of infinite grace who in the
words of Paul practices the art of love which "vaunteth
not itself." Later she was to earn a place for herself where
her literary talents could be put to good use. She was for
many years the editor of the *Outlook,* the official publication of the National Women's League of the United Synagogue of America. She was ably succeeded by Zillah Kohn.

One of the many problems which Carrie Davidson
describes is that of overcoming status barriers within Jewish ranks which are based on geographic origins. These
have always existed in America—between Sephardim,
Jews who were largely Iberian in origin, and Ashkenazim,
those who came from other European lands. Within the
latter, geography played a significant role in conferring
or withholding prestige. The Russian and Polish Jews
had their own criteria of eminence, of authority and dignity. Vilna was a place venerated for its scholarship.
Odessa for its creativity. The village of Salant was renowned for its famous rabbi Israel Lipkin and it was
enough to identify him by saying "the Salanter" to recall
a way of life which this nineteenth century mystic introduced—the "Musar" movement stressing ethical living,
prayer, contemplation, meditation. In transplanted com-

munities in America, people clung to each other because of a common geographic origin. They had terms of opprobrium and contempt to express social distance for strangers. They had unfailing warmth for the *landsman*.

The Promised Land, the autobiography of Mary Antin, dedicated to the memory of Josephine Lazarus "who lives in the fulfillment of her prophecies" is a graceful summary by a gifted woman of the process of acculturation and accommodation in a strange, new and wonderful land. "I was born, I had lived, and I have been made over." This is the formula for Americanization which may be repeated a hundred thousand fold. Her credo is a universal one: "To be alive in America, I found out long ago, is to ride on the central current of the river of modern life; and to have a conscious purpose is to hold the rudder that steers the ship of fate. . . . A characteristic thing about the aspiring immigrant is the fact that he is not content to progress alone. Solitary success is imperfect success in his eyes." This clannishness is one of the universal characteristics of the Jewish family. They climb the ladder together.[55] For Mary Antin, social distance from the host culture was an experience but not a trauma. Her recollections of the slums she knew and lived in did not corrode or degrade her. "It was good to get out of Dover Street. . . . But I must never forget that I came away from Dover Street with my hands full of riches. I must not fail to testify that in America a child of the slums owns the land and all that is good in it. All the beautiful things I saw belonged to me . . . I had only to be worthy, and it came to me, even on Dover Street . . ."[56]

The slum was in Boston, but Mary Antin spoke for all slum-dwellers. This woman whose life began in Russia in 1881, who had her rebirth in America in 1894, until her death in 1949 managed to convey her joy in her

adopted country, her gratitude for its unlimited opportunities, her flowering as a human being, as a Jewess and
as an American.

The barriers that others felt she leaped over.

The Psalmist had said it millennia before:

> Yea, thou dost light my lamp;
> The Lord my God lightens my darkness.
> Yea, by thee I can crush a troop;
> And by my God I can leap over a wall.[57]

Another autobiography titled *My Portion* differs in
spirit and content, in mood and self-revelation. Yet, as
Henrietta Szord points out in her introduction to this
book published in 1927 "Jewish literature is singularly
wanting in personal reminiscences." This makes every
personal statement one to be studied with care. Miss Szold
recalls the sensation caused by the publication of Glückel
of Hameln's Memoirs which had "lain hidden . . . in
family archives . . ."[58] History for Jews was swallowed up
as were the lost children who followed the Piper of
Hameln. Miss Szold dwells with characteristic eloquence
on the obstacles which the immigrant faces, the hurdles
he must overleap in order to preserve and record his
memoirs. "And if the immigrant is a woman to boot, then
the tale thrills with the threefold interest of victory over
hindrances barring the path of the Jew, the immigrant,
and the woman."

There were other feminine chroniclers. The tale Rebekah Kohut unfolds is indeed strange and different from
other available memoirs. The facts of her life are unusual
and totally without precedent. It is as if some spinner of
strange tales in Hollywood had triggered his imagination
to contrive a plot hitherto never told. She was born in
Hungary in 1864 and was brought to the United States

in 1867. She attended the University of California and aroused "considerable objection" from the trustees of the congregation which her father served as rabbi. Her father championed her right to a university education. She persevered making many friends among both co-religionists and Christians. With such a father and such good friends she writes, "I became spiritually stronger than I had expected. Pride was felt in one's race, glory in one's religion, sublimity in its martyrdom."[59] In 1886 her family moved to Baltimore. On a visit to New York she met and married a distinguished rabbi and scholar, Alexander Kohut. It was a strange, almost an unbelievable romance which caused much concern in the minds of her family and friends. Not only had she married a man twenty-two years her senior, but a widower with eight children! From their marriage in 1887 until her husband's death seven years later, Rebekah was wife, collaborator, stepmother. She rejoiced in her husband's scholarship: "He was a Marco Polo of philology. . . . Words to him were not shop-worn instruments of a single use, but virtual planets, with light and heat and relativity . . ." On the fourth floor of their Beekman Place brownstone overlooking the East River, with the slowly drifting boats and the reflected lights moving in the dull sluggish water, with Blackwell's Island casting a sinister shadow, the great scholar and his ebullient young wife collaborated in countless ways. He on his *Aruch Completum,* a Talmudic dictionary, she as his amanuensis and as hostess to his many friends. "The two blocks constituting Beekman Place were a little world in themselves." Within that small world was contained the large and boundless world of scholarship.

Suddenly the boundaries of that world were stretched, "both of us received a 'call' to another part of America— Chicago, where the World's Fair was to be held. The committee in charge of the Congress of Religions . . . invited my husband to deliver an address . . . I was invited to read a paper at another Congress at the Fair, the one invoked by the Jewish Women of America. . . ." Her husband was ill and she could not leave him. Her sister was delegated to read the paper she had prepared. "Afterward, when I heard about the gathering of Jewish women, and of the splendid material for social service brought together by Hannah Solomon and Sadie American . . . I was sorrier than ever that I had not been present."[60]

9

The call which Rebekah and her husband received came at a dramatic time in American Jewish history. The cornucopia from Europe was overflowing. Immigrants were spilling over the seaports of America and pouring into the great plains and beyond. Even neighboring Canada was similarly affected. Growth was phenomenal. "The first mention of Jews in an official census in Canada is found in Lower Canada in 1831, when 107 Jews were recorded as living in that portion of the country. . . . By 1901 the Jewish population of Canada had increased to 16,401, and from then on it grew rapidly until it numbered 156,726 in 1931, forming 1.5 per cent of the total population."[1] But even before 1831, Jews had a vital share in significant moments of Canadian history. A Jewish family of Bordeaux is credited in the early part of the eighteenth century with having played its role in the development of early French settlements. Indeed, the Gradis family had done more "to protect and represent France than royalty itself."[2]

Abraham Gradis had founded the "Society of Canada" in 1748.[3]

In 1760 the first Jewish settlers of Canada were officers in General Amherst's army. Seventeen years later, Montreal saw the establishing of the first Jewish synagogue. Congregation Shearith Israel of Montreal was the fifth organized Jewish congregation on the North American continent, being preceded by New York, Newport, Savannah, and Charleston. In many ways Canada's Jewish history shows parallel trends to the history of their coreligionists in the United States. Its earliest settlers were Sephardim. By the second quarter of the nineteenth century Ashkenazim began to arrive—at first in small numbers, gradually increasing as the pressures of anti-Semitism mounted in Germany and Poland and Russia. They succeeded in organizing an Ashkenazic congregation in 1858. In Toronto the Holy Blossom Congregation had been founded six years earlier. As in the United States, the Russian pogroms of 1881 swelled the Canadian tide of Jewish immigrants, the majority being overwhelmingly Orthodox. New congregations were established in a number of Canadian cities, in Hamilton in 1882; in Halifax and Ottawa in 1895. Because of the Orthodox emphasis on men as communal leaders, few Canadian women have made recorded history. Although in the accomplishments of synagogue-sponsored activities they were indefatigable.[4] Indeed one woman, Mrs. A. J. Freiman, distinguished herself in her efforts to help Ukrainian orphans. But by and large it was the history of anonymous women. The vast increase in numbers, the establishment of new congregations, the importation of rabbis trained in seminaries in the United States as well as Europe, the proliferation of Jewish newspapers and periodicals has gradually led to a more noticeable participation by Canadian Jewish women in philanthropic and communal undertakings as well as overseas relief and a definite commitment to the needs of Israel.

It was the National Council of Jewish Women which made the greatest impact on the early history of Canadian Jewish women's activities. Without a doubt, its influence on Jewish women on both sides of the border was a dramatic and significant one, a wholly unprecedented experience in their history. "The Jewish women who had convened the congress during the World's Fair had invited me to join in forming the organization that was the outcome of the congress," writes Rebekah Kohut, referring to the National Council of Jewish Women. "But for fourteen months I never left my husband for an hour, and learned of the first tumultuous meetings of the women only from hearsay."[5] She continues: "As I have already said, a new factor had come into the life of Jewish women in America, the National Council of Jewish Women. . . . I was later told of the clash that had occurred at the meeting, of the dissension between women of Orthodox and Reform beliefs, and the gloom over the differences . . ."[6]

We come now to that "tumultuous moment," and to "the gloom" and to the rejoicing.

To Rebekah Kohut, Chicago was "another part of America." It is and was a common provincial point of view held by the Jews of the Atlantic seaboard. Its tempo differed from that of New York and Baltimore and Philadelphia. It had never known a Sephardic aristocracy. But it had as arrogant a group of status-conscious German Jews as was to be found in any part of the country. East European Jews were the "untouchables," and between the earlier immigrants and their immediate descendants the caste system was practiced with a rigidity and an overbearing manner which took a long time—and a flight to the suburbs to overcome. Why the children of peddlers

grown prosperous held in contempt the children of peddlers still making their way is not too clear. The autobiographies examined show that privation, inability to
speak English, humiliating penetration into areas where
Jews were unwelcome—all of these factors existed in every
generation. Acceptance came more readily when these
immigrants were few in number than when they deluged
many cities, crowding into areas where rent was cheap,
employment of sorts available, synagogues were within
walking distance and kosher foods to be bought. The first
Jewish congregation in Chicago, founded by German Jews,
was established in 1847. Five years later, according to
Rabbi Emil G. Hirsch, because of the "aloofness" of the
"Bavarians" toward the "Pollacks," a second congregation
was started.[7]

In the field of organized philanthropy the arrogance of
the donors came into sharp conflict with the pride of the
recipients of charity. The German Jews established and
administered The Associated Charities of Chicago, which
embraced, among other institutions, a hospital, an orphanage, a settlement, a Home for Jewish Friendless and
Working Girls, an old people's home. The East European
Jews for whom these social service groups were established
avoided the services they were badly in need of because
no provision to serve kosher food was made. So gradually,
and at tremendous personal sacrifice, the despised East
European Jews established their own organizations under
the name of the Federated Orthodox Jewish Charities.
A dual charitable system was operated and the "Bavarians"
and "Pollacks" like the Capulets and Montagues were in
two separate camps. "Many members of the Chicago German-Jewish community resented the influx of Russian
Jews into 'their' city. They feared the criticism by the
general community of the poor and peculiar aliens . . . an
attempt was made to remove the immigrants throughout

the Middle West."[8] The Society in Aid of the Russian Refugees was formed in 1891. It did help several thousand impoverished immigrants "but failed to scatter them among the gentiles." There were distinct and separate enclaves in the sprawling city. The South Side of Chicago was for the Germans. The West and Northwest Side for the "untouchables."

Each group had its own congregations, societies, associations, folkways, prejudices. Gradually, the newcomers outnumbered the earlier immigrants. They had their own publications in Yiddish and Hebrew. They had a dynamic and indefatigable group of leaders who were identified with the Zionist cause. They formed labor unions led by their own zealous idealists. Their women, less sheltered and more exposed, became leaders of many causes and formed numerous study groups for learning English and for the perpetuation of the reputation of the memory of the poets and writers they had known in Europe. They had theaters that were well attended and well supported. But it took at least two generations until they had a club, the Covenant Club, to rival the Standard Club. Gradually, they made it—and eventually established some country clubs of their own which outshone in opulence and acreage those German-Jewish clubs from which they were so rigidly excluded.

Chicago was a strong, robust, brash, adolescent metropolis. And here it was that the Jewish women of America came of age.

It all began with the Chicago World's Fair (World's Columbian Exposition) in 1893. Six-hundred and eighty-six green acres along beautiful Lake Michigan were set aside and some of the authentic architectural geniuses of Chicago initiated a classical revival there.

Chicago Jewry was splintered and full of internal strife. "This splintering of the community is very bad," wrote

Chicago's pioneer historian Peter Wiernik.[9] He painted a very dismal picture of the cultural and educational life of Jews in Chicago. He wrote to the leaders of the Jewish Cultural Society in 1886 pleading that they exert some leadership in elevating the standards of the rank and file of Chicago's Jews. In the same year, on May 5, 1886, 400 Jewish immigrant garment workers began the "Jewish Labor Movement of Chicago." These workers, both men and women, were articulate, intelligent idealists. They made common cause against sweatshops and manned the first picket line which attempted to march on Chicago's Loop. Their confrontation with authority was disastrous. They were met by patrol wagons and officers who swung at the marchers savagely. They were routed. They were physically and spiritually crushed. But by March of 1890, the Chicago Cloak Makers Union was an established chartered body led by Abraham Bisno and Peter Sissman. From the first, women were numerically involved in Chicago's needle trades, eventually banding together into the Chicago Joint Board of the Ladies' Garment Workers' Union.

In 1893, from ghetto streets to South Shore Boulevard, excitement was in the air as the entire city of Chicago began to prepare for the celebration of the quadricentennial of the voyage of Columbus.[10] "The contemplated exposition filled every Chicagoan with pride and a great joy penetrated the ghetto." Two Jews, A. M. Rothschild and Adolph Nathan, were among the directors chosen to make the overall plans. One of the important undertakings was to have a World's Parliament of Religions. Here women came into their own. Mrs. Charles Henrotin, a leader of renown in Christian circles, headed the group. She invited Hannah G. Solomon and Mrs. I. S. Moses, wife of Rabbi Moses, to organize a Jewish women's section for the Parliament of Religion.

"Mrs. Henrotin manifested a rare insight when she selected Mrs. Solomon to head the Jewish section. She was young, brilliant, energetic, familiar with organization work (with) a deeprooted religiosity which gave her a keen understanding of her people."[11] A committee of fourteen Jewish women made immediate plans to launch a permanent organization. The World's Congress of Religion brought together representatives from many points of view and from many parts of the world. It was "a phenomenal success" . . . "This was accomplished mainly through the efforts of Mrs. Henrotin and Mrs. Solomon. To fully appreciate the magnitude of what these two women accomplished, a brief review of the historic status of women in general and the Jewish woman in particular, is required."[12] Bregstone states: "While the Jewish woman enjoyed greater freedom in affairs of the home, her general status was ever more circumscribed than that of her non-Jewish sister. . . . Mrs. Hannah G. Solomon was the first woman in America to weld the Jewish women into a national body, with definite purposes that stirred them on to a new consciousness and new activities." The World's Columbian Exposition, originally scheduled for 1892, had needed more time for preparation and so the opening was postponed to 1893. Hannah Solomon welcomed the additional time. She had large plans. "As a member of the Women's Board I worked during the entire winter of 1892 . . . seeing the possibility of a meeting of Jewish women organized . . . A permanent organization was the last and most important of my plans." Mrs. Henrotin in paying tribute to Hannah Solomon in a talk she gave in 1893 stated: "As the permanent effect of so much endeavor, several associations, councils and innumerable clubs were organized, of which without doubt the National Council of Jewish Women was the most successful . . . thanks to the executive ability of the chairman, afterwards its president, *a power for good not alone in America but all over the world.*"[13]

Hannah Greenebaum Solomon was a native of Chicago. She was born January 14, 1858. Her parents were among its earliest Jewish settlers. Michael Greenebaum came to Chicago from Germany in 1846. He was 22 years old at the time. His diary of his boyhood in Germany where he had been a tinner and plumber is delightful reading.[14] He married Sarah Spiegel of New York, fathered a large family and became a leading citizen of his adopted city. He continued his work as a tinner at Wheeler and Company. Other members of the family soon arrived. They all prospered. They were active in politics. Michael's brother Henry told Lincoln at a campaign dinner that "I was a strong political adherent of Douglas."[15] Michael was an ardent Abolitionist. In 1853, Michael led a crowd of citizens in an effort to liberate a fugitive slave from a United States marshal. Two Chicago rabbis endorsed this courageous act and used the occasion to condemn slavery from their pulpits. Dr. Bernhard Felsenthal even wrote a paper about Jews and slavery in a German newspaper published in Illinois claiming that the majority of Jews in America were anti-slavery in sentiment.[16]

The Greenebaum family made most significant contributions both to Chicago's civic life and to its Jewish communal life. Michael, Hannah's father, was a founder and first president of the Hebrew Benevolent Society in 1851. Six years later, he helped establish Ramah Lodge Number 33 of the B'nai B'rith, the first lodge in Chicago of that organization. He also founded and was first president of the Zion Literary Society, "a cultural center for the community." He was an officer of three congregations and served on a number of civic committees. Of his surviving four sons and six daughters, Hannah was imbued with his energy, zeal and loyalty to faith which made

her as long as she lived a delightful, charming and ir-
repressible person. When she was in her seventies, she appeared as a speaker before the Council of Jewish Women
dressed in a white costume dating back to the World's
Fair, complete with ruffles and flounces and a train drag-
ging the floor. She wore a large and very decorative picture hat, carried a little ornate parasol. She looked like a
dainty porcelain figurine of another era. Her voice was
young and her blue eyes sparkled. "This," she said with
a regal air, "is the way we used to dress when we went
out to inspect the city's garbage scows and the city dumps.
They were a disgraceful sight, an offense to our citizens."
Her voice was resonant, her delivery relaxed and punctu-
ated with many side-splitting anecdotes. She had total
recall. She had also a zest for youth, an ability to make
friends with women of other faiths, of other generations,
as well as to work with those of her own who were
separated from her by custom, origin, habits and outlook
—the "separated" sisters whose ancestry was of the East
European communities.[17]

Like her father and uncles, she was a "joiner." She was
a member of the Chicago Women's Club from 1878 and
active in the Woman's City Club. When she was elected
president of the Illinois Industrial School for Girls, she
was instrumental in moving the school from its Evanston
location to a farm in Park Ridge. She was the founder,
the first president and the honorary president for many
years of the National Council of Jewish Women. In 1904,
she represented both the National and the Chicago sections of the Council of Jewish Women at a meeting of the
International Council of Jewish Women held in Berlin.
She considered her invitation to occupy the pulpit of her
own congregation in 1897 as one of the signal honors she
had ever received.

Of the men who read learned papers at the Parliament

of Religions we can read descriptions in the Chicago *Tribune* which convey an atmosphere of conspicuous scholarship delivered to a somnolent audience and indifferent captive reporters. Of Isaac Mayer Wise's speech the *Tribune* said: "Rabbi Isaac M. Wise of Cincinnati delivered an address upon the fundamental doctrines of Judaism which was a profound paper, but rather over the heads of the majority of the audience, some of whom went to sleep and were playfully rebuked by the speaker." One bored *Tribune* reporter wrote: "The attendance of the Jewish Congress yesterday morning did not serve to more than half fill the hall. The papers were prosy and the audience was undemonstrative." Being held an unwilling captive by his assignment, the reporter revenged himself by describing the facial adornment of the speakers: After the invocation ". . . Rabbi G. Deutch of Cincinnati, a man of medium size, with heavy whiskers, gave a concise digest of the history of the Jews . . . Rabbi L. Grossman from Detroit, Michigan, a young man with a mustache of intensely black hue, described the attitude of Judaism to the science of comparative religions." There were four days of this. The women had their day later. It was another story and a highly successful one.

The Jewish Women's Congress, the first ever held, opened on Monday, September 4. So many people pressed to get in that it was necessary to provide for an overflow. The *Tribune* reported: "Women elbowed, trod on each others' toes, and did everything else they could without violating the proprieties, to gain the privilege of standing edgewise in a hall heavy with the fragrance of roses." In her keynote speech, Hannah Solomon said: "Living as we do in this renegade city, belonging to radical synagogues, thoroughly in sympathy with all endeavors to break down barriers, we are loyal to our history and to the traditions of our families."

Among the women who helped Hannah Solomon was one who is known as Sadie American, also a native of Chicago. She was educated in Chicago's public schools and became a social service worker. She is described as a "pre-eminent figure" who seems to have devoted her life to good works and many organizations "the list of whose official activities includes over a hundred separate affiliations."[18] She became an expert in the developing field of vacation schools and playgrounds and lectured in the United States and abroad. She was Hannah's right hand in the founding of the National Council of Jewish Women and acted as secretary of the Jewish women's section of the Congress of Religion.

The anonymous woman had now become a club woman—it took four centuries in the Western Hemisphere. Little did Columbus dream of such an eventuality when he wrote to Juana de Torres, a woman very influential in the royal household of Prince John of Castile that he was harassed by "wicked Christians." That was in 1500. Juana de Torres was probably a member of the same family of marranos to which Luis de Torres belonged— and Luis was one of the two men whom Columbus chose to explore the newly found land. Of Luis, Columbus had written that he "had been a Jew, knowing Hebrew, Chaldee and even some Arabic . . ." In the Columbian letter to Juana we find this telling sentence: "Our Lord, who rescued Daniel and the three children, is present with the same wisdom and power as he had then . . ."[19] Now, four-hundred years later, a Chicago native, an American Jewess whose true family name has not as yet turned up, but who gloried in being an American and is known as Sadie American, affirmed it with membership in one hundred philanthropic and social welfare institutions, a busy spinster, a loyal Jewess and a dedicated American!

It is one of the anomalies of history that Olympian predictions are often reversed. "The stone that the builders rejected becomes the cornerstone," says the Bible. So it was with the Olympian Isaac M. Wise and the woman who had studied under him and was rejected by him for the rabbinate for want of eloquence.[20]

Wise wrote in 1892, just a year before the World's Columbian Exposition: "In the Hebrew Union College, among the different female students, we had one who heartily wished to prepare herself for the pulpit. We discouraged her, because it appeared to us, she had not the requisite oratorical capacities and without them success in the pulpit is not very likely. We can only encourage Miss Ray Frank or any other gifted lady who takes the theological course, to assist the cause of emancipating woman in the synagogue and congregation."[21] At the World's Parliament of Religions it was Wise who put his audience to sleep and Ray Frank who stirred those who heard her to a deep emotional awareness of their faith.[22]

Of her life, Professor Simon Litman of the University of Illinois had written that it was "a life dedicated to a search for truth and beauty, to the expounding of what she considered divine in religion and art, a life which enshrined her in the nineties of the last century as a modern Deborah, as one of the outstanding personalities on the Pacific Coast, a life of lecturing, preaching and writing, whose eloquent sermons brought harmony on many occasions. . . ."[23]

Ray Frank was born in San Francisco in 1865. Her father was a lineal descendant of Rabbi Elijah, the Gaon (genius) of Vilna. Bernard Frank was a deeply religious Jew, rigidly Orthodox in belief and practice. While serving as an Indian agent in the sparsely settled West he never missed his daily prayers, often pitching his tent on a Friday so as not to be late in celebrating the Sabbath.

Her mother, too, was a devout woman who "was fond of reading the Bible. . . ." Ray was educated in San Francisco's public schools and attended the University of California. She taught school for six years in Ruby Hill, Nevada, where her pupils were miner's children. But even then, she went beyond what was expected of her and organized night school classes for the parents. From the first, she had in addition to a personal, uncompromising rigidity in Orthodoxy, a sense of communion with sincerely devout Christians. It was faith in God she cherished and respected. When at Christmas her friends would send her flowering plants and wreathes of evergreens, she displayed them out of a knowledge that it was an act of affirmation and of friendship. Her Bible which brought its message to Christians as well as Jews she used as a text when she addressed groups of Sunday school children in the Methodist Church. So deep was her respect for the religion of others that she made of some of her husband's Christian colleagues at the University of Illinois, eloquent interpreters of the Bible as she knew it. It was not in the spirit of once-a-year observance of Brotherhood Week that she emphasized the cherished heritage of Psalmist and Prophet. It was as a prophetess whose own soul glowed with incandescent faith that she illumined these interfaith contacts. When in the little world of academe which was Urbana-Champaign, the Jews decided to build a temple, it was a loyal friend of the Litmans, University President David Kinley, a Scotch Presbyterian, who gave the first generous contribution to the building fund.

What was our protagonist like in the 1890's? We have a contemporary description titled "*Ray Frank* (A pen portrait)," by C. A. Danziger.[24] It was published in the *American Jewess,* a periodical edited by Mrs. Rosa Sonnenschein. He begins with a lyrical and somewhat exaggerated tribute to her outward appearance: "Straight as a Trajan column, a small, finely shaped head, surmounting a gracefully curved neck, a delicate oval face, the chin firm, the mouth well formed, mobile . . . large, dark lustrous, eloquent eyes, with dark, full pencillings; amply and clearly browed and crowned by black, plainly-parted hair, all evincing a mind soaring aloft . . . this is Ray Frank." He admits that there may be other women with personal charm and good minds and fine education. But "There is no word in the English language at my command that would adequately tell of the quality of her genius . . . (or) convey a reason for that phenomenon which startles us when Ray Frank speaks. . . . The vanity of most people would not permit them to acknowledge that there can be a being as grand, and as incomparable as Ray Frank." There are many more columns of such tribute. The article concludes: "Women like Ray Frank are not to be classified, compared or analyzed; they are developed by conditions, as was Confucius, and Moses, and Buddha, and Christ; they grip mankind's heart and lift its soul to the divine." The anonymous Jewess in America had reached in Ray Frank the Olympian heights. She was known and acknowledged and acclaimed.

One would wish to linger over her many personal triumphs and drop many names. It is a privilege to have read and made notes on all of her voluminous correspondence including some intensely fascinating letters which Ambrose Bierce wrote to her.[25] "Small bits of her past became well known to me. That she had been on a Chautauqua circuit with William Jennings Bryant. . . . That she had opened the Women's section of the World Congress of Religions in 1893 and with Hannah Solomon and Sadie American had helped to found the National Council of Jewish Women. That she had lectured extensively both here and abroad. . . . I have seen her notebooks. I have read newspaper accounts of her speeches—lyrical extravagant descriptions of how she could hold vast audiences spellbound . . . of how men and women wept when she talked of the sufferings of her people. Frenzied enthusiasm, deep emotional response. . . . She must have been in the great tradition of orators."[26] In the year of 1893 when Ray Frank helped in the first historic deliberations of the Jewish women of America, the Cincinnati *Star Times* referred to her as "A famous Jewess who has been called a female Messiah." Her speech in Chicago contained this exhortation: "As mothers of Israel I appeal to you to first make of our homes temples, to rear each child as a priest by teaching him to be true to himself." She returned to her home in California to ringing acclaim. She had indeed done well. Her triumphs continued. She met a man most worthy of her, Simon Litman, "and they lived happily ever after. . . ."

These were strange times, these years of the last decade of the nineteenth century. In 1893 the Jewish women of America could glow with justifiable pride in their accomplishments. A year later, December 22, 1894, a French Jew, Captain Alfred Dreyfus, was found guilty of treason to his nation. Then the bells tolled for Jews all over the world. And Lucie Dreyfus wrote the following day to her husband, "You will be vindicated. . . . Your children will worship you. . . ." Her husband answered from prison: "Your heroism conquers me. Strengthened by your letter. . . . I feel my courage reborn. . . ."[27] He was at long last vindicated and the civilized world rejoiced.

The new organization that was born during the meeting of the Congress of Religions has continued with undiminished vigor to this day. It had significance because it provided a meeting ground for women of all geographic and economic backgrounds; because it formulated a socially desirable program; because it gave numerical strength and influence to previously scattered and local organiza-

tions; because it defined opportunities for social service
and addressed itself to concrete solutions; because it
pointed the way to a sphere of influence beyond the home,
the synagogue and the local community; because it created
and reaffirmed bonds of kinship with coreligionists all
over the world. Specifically, Hannah Solomon and her co-
workers blueprinted a five-point program: 1) an active
participation in contemporary Jewish affairs; 2) international relations; 3) social legislation; 4) social welfare;
5) service to the foreign-born. These areas are self-explana-
tory. They have grown with the expanding population
and with the growing needs created by crises during the
black years of the extermination of millions and the physical and mental and moral assault on uncounted millions
more.[28]

Rebekah Kohut, another dynamic leader of the National Council of Jewish Women almost from the days of
its inception (being prevented from sharing in its creation by her husband's illness) and who was president of
its New York Section, summarizes in her autobiography
many areas of its significant programming. One aspect
which most appealed to her and which is not clearly
spelled out in other autobiographical memoirs needs to
be noted. Rebekah Kohut writes: "It made me happy
that the Council gave a strong impetus to Bible study
and that by getting to know religious history, Jewesses
who had perhaps regretted that they were born in the
faith and were carrying the Yoke of the Torah, became
ardent advocates of synagogue services and ceremonial
observance in the home."[29]

The *Proceedings of the First Convention of the National Council of Jewish Women,* which summarizes its
deliberations in New York from November 15 through
November 19, in 1896, is an impressive volume. It runs
to 420 pages of solid information. It summarizes the

phenomenal three-year growth of the organization. For
by 1896, its officers included women from many states
and one from Canada, Mrs. Mendola De Sola of Montreal. The Council had a special hymn written for the
occasion by H. P. Mendes of New York, sung to the
tune of "My Country, 'tis of thee . . ." The Council's
motto is included in the text of the poem:

> When we from Egypt's land
> Marched forth a rescued band
>   To Liberty,
> Then Freedom, noble word,
> By mankind first was heard
> And human hearts were stirred
>   To turn to Thee!
>
> Since then throughout the world
> Our flag has been unfurled
> For Thee on High!
> Justice, Love, Modesty,*
> Duty, Fidelity,
> "Faith and Humanity"†
> O, hear our cry!

In 1896, the Council had come of age. It has had a
phenomenal record of growth to this day.

Hannah Solomon's Presidential address referred to this
almost unbelievable record: "We represent twenty-two
States and fifty Cities, and I know that all of you join
me in extending a special greeting to our sisters from
Montreal and Toronto, who represent our first flight
across the border."[31] She closed with this exhortation:
"Let us realize the power of individuals, joined for good
purposes."[32] The anonymous woman had discovered the
power of numerical strength. Christian women were also

---

*Micah.
†The Council's Motto.[30]

heard from. One of them was Mary Lowe Dickinson, president of the National Council of Women. She spoke not only for American women but for those of England, Denmark, Germany, Switzerland, Italy, New Zealand, and New South Wales. "My heart prompts me to speak to you of all these women, in a sense outside women, yet there is another and a grander sense in which no woman and no class of women can be outside of that great warm throbbing heart of womanhood that is making of itself a bulwark against the evil and the sin and the shame of the world. We are all of one family, and there is no possibility of making any of us orphans . . . we have learned . . . to work for womanhood through a national council of women everywhere."[33] At that meeting and in countless other meetings to come, these women had found a universe of discourse. There were of course differences among the members. There was a brief and very telling public dialogue which should be recorded. Here it is verbatim:

> Mrs. De Sola of Montreal, Canada: It seems to me that the first need of the Council is that every member of the Jewish Council of Women should keep the Sabbath. The President: The time has now expired for discussion of the paper . . .[34]

Summarily dismissed, yet to be brought up again many times!

10

A new age had been inaugurated in 1893, a time of manifold organizational activities of women. For women banded together are an army with banners. The anonymous woman had discovered her numerical strength. Generation succeeded generation. "Faith and Humanity" —this was the slogan of the National Council of Jewish Women. There are many protagonists who exemplify the affirmation of this credo, in this and in other organizations. The Council had a succession of endowed leaders. One noted example is Fanny Fligelman Brin. She was born in Rumania in 1884 and was brought to the United States as an infant. Her family settled in Minneapolis where she was educated. She later attended the University of Minnesota where she had a brilliant record. She was elected to Phi Beta Kappa and taught school from 1906. In 1913, she married Arthur Brin, who shared her concern for the social welfare of his fellow-Americans of all faiths. He was president of the Minneapolis Council of Social Agencies, after seventeen years as chairman of its budget committee and was a founder of the Associated Jewish Charities.

At the Minnesota Historical Society, there are twenty-five huge boxes of letters, papers and other memorabilia of this gifted woman. These are records which illumine an era of great social change, of war and its aftermath, of assault on life and human dignity and mass extermination of Jews, the victims of the most cruel and evil plan to exterminate a religious group that the world has ever known. Through those bleak and anguished years, this gentle woman wrote thousands of letters, traveled tens of thousands of miles, dedicated her life and all of her energies to an unyielding effort to assuage, to remedy, to improve the lot of the escapees from terror. In this, she had the full support of Arthur Brin and of their three children, Rachel, Howard and Charles. Her record is imperishable. Here are the outlines of selfless greatness. She was quiet and soft-spoken. Her manner was reticent, almost withdrawn. She listened with an undeviating and courteous attention, a creative kind of listening seldom encountered in club women. She met many congenial souls in all walks of life and from many backgrounds. The evangelist Sherwood Eddy was a close friend and Mr. and Mrs. Brin made a momentous journey to Palestine with a group that included that eminent Christian clergyman. While there, they established the Brin Scholarships at the Hebrew University. In the bulging files of the Minnesota Historical Society where the Brin papers repose, one may find not only the materials for a rewarding biography of a great American Jewess but enough of other social data to illumine the bleak decades when Fanny Brin rose to heights of heroic leadership. The custodian of these archives summarizes some of them as follows:

"Among the many organizations Mrs. Brin served, the

National Council of Jewish Women is most amply represented in her papers. The Council, Mrs. Brin believed, had a vital role to play in the nation's life . . . Over the years the Council sponsored a broad program . . . One of the early programs of particular importance in American life was the Foreign Born Department, established in 1904 at the request of the United States Government. The government's concern was due to the activities of white slave procurers and sweatshop operators, who preyed upon newly arrived immigrant women. . . ." After 1933, "she was concerned, particularly, with the placement of European Jews uprooted by the persecutions . . . Her activities included providing scholarships and positions for German-Jewish scholars, bringing . . . Jewish children [to the United States] sending food and clothing to the needy, and promoting the cause of education in Palestine." Even this summary as provided by the Minnesota Historical Society as well as by conversations with her daughter and other members of her family, visits to Minneapolis, knowledge of the magnitude of her work for refugees, do not begin to convey the scope and power of that selfless life, those endless vigils in behalf of others.[1] "She served the cause of women's rights . . . in two ways; the commanding place she took in American Jewish life through her abilities and dedication to work won recognition for her sex as well as for herself . . . she participated in the Women's Centennial Congress, the International Congress of Women, the International Assembly of Women, and the Committee on Women in World Affairs. She served as National President of the Council of Jewish Women and as an alternate consultant on the United States Delegation to the United Nations Conference in San Francisco. Mrs. Brin served as Minnesota State Chairman for the National Conference on the Cause and Cure of War and was active in Hadassah, the League of Women Voters

and the National Conference of Christians and Jews."
To all of these causes she gave herself unsparingly. There
are many men and women who keep her memory green.

In addition to opening avenues of social service to
thousands of its members, the National Council of Jewish
Women provided a forum where Jewish scholars and
specialists in history and sociology and the arts could speak
of their years of research. For an audience is as important
to a lecturer as a reader is to an author. We cite briefly
but one example of such programming opportunity. On
November 21, 1905, a respected scholar in the field of
American Jewish history was invited to deliver a paper
before the New York Council of Jewish Women. Leon
Huhner delivered a brilliant address on "The Jewish
Woman in America." He found to his great surprise, he
told his audience of women at Temple Emanu-El, that
although "students of Jewish history have written on a
great variety of subjects, there appears to be no essay or
even any attempt at one, upon so important a topic." He
then covers the very earliest records and the very most
tragic of heroines, the victims of the Inquisition. "Nor
were these women elderly matrons whom time and adversity had inclined toward religion; quite a few were in
the very bloom of youth . . ."[2] He traced the evolution of
the history of Jewish women in the Western hemisphere
giving numerous examples now well known, then totally
unknown. He does not fail to mention the poets and
writers, the actresses and social workers. He names a Miss
Katherine Cohen, "the gifted pupil of St. Gaudens, who
has exhibited her sculptures at the Paris salon," a name
hitherto not encountered elsewhere. He is gratified by
the fact that hundreds of Jewish women have entered the
teaching profession and social work. He concludes with
this appeal: "It is for you of today to show the same
zeal that animated Emma Lazarus, so that the story of

the Jewish woman in America, which begins with the gloom and darkness of the Inquisition in Mexico and Peru, may grow resplendent with the sunshine spread by the American Jewess in helping the distressed in every land." In the following year, in far off Minnesota, Fanny Fligelman began her long years of "resplendent" service.

Members of Hannah Solomon's family in her lifetime and to this day continue her work. Hannah Solomon's niece, Rose S. Alschuler, has won a place for herself in the annals of Jewish women of America. Her gifts were largely expressed as an individual and not through a group. But Hannah's torch was passed from hand to hand. In Rose Alschuler's autobiography, titled *Bits and Pieces of Family Lore,* published on her seventy-fifth birthday, December 17, 1962, there is a detailed genealogy which goes back to 1719 and which is important to future students of American Jewish history. Certainly, it adds to our knowledge of the antecedents of Hannah Solomon. It also points up the importance of the safeguarding of Jewish family records while there is still time.

In one of his sermons titled "The Religious Basis of the Family" one of the militant founders of the Reform movement, an outspoken and often uncompromising foe of Orthodoxy, Emil G. Hirsch, under whose religious umbrella the German Jews of Chicago took shelter, has some rather interesting things to say about Jewish women and particularly those who were members of the Council of Jewish Women.[3] It was this man who shaped both Hannah's and Rose's early opinions and instilled the rigid and unyielding attitude which Mrs. Alschuler held —and forsook—as a mature woman. The story of her "conversion" is as dramatic as any found in American Jewish annals.

Hirsch begins: "Were I a member of a women's organization . . ." and continues: "But unfortunately I am not a member of the Council of Jewish Women and therefore I have not that fulness of wisdom and I do not believe everything that is written down in the Bible the way apparently they do. If I make that statement it is because recently I read some of the papers that were delivered at the convention of the Council of Jewish Women and to read those papers is enough to make one who has been teaching in Jewish congregations for over forty years disappointed in himself." His disillusion is boundless. "There isn't the least trace that the Council has taken even notice of the position advanced by me and others of liberal mind in the Jewish pulpits. We still hear, as we heard fifty years ago, all about the beauty of orthodox religion, all about the poetry of orthodox ceremonials . . ." Was Rabbi Hirsch reading the handwriting on the wall?

This man had a profound and indelible influence on Rose Haas, later Mrs. Alfred S. Alschuler, as well as on her aunt Hannah Solomon. Her earliest biographical anecdotes involve both the dynamic little aunt and the lusty, uncompromising and determined rabbi. Her "earliest memory" was in "World's Fair year (1893) ." She had fond recollections of Emil G. Hirsch and respected him for instilling into her an undeviating allegiance to Judaism. The comfortable home in which her childhood and youth were spent was in a different world from the overcrowded streets where dwelt the East European Jews with whom she was for a great part of her life to have had no contact. Her father prospered. Toward all of her family, Rose's mother showed undeviating love. It was in her own mother's dying hours that Rose came to have the great "transcendent experience" of her life—an authentic religious illumination which enriched all of the years that followed and brought her into activities and social services which she had hitherto considered foreign and alien to her. It brought her actively into the ranks of those who helped develop the State of Israel.

This is the way she describes her mother's death:

> The illumination that enveloped me immediately preceding her death has been a beacon light throughout my life, and in a unique way has made the intervening years meaningful. Through her death, forty-six years ago, the spirituality of the universe was revealed. That we are all part of the Universal Spirit, today remains for me the only unchanging reality. Fulfillment by each one of us of our greatest potential is our day-to-day function and obligation.
>
> I live knowing and feeling that Life and Death are a continuum. Death is but an incident in the continuum of Life. . . .
>
> We may grieve for the way of the world, for burdens suffered by those we love—and for our own loss when some beloved person has gone from among us. But Death is as natural as Life—and both are blessed. We are fortunate if Death comes not too soon to those we cherish, nor tarries too long before beckoning us away.[4]

This is her credo. It enabled her to become an educator, author, philanthropist, and a recognized and honored contributor to the development and growth of Israel. It set her feet upon hitherto untrodden paths. For little children in her own home and in the home of her parents there seemed to have been but one climate—that of love. What makes Rose Alschuler unique is that she has brought that spirit to countless little children in many parts of the world. She is known for her pioneering educational accomplishments in Winnetka and in Washington, in Oslo and in New Delhi. She has been called to White House Conferences and has slept in Gandhi's ashram.

It all began in the twenties at a time when Freud and his concepts and his vocabulary were doing much to reinterpret human motivation. It was an era of significant discovery, of new insights. In the little village of Winnetka, Illinois, Rose Alschuler became a pioneer in the field of nursery school education. She had served her apprenticeship under "Uncle Julius"—a courtesy uncle and longtime family friend, Julius Rosenwald. He had endowed and Rose Alschuler had established and directed two Nursery Schools in a housing development on the South Side of Chicago known as the Garden Apartments. Junior kindergartens were established in Winnetka. In a tree-shaded area adjoining Skokie School, Alfred and Rose Alschuler built and donated a magnificent school for little children, one of the most modern in the world. To this school came educators from every part of the world to become a part of the teacher education program for nursery schools. After her husband's death, Rose was summoned to Washington where for a number of years she was active as the Chairman of the National Commission for Young Children.

In 1943, she became a consultant to the Federal Public Housing Authority. She helped plan and select equipment for nursery schools built in connection with war housing projects. She served as director and member of executive boards of a number of educational associations, taught and lectured in several American universities and received countless awards and citations for her pioneering work in nursery school education. One of her books, *Two to Six,* is considered a classic in its field. Another major undertaking was a two-volume book called *Painting and Personality,* which she wrote with L. W. Hattwick. The book was the result of new psychoanalytic and psychiatric techniques presented at a meeting in Mexico City in 1935 at which it was claimed that the paintings of little children reveal in depth their major experiences, traumatic and other, which they cannot verbalize but which give insight to their problems and personalities of which educators should be aware. Having done so much for the cause of liberating the minds and souls of small children both in deprived and suburban areas, Rose Alschuler embarked on a process of self-liberation which was equally epic in scope.

Her horizons had been expanding over the decades. She had abundant religious loyalty and never forsook her roots. She continued to express her esteem and affection for Rabbi Emil G. Hirsch. Yet she found in the ceremonials and traditional mode of worship of the Conservative synagogue which she attended near her home (while maintaining her membership in North Shore Congregation Israel of which her husband was the architect and founder), and in the sermons and services of Rabbi Philip L. Lipis, something so vital and so precious to her that she became a fast friend of Rabbi and Mrs. Lipis and of the many causes they espoused. She had been brought up to consider Zionism as a project that appealed only to East European Jews. She visited Palestine and then Israel several times and was overwhelmed by the spiritual significance of the dedicated idealists who had long planned and dreamed of a refuge for homeless Jews and were at last triumphantly vindicated. Their vision and ideology became hers. With the courage of greatness she reversed her previous opinions and acclaimed the new state and its accomplishments. She brought down scorn and contumely upon herself. With an Olympian serenity she shrugged off her critics and continued to write and lecture about the new hope of Israel. In turn, the leaders of the state of Israel have honored her.

Gentle, serene, dedicated and worthy, this daughter of Israel symbolizes a spiritual journey which began for her

at her mother's bedside in the last flickering hours of
that life. She writes of that threshhold vigil: "Life was
gradually ebbing away. I knew we were getting to our
journey's end. We traveled ever onward and upward, now
one halting and then the other. . . . Our souls were ever
traveling together, until we finally emerged.—I hesitate
to write this for thought of your unbelief—but we were
immersed in a wonderful glorious, more than earthly
light. When my vision was at last blinded by the glory
of it, I realized that I was there alone. She had entered
the Great Gates. I had gone with her as far as it is given
mortals to go. I live but to follow her worthily."[5]

The half century that elapsed since these words were
written has vindicated the vision. This may seem strange
and arcane to the skeptic. But there are those among
Hasidim and other devout souls, both Christian mystics
and Jews, who will believe in the vision. It requires, says
Professor Heschel "spiritual delicacy" to share such an
experience.[6] The roots of the "higher faith in God are
not in the realm of reason but in the divine soul . . ."[7]

So Rose Alschuler stands tall with other articulate
Jewish women in America. Yet in a strange and wonderful
way she is also the Shunammite, the anonymous benefactor
of mankind. For her gifts and her skills, her visions and
her accomplishments have been largely practiced in secret.

"There is a river whose streams make glad the city of
God." So sang the Psalmist millennia ago. There are
times when the contemplation of the history of the Jewish
people makes these words imperishable, shining truths.

Blueprints for biography are infinite in their variety.
Endlessly challenging the chronicler are thousands of
heroines each fulfilling her destiny after her fashion.
Sometimes one of our protagonists in the development of
her personality and the gifts she freely offers her country,

seems to be fulfilling a long chain of events carried in her biological stream which flows from generation to generation. Such a person was Dr. Minna Libman Emch, brilliant psychoanalyst who brought as her oblation to her times, not only the gift of a brilliant mind, a dedicated urge for service—but also a continuation of the dreams and hopes and goals of a brilliant and saintly ancestor. She was a lineal descendant of Rabbi Israel Lipkin, known as "the Salanter" for the little Lithuanian village where his dream was born and nurtured. During his lifetime (1810-1883) he became an exponent of the Musar movement which called upon his disciples "to strive to attain moral elevation by means of self-renunciation and mental discipline." A life of ascetic deprivation led to his undergoing psychiatric treatment. It was as a physician and psychoanalyst that Dr. Minna (1904-1958) fulfilled her destiny. The Salanter's infinite patience, compathy, gentle wisdom were hers in full measure. She could be summarized by the Biblical injunction

"Say to wisdom, 'you are my sister'
and call insight your intimate friend."[8]

Ten years after her death in a book published in 1969, and largely a tribute to her, Lucy Freeman wrote of her "great dependence on Dr. Emch," of her empathy toward her patients.

"It was this rare ability to block out everything—the outside world, her life, all else did not matter—that in part permitted her to have such empathy. My life became hers for those few moments in time. She somehow reached inside my mind, absorbed my emotions. She felt as I felt, thought as I thought."

At her death Miss Freeman wrote "I loved her because she gave me the feeling of worth and dignity . . . I loved her because she desired to ease the suffering within me."[9]

And Ben Hecht in eulogizing her said of her "She had

a sort of reverence for the mind of man . . . And she turned her own mind as a searchlight on all the evidences of existence. Music, art, literature, philosophy, history and all the provocative findings of science delighted her . . . Dr. Minna Emch was a brilliant psychoanalyst whose work was touched with genius. Many honors came to her. Her multitude of patients sounded her praises in all parts of the earth. And the leaders of her profession esteemed her as one of their keenest and most talented."

So "wisdom had built her house" and she taught countless people "to walk in the way of insight."[10]

It would obviously be impossible, short of writing a work of many volumes, to cover adequately the organizational activities of an army of women serving under many banners, all dedicated to good works, to social meliorism, to interpreting their concern for others. It is equally impossible to name the hundreds of women whose names are recognized and whose contributions are saluted by Americans in every walk of life. Indeed, some of these women are better known to the Christian world for services they have rendered, for talents they have nurtured, for the enrichment they have brought to the larger community. There are women who transcend parochialism. There are women who shine in "the great society." It is not our purpose to list or to extol them all.

In a 1959 issue of the Publications of the *American Jewish Historical Society* there is an interesting notice which enlarges this point of view. Under the heading, "Notable American Women 1607-1950," we learn that "Radcliffe College is sponsoring the preparation of a biographical dictionary of American women."[11] The editor is Dr. Edward T. James, previously associated with the Supplement of the *Dictionary of American Biography*. He lists the names of American Jewesses who may be

found in the *Dictionary of American Biography*. It is an
edifying inventory and the reader is referred to the source.
There are fourteen names:

> Sophie Breslau
> Rose Eytinge
> Alma Gluck
> Emma Goldman
> Rebecca Gratz
> Emma Lazarus
> Sophie Irene Simon Loeb
> Adah Isaacs Menken
> Penina Moise
> Belle Lindner Israels Moskowitz
> Ernestine Louise Sismondi Potowski Rose
> Rose Harriet Pastor Stokes
> Lillian D. Wald
> Fanny Bloomfield Zeisler

In December of 1965, the B'nai B'rith, seeking to honor
"Jewish Women in American History," drew up its own
list of fourteen great American Jewish women. Some of
the names appear on both lists. Others are omitted from
the earlier list to make room for new honorees. On the
B'nai B'rith list these are the new names:

> Henrietta Szold
> Rebekah Kohut
> Hannah Solomon
> Fanny Brice
> Edna Ferber
> Fanny Hurst
> Bertha Kalisch
> Lillian Hellman

Countless other lists may be compiled. One need only
define standards and criteria.[12] A number of European
Jewesses had a great impact on American Jewish women,
forming a trans-Atlantic sisterhood. One such great English woman, like Grace Aguilar, was Lily H. Montagu,
who in her lifetime was Honorary Life President of the
World Union for Progressive Judaism. In feminine theological circles she is preeminent. Lillian Helen Montagu,

daughter of the first Lord Swaythling, was "one of the founders and most enthusiastic supporters of the Liberal Jewish movement in England," the only woman to achieve such distinction at any time. One of the prayers she composed summarizes her own philosophy and that of her sisters on both sides of the Atlantic:

"O God, be thou praised. All around us are revelations of Thy loving kindness. . . . We fix our minds on the day when Thou wilt make Thyself known to all nations of the world, and all men will seek together to do Thy service."

Here was the concept of universal Judaism which Solomon Schechter and his brilliant wife promulgated and to which she dedicated a lifetime of service, ". . . for kinship with God implies the ultimate perfectibility of man." It is the sense of "kinship with God," that led to the inception of many women's organizations.

What applies to individual women holds true of organizational life in America—Canada, Mexico, the United States, and South America. For out of the sheltered areas in homes and synagogues they have enlisted in vast groups identifying themselves with countless causes. Serving the larger community, they also served themselves. There was strength in numbers and they wielded it. There was comfort and reassurance in group contact and they discovered it. There was balm in leaving the narrow confines of the home and entering a larger sphere of action. Meetings were the antidotes to loneliness and isolation which every housewife has experienced. Talents, skills and abilities long held dormant were discovered. There were gratifying moments of self-discovery when oratorical skills hitherto unsuspected were like subterranean streams let loose. "All the great speakers were bad speakers at first," said Emerson. There was the unguent of applause and approbation. There was always the opportunity to do good, to help those less privileged. There were the legitimate claims of oppressed kinsmen in need of an immediate place of refuge, of food and clothing, of medical care. So for reasons altruistic and selfish, women joined clubs, societies, associations, *landsmanschaften*. It was James Bryce who said of the immigrant in America that he seems to melt in it (the new environment) "as a lump of sugar melts in a cup of tea."[13] Clubs for women were their cup of tea.

It is a strange fact that the same motives and methods of group life operate in every stratum of society. Whether in country club or self-imposed ghetto, whether native or foreign-born, whether speaking flawless or fractured English or Yiddish—the pattern repeats itself endlessly.

Geography and language made no discernable difference in group activities. In January of 1966, out of a total Jewish population in Canada of 267,000 Jews, more than 82,000 claimed Yiddish as their mother tongue. Within these Yiddish-speaking Canadian groups, women expressed themselves with equal eloquence whether for the general good or for self-enhancement. Club politics in country clubs and in WIZO meetings follow the same overt and covert procedures.[14] They overleap geographic and national boundaries. In August of 1953 there was a Conference of the Associated Countrywomen of the World which met in Toronto. "This non-political non-sectarian organization has as its aim the raising everywhere of the level of housing, health, education, food and agriculture. At this conference the focal point was the development of a programme of assistance to underdeveloped countries."[15] Branches of WIZO of Canada and Israel participated in its deliberations.

It may not be amiss at this point to call attention to the phenomenal growth of the Jewish population of Canada in the last thirty years, which reflects itself in the

activities of its Jewish women. The Jewish population of
Canada increased vastly between 1901 and 1931. From
1931 to 1961 it increased by more than sixty-two percent.
"The greatest numerical increase during the thirty-year
period from 1931 to 1961 has taken place in Ontario
(47,250) . . . and the greatest percentage increase has
taken place in British Columbia . . ."[16] Competent reporters of the Canadian Jewish scene stress the fact that
Orthodoxy and the Conservative movements have a greater
appeal there than does the Reform movement. Sherman
points out the correlation between adjustment and language: "The Yiddish language, instead of being a hin-
drance, was actually an important means of adjustment."[17]
The large influx of Jews into Canada and the widespread
uses of Yiddish as recently reported there are related
phenomena.

Canada was like Chicago, "another part of America."
Yet in group life, in folkways and mores, in philanthropic
and religious organizations, in the use of Yiddish, in the
shepherding of children into religious schools to learn
Hebrew, in loyalty to kith and kin, there were many
similarities. And in the Canadian branches of women's
organizations which originally were established in the
United States, one finds similar group patterns in communal, civic, and religious activities.

As the decades roll on, women in organizations begin
to feel and to wield their power. We are not always concerned here with the "great" women who through special
talent, skill or genius, bring their gifts to the great society.
In literature, in science, in government, in the professions
they are forging ahead. Often these noted Jewish women
have lost contact with the group and the society which
nurtured them and shaped their genius. One considers
the bleak and sorrowful years, the years of mourning for

six million martyrs, and wonders where their voices and their sentiments were. Their silence becomes oppressive. In those burdened years when their unknown sisters affiliated with countless causes, by sheer weight of numbers rescued children, provided visas for families, sheltered individuals in their homes, worked tirelessly collecting money, clothing, signatures for visas for those who were stripped of all dignity, honor, possessions—the persistent question remains as to the whereabouts of some of the famous ones, as to their contributions to the dispossessed. To be counted, one enlists in the ranks with the disinherited. The seeker of glory for glory's sake must be content with her wages—fame, success, ivory tower eminence, Olympian heights, money, public acclaim. The anonymous woman joins ranks with her own kind. The goals she serves are socially useful. Her time and her energy are devoted to objectives which enhance others. If, in the process, she discovers her own talents, if she can wield a gavel with authority and address her peers with eloquence, if she becomes known in her community for her good works, she is only fulfilling the role which the Bible exalted—she is then a woman of virtue—and "she is far more precious than jewels." "The fruit of her hands" is in the roll call of women's organizations dedicated to the common needs of others.

Hadassah and HIAS and ORT and Pioneer Women and Women of the American Jewish Congress and Women of B'nai B'rith and women who have founded synagogue and temple sisterhoods and the National Women's League of the United Synagogue of America—these are some of the organizations which have chosen a critical area of social service and have brought their numerical strength to bear on the steady climb toward amelioration of social conditions. We propose to rescue from oblivion some forgotten feminine soldiers in the ranks who have fought

the good fight. In this we are often joined by women of
other faiths. For "Women have a heritage in religion to
regain, develop and carry forward," writes Margaret Brack-
enbury Crook, reminding us also that "Women have an
important place in the early history of Israel."[18] Professor
Crook then recalls Miriam's searching question: "Has the
Lord spoken only through Moses? Has he not spoken
through us also?"[19] And the Psalmist has added:

> The Lord giveth the word;
> The women that publish the tidings are *a
>   great host*.[20]

A woman who "published the tidings" as the nineteenth
century was speeding to its close was Rosa Sonnenschein
of Chicago, whose magazine had a brief span of life. The
American Jewess sold for ten cents a copy, or one dollar
a year and was surprisingly literate and attractive in content. In view of the great merit of the periodical, of its
splendid articles mirroring the times, it is strange that
it has been so completely overlooked. Recently a Hebrew
journalist, writing in *Hadoar* in an article titled "In the
Footsteps of the Generations," discussed the career of this
amazing and undeservedly forgotten journalist.[21] She was
of a thoroughly independent mind and did not in her
long years, as journalists often do, say or write the pre-
dictable. She was not a political Zionist. Nor did she
belong to *Hovevei Zion,* the early Zionist organization.
She wrote essays and reports for a number of English,
American and European periodicals. She traveled widely
and was in touch with some of the early leaders in Europe
who were eventually to direct the Zionist movement. Both
Herzl and Nordau influenced her thinking. On an impulse
she wrote to Herzl. He answered her May 8, 1897. Rosa
Sonnenschein attended the First Zionist Congress as an
observer and was most favorably impressed by Herzl's

personality. She was deeply moved by the gathering of her dispersed kinsmen and by the spirit of the proceedings and the decorum and sense of mission which prevailed. Nordau's prophetic address on opening day was for her an unforgettable experience. With twelve other women, delegates and observers, Rosa was photographed and on her return described both the proceedings and her own impressions.

Rosa was born in Hungary on March 12, 1847. Her father was a rabbi. The family came to America in 1869. She plunged into an active life as a journalist, and served as a special correspondent for St. Louis and Chicago newspapers while attending the Paris Exposition. Her life in America was both tragic and eventful. She married Rabbi Solomon H. Sonnenschein. He belonged to an extreme Reform group and was totally and unalterably opposed to Zionism. They had four children—and all predeceased their parents. It became ideologically and physically a barren union. Perhaps the grim happenings of her day-to-day life drove her to her literary labors. Originally, *The American Jewess* was published in Chicago. Some of the later issues appeared in St. Louis and in New York. All the Anglo-Jewish periodicals and many general newspapers and magazines welcomed this new publication "dedicated to the Jewish woman in America." And as one turns its crumbling pages, the thought arises that the Jewish woman of today could well use such a journal to chronicle her activities, to describe the countless philanthropies and causes she supports.

Rosa claimed that her journal had 29,000 subscribers. In a notice to her readers she stated that it was the only Jewish periodical which had many Christian readers as well. She added that *The American Jewess* was the only publication of its kind in the world dedicated to the interests of Jewish women. She espoused two principles:

Her magazine would always "uphold the Sabbath. It would continue the campaign for equal rights for women in their religious life." To her critics—of whom her husband was one—she addressed two questions: "Why should one Jew despise another because he wishes to continue his ancestral customs?" And "Why does Reform Judaism put so many obstacles on the road to Palestine?"

It was with deep personal sorrow that she announced that the periodical had passed out of her hands. In 1899 its publication was discontinued. When her magazine died, Rosa Sonnenschein went into "a personal eclipse." Her name was forgotten even by her erstwhile associates. She died at eighty-five in St. Louis. On March 5, 1932, Rabbi Ferdinand Isserman spoke the traditional words of prayer and of eulogy. It was the end of a life of valor and of tragedy. Her literary remains repose in a warehouse—and she is buried in Har Sinai Cemetery in St. Louis.

One cannot really know what the woman of that era was like, what interested her, what intrigued and concerned her without reading this magazine. It served many purposes. One of them was furnishing a sympathetic forum for the budding authoresses of the day. Among them were Rebekah Kohut and Ray Frank. Rebekah contributed "An Autobiographical Fragment." Ray Frank wrote on "The Arch Enemy of the Jew" and discussed the pathetic weaklings who run away from their ancestral moorings and spend their lives despising themselves. "Is there anything," Ray Frank asks, "more profoundly pathetic, more grimly humorous, more piteously contemptible than he who denies his father and is in turn rejected because he avows he is not that which he is? . . . Of the sincere convert from any one creed to another, I am not speaking. . . . I criticize only the descendant of Jacob who, for no better reason than a sordid ambition, is ashamed of, deserts, aye, hates his own people." There must have been good and cogent reasons for Ray Frank's moral indignation. She did not tilt at windmills.

At a "Literary Tea" described at length in *The American Jewess,* there was an "Aguilar Library Table." Autographed copies of books by other popular authors were offered for sale, as well as signed photographs of President Cleveland and all his Cabinet. The description of the party could have been written today, except for the authors honored: Kate Douglas Wiggin, Frank Stockton, Charles Dudley Warner. . . . Throughout these volumes sketches of Jewish women of rare beauty illumine the pages. Personalities of significance are described. Baron de Hirsch's death is mourned and his beneficence saluted. "Most remarkable is the fact that his philanthropic and sentimental nature evidenced itself by a misfortune, which, as a rule, is calculated to make of ordinary men misanthropes." The reference is to the death of the only son of Baron de Hirsch. In July 1896, a serial titled *Jewish Blood* has the leading place. Club notes and news of meetings and literary events become more frequent. The Young Ladies' Aid Society of Chicago gets full and detailed coverage. It is the boast of its members that "Every project that has for its object the good of humanity meets with careful consideration . . . Thus, at the time of the wonderful World's Fair . . . the members of the Young Ladies' Aid Society threw open their doors to the Committee of the Congress of Jewish Women and made propaganda for the work."

In addition to fashions, book reviews, exhortations to cherish the faith, nudgings of all kinds to duty and conscience, one finds articles on many subjects that are arcane and mysterious which presage the interest in psychoanalysis and extrasensory perception of our day. Long before Freud's work was known in this country, a Dr. Carl Simon wrote about "Peculiar Latent Faculties of Mind." Here are discussed "the vivid and startling hints of the soul's omnipresent connections . . ." through such phenomena as "unconscious cerebration." He writes as if he had looked into the scientific journals of fifty years hence. "The mistake made is to apply to the soul the conditions which control gross matter."

Casual biographical sketches as well as salutes to women of renown were often included. Always the fact of pulchritude was stressed as if it were a peculiarly Semitic characteristic. Of Rachel Felix, "the Queen of Tragedy" it was written: "She is described as having a face of refined Judaical character . . . The physical traditions of her race found expression or incarnation in her." A gentleman submits a poem titled "The American Jewess," saluting a youthful heroine:

> O youthful daughter of thy ancient race,
>   In thy behalf great progress has been wrought . . .
>   In this free land of stirring act and thought . . .[22]

Chauvinism abounds. It is an antidote for self-rejection from which so many second-generation Jews suffered. There were subtle rabbinical blandishments and exhortations, as when Rabbi David Philipson attributed to Emerson a remark he probably never made: "I believe it was Emerson who said that a woman without religion is like a flower without perfume." This in connection with a tribute to Queen Esther, "The Ideal Jewess." Jewish women as heroines of history, as celebrated in Bible and Talmud, were ever-present space fillers. Only occasionally was there a hortatory note. In a fairly regular section of the magazine there was a section titled "The Woman Who Talks" devoted to lady lecturers. "Never in the history of American Jews have its young disciples quenched their thirst for knowledge as during the past winter." From some of the announced lecture topics one must deduce a powerful yen for knowledge and an inexhaustible supply of orators. Sometimes in one issue one can find an editorial on "Biblical Humor," or on "Jewish Women in Talmudic Times," and sandwiched between, an editorial on the benefits of "Malt-Nutrino" made by one of the firms that advertised in the journal. Only rarely, however, does Rosa obtrude with personal opinion or propaganda for Zionism. In 1898 she wrote on "Anti-Semitism and Zionism," insisting gently, "Zionism has not only passed the stage of ridicule, but it begins to receive the public homage it deserves . . ."

One could wish to have known her—this woman of grit and valor and endless personal tragedy and exuberant talents and indefatigable labors for her people. Yet she is forgotten, almost totally unknown, as if she had never lived, or, having lived, had had her name erased by the tides of time and history. Her name does not appear on any scroll of honor. To have rediscovered her even briefly is a great privilege. To recall her, to keep her memory green, is her due.

There were other women with claims to recognition who will never make lists of the chosen in works dedicated to the exalted few. And yet to get the total woman's portrait in America, one must seek out these lost records. The top of the iceberg has often been described. But the vast unseen bulk looms beneath the surface. It is that which largely concerns us. Numerical strength rather than public acclaim. Yet here, too, we need to focus on the individual. For the organizational colossus is really a mosaic composed of small and large souls. The overall portrait achieved is vital to history. But so are the little people who compose it, who build the ant heaps and carry the burdens.

From the earliest days of their coming to America, Jewish settlers like others were concerned with immediate needs—with survival and shelter and the means of earning a living. It was enough to satisfy the primary wants. Then came the claims of the people whose lives touched them through kinship or propinquity. Finally there came the larger goals—the needs of strangers, the recognition of the rights of others, especially of the underprivileged ones in the community. That is when the anti-slavery movement gained its ardent supporters, when feminists became vocal, when labor unions enlisted the articulate ones in their midst. Women identified with important causes soon came to recognize the inequities inherent in their own place in society.

There were isolated voices even in Colonial times demanding rights for women. A Catholic woman, Margaret Brent, helped to bring about the Toleration Act of Maryland. Abigail Adams wrote to John Adams in 1777 to remember the rights of women in the laws to be drafted. In New Jersey, women voted in 1776. "In seeking to free the slaves, radical women became conscious of their own lack of freedom." This explains the dedicated lives of the Grimké sisters, daughters of a South Carolina judge. It also places in its proper frame of reference a book published in England in 1792, titled *A Vindication of the Rights of Women,* by Mary Wollstonecraft. It was this work, as well as the Declaration of Independence, that was to inspire Frances Wright, Ernestine Rose, Lucretia Mott, Elizabeth Cady Stanton, Susan Anthony. In this tradition was Margaret Fuller, who wrote *Woman in the Nineteenth Century* in 1845. Three years later, in 1848, with revolutions sweeping over Europe, a call went out for a Woman's Rights Convention, to be held in Seneca Falls, New York. Four years after that, at a convention held in Syracuse, women demanded that the Bible be rewritten to eliminate texts hostile to them.[23] In 1869, "the most important feminist text in late Victorian times . . ." was written by John Stuart Mill.[24] It was titled *"On the Subjection of Women.*" In 1883, the anti-feminist Henry James lampooned the situation of women in *The Bostonians.* Women read books and listened to speeches and became orators and sought audiences as well as causes. Giant organizations developed from little parlor meetings. And goals were formulated and campaigns were conceived and carried out and society felt the impact and reacted with laurels or trauma, with praise or denigration. "The secret of the world is the tie between person and event. Person makes event, and event person." Thus Emerson.[25]

The celebration of the voyage of Columbus at the World's Fair in Chicago in 1893, was held against a background of economic unrest. Agrarian protest, growth of labor unions, the birth of the Populist Party, the severe panic of 1893, the coalition of jobless men marching on Washington in 1894, known as Coxey's Army, all were a part of the times. The speeches at the Congress of Religions do not mirror these conditions, nor do they presage the great social changes that were around the corner in the twentieth century. In Buffalo, New York, President McKinley was assassinated in 1901. On September 14, 1901, Theodore Roosevelt became the nation's twenty-fifth President. The following year he demanded a "square deal" for all Americans. He did more than that. By his forthright and humane attitude toward the victims of persecution in Russia, he became for Jews all over the world the voice of America's conscience. In 1905 President Roosevelt saluted the Jewish citizens of his country in these ringing words: "While the Jews of the United States . . . have remained loyal to their faith . . . they have become indissolubly incorporated in the great army of American citizenship, prepared to make all sacrifice for the country, either in war or peace . . . They are honorably distinguished by their industry, their obedience to law, and their devotion to the national welfare . . ." This

came at a time when the bells tolled the doom of the
Jews of Russia. In April of 1903, on the last day of Passover, there occurred the bestial pogrom of Kishinev.
America was aroused. From coast to coast in the United
States meetings were held to register their moral indignation. In New York, the President of Cornell University,
Jacob Gould Schurman, said, "O Christ! What crimes
have been committed in Thy name against the race which
gave Thee to the world!" Christians of conscience closed
ranks with American Jews. There was work cut out for
the burgeoning welfare and communal agencies of the
Jews of America. Its women had already discovered their
strength.

Of the birth of these groups, of their growth out of the
acute needs of their kinsmen, volumes may be written.
They need to have their stories told to point out the
patterns of organizational activities, to clarify their goals,
to describe the development of their strength through
numbers, to explain the self-discovery of the individual
woman as she worked for others and grew in stature
through her work.

Always these activities were carried on against the background of events at home and abroad. One feels an accelerated pace in the processes which involved relief and
rehabilitation of Jews overseas, of immigrants on the high
seas and those thronging the seaports. It was not only the
weight of numbers of newcomers that presented a challenge to the Jews of America. It was the moral weight of
problems which the newspapers brought each day with
their ever-increasing stories of horror, desolation, extermination. Every city had to make its own adjustment. In
1893, at the time of the Columbian Exposition, the Jews
of Chicago numbered 75,000. Refugees from Galicia and
Russia and Rumania kept pouring in. According to Rabbi
Stolz of Chicago, in two decades more than 100,000 Jews

of Eastern Europe came to Chicago and established a
"voluntary ghetto" on the southwest side.[26] Increasingly
both Yiddish and Anglo-Jewish papers covered the affliction of Jews in other parts of the world. The twentieth
century was to be a time of accelerated tragedy for mankind, of war and the threat of war, of hunger and privation, of an assault on everything that had been held dear
in the past, of a final triumph of brutality and sadism
which saw the extermination of six million Jewish martyrs. Against these crimes many Christians of conscience
had cried out. No more eloquent words were spoken than
those of Edwin Markham:

> Yes, from the trembling lips of many a seer
> The whole wide world has heard, and still can hear
> The Psalms, the Torah, and the Talmud speak . . .
> Shall not this race whose gifts have been so great
> Have some protection from the tooth of hate?
> They have not yet their safe place in the sun,
> They who knew Egypt, who know Babylon!

Even children's voices were heard in extermination
camps. And from Theresienstadt, where 15,000 Jewish
children perished, miraculously some of their faint cries
are heard in desolate songs collected in "one of the most
poignant reminders of the nightmare which the Nazis
brought to Germany." In *I Never Saw Another Butterfly*,
little children join Ann Frank in a plea to humanity.

Favel Friedmann wrote in 1942:

> For seven weeks I've lived in here,
> Penned up inside this ghetto
> But I have found my people here.
> The dandelions call to me
> And the white chestnut candles in the court.
> Only I never saw another butterfly.

> That butterfly was the last one
> Butterflies don't live in here,
> In the ghetto . . .

Events abroad of a happier nature were also found in the press. In Paris, when Baron Edmond de Rothschild wanted to mark the occasion of his daughter's marriage, he gave 50,000 francs to the Jewish community of that city, and Jews everywhere said "Mazel Tov" (Good luck!). In London a man named Louis Levy received a Carnegie medal for valor and heroism in aiding police in putting down riots "which greatly affected the Jews." In New South Wales two Jews were elected to the legislative assembly. A millionaire merchant of Port Arthur named Ginsburg offered half a million rubles "for the erection of a Jewish university in Vilna." In Chicago, on its northwest side, there was an Esther Falkenstein Home "modeled on Toynbee Hall in London." In Chicago, as elsewhere, women were being wooed from press and pulpit and podium. The *Sentinel* of that city had a department titled "The Woman and her Club," edited by a sturdy, dedicated matriarch named Nannie A. Reis. She urged women's "participation in world's work. . . ." Dr. Emil G. Hirsch preached on "the opportunities of the women's clubs. . . ." There were articles on "the influence of Jewish women in the social work of Chicago." "So many groups rushed in to fill communal philanthropic demands that Nannie A. Reis, women's page editor, discussed 'psychical research' as one explanation for the similarity of such programs on the part of many women's clubs."[27]

When Henrietta Szold came to Chicago in the days before Hadassah was founded, she spoke before two groups where Zionism was anathema, Sinai Temple and the Chicago Woman's Aid. Her subject "The New Pales-

tine—Its Hopes and Possibilities." In 1913 a roster of
great Jewish Women was published in the *Sentinel* and
Ray Frank Litman was on that list with others. The Jews
of America grieved when a gentle Jew of Atlanta, Georgia,
a native of Quero, Texas, was accused of murdering a
little Christian girl. Leo Frank was innocent. But a Southern mob lynched him and his co-religionists everywhere
were plunged into grief.

The depression spread an ever greater sense of insecurity among immigrant workers. They marched and
paraded and organized and listened to an anarchist spell-
binder, Emma Goldman. Her photographs made her look
like a witch, but a Jewish woman journalist assured her
readers that "Emma Goldman in the drawing room . . . is
full of grace and charm."

The nation was on the brink of war. In 1917 submarine
warfare was intensified by Germany. On April 6, 1917,
the United States declared war on Germany. In 1918
President Wilson announced his objectives in terms of
his famous 14 Points.

But even before these events had transpired, the Jews
of America, men and women and children, had taken new
hope with the issuing of the Balfour Declaration on November 2, 1917, which stated that the British Government
looked with favor upon the establishing of a Jewish National Home in Palestine. It promised a permanent address to the stateless, homeless Jewish wanderers. It was
the culmination of an age-old dream. It created special
areas of action for the Jewish women in America.

Social change is constant and inevitable. The impact
of outer events challenges the self. There is drama in
the interaction of self and society, self and events. When
an individual or a group is uprooted and transplanted to
a new environment, what is needed is the same scientific

care which is used in transplanting trees and flowers. The roots of growing trees need a nurturing ball of earth around them. They need a familiar climate and time to adapt to the new earth. Unfortunately, it is not given to human transplants. It takes time and faith and a generation or two to make the transition.

But eventually the need is met. And after the physical search for sanctuary and asylum is over, and after shelter and opportunity to work are found, a second stage is begun. It is the search for self-expression, for contact with new neighbors—and this means learning a new language—for recognition and acceptance and communication in the new environment. There is a craving for new status symbols, since the old ones have been erased. Yet women of means, women deprived and unemployed become fellow-workers. There is contrast. There is unity.

While Jewish seamstresses marched in picket lines, their bosoms stuffed with old newspapers to keep out the cold, the more affluent club women continued to meet, to exchange recipes, to attend musicales. Yet they also collected money for ice to keep infants' milk from souring during the summer months. They raised money to buy coal and clothing in the winter. They continued in speeches and articles in the papers to plead the cause of their disinherited kinsmen. The Conference of Jewish Women's Organizations acquired many new members. New groups were started all over the land. The propaganda mills were grinding out stories about persecution of Jews that were heart rending. Ameliorative efforts were intensified. On the eve of the First World War, the Jews of Chicago under the dynamic leadership of Julius Rosenwald, spurred by a sense of urgency by news dispatches from Russia and Poland, pledged to raise one million dollars, one-tenth of the national quota for relief abroad. Mrs. Charles Brady, a Christian woman of Rockford, Illinois, "inspired by the appeal of the Chicago Joint Relief Committee . . . took every piece of jewelry she possessed and gave it up for the benefit of the war sufferers." Bernard Baruch, Julius Rosenwald, and Otto M. Kahn were called to Washington as relief needs were intensified. The country was preparing for war, and Liberty Loan campaigns were vigorously waged. In garment factories, Yiddish speeches were made during lunch hours, and the response was overwhelming. The *Sentinel* reported "The garment workers . . . may have to receive a little instruction in the language of their adopted land but their generosity was overwhelming."[28]

11

Women begin as anonymous shadows. They evolve as vital factors in home and community. They emerge as personalities, responsive, articulate, attuned to the needs of others, pilgrims in search of service. This transformation develops from the narrow cocoon self into the butterfly ranging the wider spaces. It occurs everywhere. Women in California and in Maine and in Texas and in New York endlessly repeat this process of self-liberation and self-discovery. It is almost as if their activities are instinctual drives like the migration of birds. Perhaps in the Divine economy that is what they represent —creatures who struggle to leave the cocoon for the larger freedom.

The emergence of women as a social force, numerically strong, motivated by socially desirable goals, determined to bring about changes in society, to right wrongs, to improve conditions—these are not due solely to Quixotic impulses. They arise out of the very qualities which make them good mothers, wives and homemakers. They are motivated by love and compassion, by sympathy and tenderness. Having comforted their own, they then seek to help their neighbors. The rhythm of a woman's life is more or less predetermined. The busy child-bearing years are succeeded by the lonely stretches of time when the children are grown and are leading lives of their own. Enforced leisure is repugnant to one who has known creative household work, the joys of companionship, the morale-boosting which comes from being irreplaceable. So for idle hands, work is found. And for minds grown dull, ideas are sought and the imagination is fired. There is therapy in group work. There are new doors opening. Henri Bergson wrote that "A force of unvarying direction, which is to the soul what gravity is to the body, ensures the cohesion of the group by bending all individual wills to the same end. That force is moral obligation."[1] The Jewess accepted moral obligation as part of life.

There are hundreds of organizations large and small. They have histories as individuals do. They are the answers to social needs, to personal needs. They are articulate responses to world and national events. They are caused by the pressures of the host culture upon alien and minority groups.

Groups spring up to meet immediate problems. Hebrew benevolent associations and burial societies are an example. They are organized to fulfill religious needs and to perform rites of passage. Synagogues and temples are built. Weddings are solemnized and Bar Mitzvah and more recently Bas Mitzvah rites are celebrated. They are observed to express solidarity with kindred groups, stressing common geographic origin, as in *landsmanschaften,* or to keep alive linguistic traditions, as in Hebrew- and Yiddish-speaking groups which support theater and press. They arise from common ideologies as in the formation of labor unions. They are responses to acts of sadism, cruelty, denigration, deprivation of rights all over the world, as in the Damascus Affair, the Dreyfus Affair, the case of Mendel Beilis or Leo Frank. Campaigns of moral indignation and outrage enlist the finest and most humane Christians in the community who in their concern close ranks with Jews. So in Chicago in October, 1913, a dedicated liberal, the Catholic Judge Edward Osgood Brown, shared the speaker's lectern with Brooker T. Washington at a giant mass meeting to protest the false arrest, detention and persecution of Mendel Beilis.

"Probably every Jew is reading now about the Beilis case," wrote the *Sentinel* of Chicago. "Over in Kiev, Beilis weeps and talks incoherently, a nervous wreck from the strain of two years' unjust imprisonment. . . . Acquittal will not restore to this hunted man—hunted because he is a Jew—the strength and health that have already been taken from him . . ." Not only did the Beilis case focus attention on the precarious position of Jews in Russia. Speeches, addresses, and articles on the genius of the Russian Jew filled the newspapers all over the country.

Associations furthering the Zionist dream of a homeland in Palestine for persecuted Jews spring up everywhere. Here and there a few opposing voices formed feeble groups of congealed anti-Zionists. College quotas impeded young men and women and prevented their entering the professions. The B'nai B'rith and other organizations sought to counteract these policies of exclusion. Employment was "restricted" to non-Jews in many occupations and professions. Country clubs and summer hotels barred Jews. Anti-alienism used political pressures to keep out Jews and other "undesirable" immigrants. But vocal groups led by men and women of eloquence and vision and conscience closed ranks in their behalf. Immigrants needed help and HIAS met the need.

They needed retraining here and abroad and ORT faced
and solved that problem.

These data overflow. There are bulging boxes and
packing cases in historical archives, in libraries and in
the homes of scholars. Their contents have been summarized in books and periodicals and special interest
publications.

Wars are fought and Jewish War Veterans and their
Women's Auxiliaries apply themselves to the needs of
men who are entombed in hospitals with permanently
disabled bodies or permanently disoriented minds. Disease
threatens, and cures are sought and sometimes found in
Jewish hospitals serving their fellow citizens on a non-
discriminatory basis. Polio is conquered and two Jews are
given recognition for this victory. A hospital in Colorado
or Arkansas, the City of Hope in California, have their
supporting groups and women's auxiliaries. The deaf
and the blind and the crippled and the disabled and the
retarded and the deprived are helped. Compassion and
sympathy, love and dedication draw the privileged into
associations to help the deprived.

A composite picture of the "Organization Woman,"
a woman of concern, a volunteer who offers freely countless hours of service with no thought of recompense
emerges.

The calendar turns. The clock ticks away the saga of
new events. The echo of distant sorrows beats out its inexorable rhythm. Who can be deaf to pleas for help?
Who can stand aside in cool indifference to the desperate
cries of others? Heroines and leaders emerge. Nebulous
dreams of help and alleviation crystallize into action.
Plans are drawn and campaigns are planned and tentative
efforts become in time giant accomplishments. In 1893
at the World's Congress of Religions, Jewish women first
found their strength and program for action through the

National Council of Jewish Women. A generation later, the greatest Jewish woman since Biblical times, educated by her father, a scholar and rabbi, had an indelible vision. It was in 1912 that Henrietta Szold dreamed of bringing medical and nursing help to Palestine then suffering from tropical and other diseases. Miss Szold knew through helping others, that the American Jewish woman could be brought back to the neglected observance and practice of Jewish folkways and mores and so enrich both her immediate family and her community and nation. She knew too that what she had seen of the desperate needs of the Jewish settlers in Palestine would find an immediate and wholehearted response in American campaigns for medical supplies and for nurses and dieticians in that distant land which was so near to every Jew who knew and read the Bible.

It was in 1896 that she stated her credo speaking to a group of the National Council of Jewish Women in her native Baltimore: "To meet a people's need through a people's own efforts . . . this ideal of self-emancipation was Zionism . . ."[2] She had seen with her own eyes the crying needs in Palestine. On her return she addressed a study group of which she had for some time been a member. It met to hear Henrietta's eyewitness Palestine report in the vestry rooms of Temple Emanuel of New York. The Hadassah study circle became Hadassah at that historic meeting, February 24, 1912—with Henrietta Szold elected as chairman of the group. She believed in her cause and was not deterred by the small numbers enlisted under her banner. "Unpaid service was to have its crown of glory. Henrietta Szold enlarged the status of voluntary work, its scope and meaning."[4] The handful of women grew to hundreds of thousands.

There was a kind of magic in her personality and in her ability to influence others. Her dream was contagious.

Her vision moved thousands to response and to participation. Yet there was nothing parochial in her goals and objectives. She was as ready to enlist in other good causes as she was to claim adherents for her own. The National Women's League was soon to claim Henrietta Szold as a founder also.

Always there was magic in the dream and magnetism in the dreamer. Time did not dim or tarnish the impact. "In 1932," writes one woman who knew her, "I had the good fortune to meet Henrietta Szold . . . in Jerusalem. She lived in the Eden Hotel and my room was next to hers. Every morning . . . I was with her in the dining room for breakfast. She was small of stature with soft wavy gray hair. (She was then seventy-two years old.) She would hasten through breakfast then go off to an eight o'clock Hebrew class before starting her strenuous day's work . . . I deem it a rare privilege to have known her and this memory is one of my most cherished possessions."[5] This indomitable heroine crowned her life's work by leading a children's crusade, Youth Aliyah, in the last decade of her life. To her many of the little victims of Nazism owe their lives. She led an Exodus of orphans into the Promised Land. "She was not an American in Jerusalem . . . she invested her Americanism with the rich heritage of Jewish ethics, its moral fervor, its Messianic dedication to a greater humanity," wrote Tamar de Sola Pool who had been her aid and companion for many inspired and heartwarming years.[6]

The National Women's League derives from the Jewish Theological Seminary. It is an integral part of its ideology and history. It is identified with the Conservative Movement.

Solomon Schechter had defined "Historical" Judaism as "catholic Israel." It is to Henrietta Szold that we turn for a clear and systematic explanation of this concept. In a speech before the New York Council of Jewish Women, later published in the American Hebrew, she described, interpreted and analyzed this theme.

"Presuming on his generosity," said Henrietta Szold, referring to Dr. Schechter, "I abstract, for my own purposes, a happy term of his coinage . . ."[7] The antecedents of this philosophic concept were imbedded in Jewish history. Its boundaries rested on history past and reached far into the future. Says Miss Szold: "In 1881 the Jews of America were taught to support the arms and grasp the hand of the outcast Russian Jews. *We learned how to pity effectively* . . ." But more than pity was demanded. "Allegiance to catholic Israel requires such sacrifices, such lessons got by heart, such emotions translated into effective action—and it requires far more. The duty of the Jews tingling with the consciousness of catholic Israel extends beyond his outcast brother to the prosperous. He is, not patron, but fellow aspirant . . . He keenly feels his responsibilities toward mankind. If the Jew deserts his watchtower, injustice and pagan recklessness may undermine the strongholds of culture."[8]

It is fortunate that this concept should have had so able and so inspired an interpreter. It is no less remarkable that there were women in the early years of the twentieth century who listened and learned and absorbed the vibrant theme. It is curious too that Dr. Schechter and the Jewish Theological Seminary should have welcomed and accepted and cherished Henrietta Szold when we recall that years before the devout and devoted Ray Frank Litman was rejected in Cincinnati—and of all people, by the ardent champion and advocate of women's rights—Isaac Mayer Wise. Henrietta Szold was at home at the Jewish Theological Seminary as she was often welcomed by Dr. and Mrs. Schechter to their hospitable home.

One would wish to linger to describe in detail the hazards of those early days of the twentieth century when problems without number were created at home and abroad, when both shining faith and cold and abject indifference could be traced in the American Jewish community. When heroic dreams were dreamed and campaigns of escape were simultaneously practiced; when Jewish life in America was a burgeoning entity or a hair shirt. This story has been brilliantly told in many absorbing volumes. Biographies occupy the shelves of many libraries. Legends circulate. The romance of creative lives rising to meet unprecedented challenges exists in heroic dimensions. Hitherto this has been a one-sided narrative, a masculine saga. But now women emerge as individuals of great endowment. Shining personalities with a magnetism and power which has survived them. And behind them the anonymous hundreds of thousands of matriarchs and mothers, of childless wives and spinsters united in service, in purposeful dedication to the Jewish way of life. "How beautiful upon the mountain are the feet of him who brings good tidings," said Isaiah. These women knowing sorrow and deprivation, persecution and transplantation yet brought the good news and the glad tidings of the recaptured glory of their faith.

The National Women's League of the United Synagogue of America was founded in 1918. It began with a meeting of three women in the home of Rabbi and Mrs. Jacob Kohn.[9] Mrs. Solomon Schechter, by now a widow of three years, asked her friends to hear some ideas she had evolved in the years when with courage and dignity—but with untold anguish—she had faced her challenging task of meeting life for herself and her children without the strength and inspiration and wisdom and laughter of the great man whose life she had shared. It had been a sharing such as is given to few. Solomon Schechter in one of his essays on "Saints and Saintliness"[10] records a conversation "with a lady of the Jewish persuasion, of high culture and wide reading"—who might have been his wife, who had stated that "Judaism is the only one among the great religions which has never produced a saint . . ." Schechter demurs: "But enthusiasm and mysticism are the very soil upon which saintliness thrives best." One can almost project oneself into this dialogue, an invisible spectator at a fireside chat between a great man and his inspired and endowed life's companion. The husband speaks:[11] "The notion of Chasiduth, or saintliness, is variously described by different Jewish writers . . . The golden mean . . . has no existence for him . . ." He refers here to the mystic or saint. Then he contends with the idea of prayer in the life of the religiously dedicated person: "Hence the value the saint attached to prayer. He longs for the moment when he can pour out his soul before his God in adoration and supplication."[12]

Often Mrs. Schechter must have heard her husband speak in this vein. Where could he have found a more responsive auditor? She shared his conclusion that "truth is one of the specialties of the Jewish saint." Certainly truth was one of the most discernable attributes of what Henrietta Szold called "The Lineaments of Mathilde Roth Schechter." Solomon Schechter enlarged on the subject, describing "the period of struggle in the life of the saint, and the stage of serenity and peace following upon it . . ." He reminds us that the Torah is "the bride of the congregation of Jacob."[13] That his wife practiced his teachings, that she embodied within her person the qualities he venerated, we know from countless notes and testimonials and encomia of her contemporaries and intimate friends. Did not Hanna Marx in a tender "Appreciation" begin with describing "the influence of her serene personality?"

The continuity of such an influence, its inextinguishable light, is in the case of Mathilde Schechter, proof of the immortality, the imperishability of good works. Again Dr. Schechter speaks—this time referring to Glückel of Hameln: "After a hundred and seventy-two years of dead silence, Glückel speaks to us again. And her words are well worth listening to."[14]

So now, half a century after the little meeting over the tea cups in 1918, we recall the conversation and the momentous events that followed. Mathilde Schechter proposed a plan to three women nodding their heads affirmatively in 1918. Two hundred thousand women half a century later celebrated a Golden Jubilee. The years between hold the story of an unfolding of a dream.

What shall be written of Mrs. Solomon Schechter?

To recall another person to life is to open the door on a secret and private chamber. One must tread softly, with reverence. The whole of life, the whole of any life, is a tapestry patiently woven. The pattern does not emerge until the weaver's hands have ceased their occupation. Only then does the design come clear and the plan become manifest. And we whose loom is still in motion are not fit to judge the virtuosity of another. We can only speak the old prayer. "Endow us with the vision to see in everyone his good qualities and to overlook his defects . . ." for are we not each one as vulnerable?

What are the sources? First there are the recollections glowing and undimmed of those who knew her and who survive to keep her memory green. Those tender evocations, the warm anecdotes, are eloquent tributes to a personality which still survives, still has power to animate and kindle, to delight and to inspire. There are the involvements and contributions that she made to the life and works of her illustrious husband. There are the plans for an organization that she conceived and mothered—the National Women's League of the United Synagogue of America. There are the tributes of those who knew her and came to eulogize her and whose encomia are indelibly written in the annals of the Jewish woman in America. Finally there are two slender volumes, one which she co-authored and one which was a sheaf of heartfelt tributes to her character and performance, to her integrity and undeviating allegiance to Judaism and to an unyielding affirmation of its eternal verities.

It fell to the lot of one of her close friends and associates, Mrs. Leon M. Solis-Cohen, to summarize the story of the life and death of Mathilde Roth Schechter, a woman they had all known and whose leadership they had all acknowledged. Here considerably condensed are the words she spoke:[15]

Eight years after the death of her husband Mrs. Schechter's funeral services were held in the same room where her husband had been eulogized at the Jewish Theological Seminary.

Despite her bereavement and her personal illness—she had had a paralytic stroke which had incapacitated her for several years—she had continued contact with her many devoted friends and had been able to spend her summers in Far Rockaway. But a severe gallstone attack necessitated her removal to Mt. Sinai Hospital and she died there on the 27th of August . . . The brief service was impressively simple . . . Dr. Finkelstein read two Psalms. Rabbi Elias L. Solomon delivered a beautiful eulogy and recited the El Mole Rachamim (traditional prayer for the dead). She was buried at Mt. Hebron Cemetery and many attended as a last tribute of sorrow and respect. She left three children. A son,

Frank I. Schechter and two daughters, Mrs. Ruth Alexander, and Mrs. Amy Kweit . . .

We are too close to grief to analyze and dissect Mrs. Schechter's life for the secret of her charm and power . . . Born in Breslau sixty-five years ago, she received a splendid education along both secular and religious lines. She was. greatly interested in art and went to London for further study. There she met Dr. Schechter and their common love for Judaism and Jewish literature and learning drew them into ever closer companionship. They were married in London on June 22nd, 1887 and settled in Cambridge . . . [Their life in England is then described.] At their farewell dinner given them before their departure from England, Mrs. Schechter wittily, and with characteristic modesty, described herself as "an Appendix to the precious Book of Wisdom you have all grown to be so fond of." But she was much more than that—she was an integral part of that Book itself . . . Mrs. Schechter entered heartily into New York communal life and served on the board of many institutions. She was deeply interested in synagogue music . . . With her, however, as with her husband, the United Synagogue came first in affection.

Devoted and loving companion that she was during life, she was equally devoted to Dr. Schechter's memory after death. Her ardent desire was to give to the world a real biography of her husband so that the man who had done so much for Jewish learning and for Jewry might be better understood. Failing health made the completion of this task impossible . . . She realized the necessity of bringing Jewish women of conservative tendencies together into an organization similar to the United Synagogue that the work of one might supplement the other . . .

. . . The Students' House was especially dear to her . . . And it was this Students' House which became the first Hostess House for the Students' Army Training Corps at Columbia University in the days of the War.

Mrs. Schechter in her magic sleight-of-hand fashion being able to transform it and get it into action before even the Y.M.C.A. appeared on the Campus.

The same magic personality was evident in all she did. Young and old, rich and poor, wise and simple, delighted to serve her, felt it indeed a privilege to be allowed to do so. They rejoiced that they might call her friend and feel her sincere interest in their welfare. Always occupied, she was never too busy for some sweet act of kindness . . .

Mrs. Schechter is dead, but she leaves a precious heritage to the Women's League. She loved the League dearly and had high hopes for it, as all the workers who had the privilege of personal contact with her know. When failing health compelled her to resign the presidency she said: "I thank you all and treasure the common memory of each step in the hard, uphill work of this new organization which we built up together in sweet comradeship. I shall always be the happier for having known you and having worked with you. . . .

She went on: " 'There is a secret city,' says the proverb, 'in every man's heart.' It is at that city's altars that the true prayers are offered. And it is there that I offer my prayer for the future of the success and the spiritual growth of our beloved United Synagogue."

Her final words were: "We Jews must become again a moral influence, indeed *the* moral influence in the world of Other-Wordliness."

We have photographs of Mathilde Schechter. She was the sort generally described as "motherly." She had an innate dignity and serenity and composure which drew people to her. Henrietta Szold who was very close to Mrs. Schechter said: ". . . always her eyes are suffused with tears and always a smile hovers upon her lips." She had an unusual gift which endowed her with empathic understanding and which made her able to reassure the shy and reserved people who came her way. She was, said Henrietta Szold, "above all, a homemaker. Even when she went beyond her four walls . . . as when she founded this Women's League of the United Synagogue, she still remained the homemaker . . ." Gratitude filled her heart always. Even at death's door she said, "God is merciful to my evening."

Perhaps it was because of her unfailing belief in immortality that she found her spiritual strength. Even after the death of Solomon Schechter—again it is Henrietta Szold who is speaking: "She spoke of him . . . gently indeed but not sadly, spoke as though he were still at her side, among the living. He remained with her—he and his sayings and his doings."

It is difficult to choose among the women who rallied around their leader. And yet perhaps a few very brief biographies will serve to illumine the Women's League's early history and to explain its phenomenal growth. Augusta Hirsh Kohn, wife of Rabbi Jacob Kohn, hostess at that momentous first meeting, died a little more than a decade ago.[16] She was seventy-four at the time of her death. Her activities stretched from the Atlantic to the Pacific. She knew and loved the land and its people. All of her life she combined innumerable organizational tasks with the arts of a gracious homemaker and hostess. She made friends and kept them for life. Those who attended her husband's synagogue were drawn into the orbit of her family. The great and the small were welcome at her table. Once the friendship was established, it was firmly maintained. When on a transcontinental trip in 1945, she thought nothing of stopping off to pay a condolence call in Chicago, on the mother of a young soldier who had recently died in combat.

She was an attractive woman, calm and serene and gracious in bearing. She was a gifted listener and in her

silent response one found strength and renewal. Somehow she had a wealth of equanimity to share with others.
She was always available to those who needed her. When
Henrietta Szold, who was a regular worshipper in Rabbi
Kohn's Temple Anshe Chesed of New York, came to
know Augusta Kohn, she became "a dear friend of ours."
Her husband writes: "Augusta was one of the thirteen
women who became the charter members of Hadassah
under Miss Szold's leadership. Lotta Levinson, Jessie
Sampter, Mrs. Seligsberg, Rose Zeitlin were among the
other members of this League who frequently came to
worship in the Temple on Sabbath mornings. Augusta
also assisted Mrs. Solomon Schechter in the founding of
the Women's League of the United Synagogue, and became the president and later the honorary president of
the Pacific Southwest Branch of the Women's League of
the United Synagogue."[17] Augusta Kohn also was president of her Sisterhood, served on the Board of Directors
of the Council of Jewish Women, and took an extremely
active role in the work of the League of Women Voters.

At a Conference of Women's Organizations, a nonsectarian group, one of the members in memorializing
her said that she could "lead us on in her calm, kind and
cultured way to high thoughts and altruistic deeds." Yet
she had left instructions that she wanted no eulogy at
her funeral. Her husband writes: "When someone asked
me why she insisted on a prayer service, omitting the address, I could only say, 'She was too humble a woman to
want it, and too great a woman to need it.' "

There was a drawing together of Canadian Jewish
Women with their sisters in the United States which
augured well for both groups. It emphasizes too the far-
sighted approach of the founders of the National Women's
League. For it can be of great help where there is nu-

merical weakness and it can unite into a vast cultural entity the women of both nations. Canada has the sixth largest free Jewish community in the world and the third largest in the English-speaking world. "No longer able to draw upon European Jewry for leadership, the Jews in Canada must find themselves thrown to an increasing extent upon their own resources."[18]

In *Maclean's Magazine,* in an article titled "The Jew in Canada, Where Does He Stand Today?" the Jew is saluted as "our proudest minority." The author, Phyllis Lee Peterson, maintains that although this minority numbers "only a quarter million and is likely to decrease . . . they've given Canada priceless gifts in nearly every field from nuclear physics to TV comedy." Numerically diminishing yet spiritually accelerating their growth and institutions—much of it may be due to the dedicated Canadian Jewesses whose quest for ethical values and for rediscovery of ancient Jewish tradition has sparked the many changes noticeable in the life of Canadian Jewry. "A new Judaism is emerging, indigenous to Canada and characterized by healthy self-criticism, bold experiment and vigorous activity."[19]

This "new" Judaism is the rediscovery and practice of ancestral practices and rites and daily prayers and daily meditation and the need for performing good works which have for centuries characterized Jewish women's attitudes and activities. These practices were lost sometimes, hidden at other times. The Inquisition records eloquently and tragically portray the practice of crypto-Judaism. Religious devotions were submerged or abandoned when pogroms and flight made the problem of survival overwhelming. They were lost when children rebelling against the dank basements and the wretchedness of their Hebrew schools, the cold-water flats and the deadly round of poverty, and the association with parents and other rela-

tives who were overwhelmed like so many candles snuffed
out, escaped Judaism by various devices—escaped and were
lost to all that could and should have sustained them.
Now the old values were beckoning.

In Chicago which was the geographic center of both
the nation and much of the work of American Jews, the
local press began to examine this new type of feminine
crusade which combined religious dedication and observance with synagogue and temple membership. Nannie A.
Reis, writing a column titled "In the World of Jewish
Womankind" in the *Reform Advocate,* referred to Mrs.
Benjamin Davis as "the Dean among the Jewish women
of the Conservative group" and examined the sudden
interest in Jewish education "which is sweeping or creep-
ing, as the case may be, over our land and into the consciousness of American Jewry." Mrs. Reis concludes her
column with the observation that "Conservative Judaism
is endeavoring to revivify and strengthen Jewish life by
new interpretation founded on old tradition . . ."[20]

Under the leadership of Mrs. Benjamin Davis who became president of the Chicago Branch of the Women's
League, things were really humming. By 1923 there were
13 Sisterhoods affiliated with the national organization.
Under a 1924 directive from Mrs. Davis we read: "We
are now arranging for a joint meeting of the Women's
League and the members of the United Synagogue . . .
The Sisterhoods desire assistance with the monthly programs and a Speakers' Bureau . . . The religious schools
require a supervising committee . . . These schools take
the Jewish children from the Christian missions and hold
them within their own fold . . . What we need most are
competent officers to take the work in hand . . ." The
scrapbooks of Mrs. Davis are full of such appeals and
notices going back to the founding year, 1918. A letter
dated November 14, 1918, is written on official imprinted

stationery of the Women's League, Chicago Branch, and bears the name and address of its first regional president. In it Mrs. Davis writes that she is waiting to hear from Mrs. Max Margolis, "for some printed literature or instructions." In the United Synagogue *Recorder* of 1927, Mrs. Samuel Spiegel, national president of Women's League, pays tribute to its national vice-president. "We of the Women's League are grateful to the Midwest Branch for it has given to us an outstanding leader . . . who . . . has endeared herself to us for all time . . ." For by this time, Mrs. Davis's voice was familiar to audiences in many cities. She preached and exhorted and celebrated a dynamic Judaism. Speaking in Atlantic City in 1927, Mrs. Davis said: "The true Jewish life is full of joy, if we but establish it in our home circle. Every day, each week, each month and year is made colourful by the various beautiful ceremonies connected therewith, each bearing its own message of hope and cheer to old and young alike, if we know how to interpret and impart it." She had that rare gift of infusing joy into her religion. In return, again and again, she was saluted for her leadership. The United Synagogue *Recorder* wrote of her: "Unlike those of our women who must gather their laurels of achievement in the larger world before being idolized by their own, Jeannette Isaacs Davis has been content to lay her gifts at the shrine of her own people . . ." In a sense she captured the spirit of the resurgent movement which was calling to its people to come back and in returning to rediscover its spiritual riches.

Had not Isaiah promised that "in returning . . . ye shall be saved . . ."? It was the only answer to the erosion in the ranks of American Jews, to the process of attrition which had depleted them. For the escapees were running away from bleak childhood memories. The status-seekers were looking for new and more fashionable addresses to go with the new Anglo-Saxon names they had chosen. The blandishments of the missionaries and evangelists were increasing and little children were being enticed from the fold in countless ways. The young men and women who managed to get to college were "emancipated" from dogma and folkways and were finding Christian mates among their classmates. In the business world as contacts with other groups increased and prospered, non-Jewish wives and husbands made new patterns of family life. Exogamy meant as a rule, loss of children. It was a process which began in the early history of Shearith Israel and has continued to the present day. It was for this that the Conservative movement was established to create a bridge between Orthodoxy and Reform, hoping that the middle way which combined adherence to ancient folkways and customs and rites and ceremonials with a more yielding attitude toward the position of women, toward the host culture, toward youth, would preserve the group and strengthen it. The Conservative movement developed and knew its largest growth at a time when the anti-alien sentiment in this country had reached its zenith and immigration which had formerly replenished Jewish ranks was at a virtual standstill. No longer were scholars and rabbis coming here in large numbers bringing their disciples and congregations with them. Depletion loomed large. Jewish ranks were diminishing at a time when mass annihilation in Europe was being unleashed. The challenge was crucial. The Jewish Theological Seminary faced these issues squarely. The masses, silent and inarticulate, yet aware of the threats, were ready for leadership.

In June of 1954, the Women's League *Outlook* saluted Mignon Levin Rubenovitz, whose antecedents present some interesting sidelights. Members of her family came to Charleston, South Carolina, in 1838 and were known as "ante-bellum Poles." Her father had served in the

Confederate Army. She was educated in her native city of Baltimore and later went on to New York. "Her association with the immortal Henrietta Szold was another determining influence in her life." In 1915, she married Rabbi Herman H. Rubenovitz of Boston. Now her proclivities and talents had full scope. She stood beside Henrietta Szold at the founding of Hadassah and became the first President of the New England Region of Hadassah. The National Women's League involved her from its inception. She wrote for publication, she taught, she organized women's branches of the National Women's League, she established a splendid congregational library and founded "a unique Jewish Museum." Her book, *Altars of My Fathers*, expresses her philosophy of life in terms of a viable Judaism.

From the hundreds of letters, personal sketches, clippings from the press, there emerges a collective portrait which is strange and unbelievable. Here are women toiling in the vineyards, conquering insurmountable obstacles, having their brief hour in the spotlight—and returning to the anonymity which is their permanent destiny. To recall them to life, to recount their deeds, to trace their biographies, is to relate them to the Shunammite "whose guest room was available to the tired prophet Elisha."[21]

On a scrap of paper is a little handwritten poem, some lines altered and scratched out. It is an attempt by one club woman to salute another. Its eloquence lies in its naive unpretentiousness. It honors Mrs. Benjamin Davis, a founder of the National Women's League on her seventy-fifth birthday.

> Open wide the portals
> Wreathe the posts with flowers
> 'Tis but fit that mortals
> Mark the joyful hours!

> Hours that in the glory
> Of the sunset's fires
> Tell a radiant story
> Which our heart inspires.
> Tell of hallowed duty
> As daughter—wife—
> Mother—love and beauty
> Crown a worthy life.[22]

The woman who wrote the poem was herself the epitome of the dedicated "organization woman." She was Nannie A. Reis whose editorial work for the Anglo-Jewish press has been noted. The scrap book in which this bit of verse was found has this comment by the daughter of Mrs. Davis: "Through long years of close association, Mrs. Reis became one of Jeannette Davis' most ardent friends and admirers." Its importance lies in what is implied. It joins the performance of woman at home with her contribution to the community as "hallowed duty." It describes with sincerity the possibility for women of developing meaningful and rich friendships outside the home. It speaks eloquently of the continuing satisfactions lasting well to the end of life, of what the novice only glimpsed when she entered the volunteer ranks. It discloses the depths of a personality which is involved in family and communal affairs. A woman columnist of the Chicago *Tribune* and a great admirer of Mrs. Davis, Dr. Bess Sondel, wrote to the latter: "How, Grandma Nettie, do you come by your philosophy?" On February 20, 1941, Mrs. Davis upon whose shoulders devolved much of the Midwest work of the Women's League, answered the query as follows: "Prayer is a personal manifestation of human expression. If we earnestly seek it, by meditation and study . . . we will reap the reward of understanding more of life's problems . . . My Creator speaks to me through my soul-conscience . . . This mystic message is to *me* personally, and if *I* fulfill it, *I* am happy . . . We cannot expect to be exempt from suffering, nor is our joy individual—we share both with our fellow beings as we do our responsibility."

Here is the simply stated credo of a great woman who has not made a single list of "noted" Jewish women in America, whose long life exhibited an undeviating, single-hearted sense of responsibility to God and to society. She found her way to a personal philosophy of service as a very young woman. Among her memorabilia is a frayed, browned-with-age document stating that Jeannette (sic) Isaacs had "completed with honor the course of studies required . . ." by the Jersey City Normal School of Hudson County, New Jersey. It was dated April, 1874. She became a teacher and joined the Teachers' Association of Jersey City. By April 6, 1880, the principal of the school where she taught wrote of her "Miss Isaacs is a young lady of more than ordinary intelligence, and I consider her to be one of my best teachers." Within the next decade she married, moved to Chicago and became a contributor to Anglo-Jewish periodicals. Her portrait taken the following year shows her with hair piled high on her head, a beruffled gown cascading to a long train on the floor, the pinched waist and the bouffant sleeves of that era enhancing her pretty little frame.

She became a prolific contributor to the Anglo-Jewish press. Her main concern was the education of young children. She insisted that "our children lack proper instruction in the explanation of our Law and the history of our people." In the *Reform Advocate,* she again wrote that ". . . even Hebrew can be taught successfully in small classes, if there be no opposition from parents."[23] She and the editor of the *Reform Advocate* were in strong disagreement with the editorial policy of that publication. Among its objectionable editorials was one which de-

clared, December 26, 1896—"The Talmud teaches, that
he who imparts the Thora (sic) to his daughter, teaches
her blasphemy." Vigorous objections from Mrs. Davis!
She found another periodical, the Chicago Israelite, a
welcome outlet. It took courage to criticize the Chicago
Council of Jewish Women of which she was a most active
member, for violating the Sabbath, ". . . it must have
been a rude shock . . . to find the mother section of the
Council trampling under foot the most sacred principle
of the organization . . ." In an article published in the
Jewish Comment of Baltimore titled "Notes from Chicago" she was unhappy to report that the Bible class of
Isaiah Temple led by Rabbi Stolz had attended a lecture
of Professor Breasted devoted to the recent discoveries of
Dr. Flinders Petrie.

She threw herself heart and soul into the work of the
Women's League. She continued to take issue with the
Council of Jewish Women and its founder, Mrs. Solomon,
who had stated in the National Convention in New York
that the "ultra-orthodox" wing was too vocal: Said Mrs.
Solomon: "They must have had well-developed chests and
strong lungs, for they spoke loud and long." And these
are the people, observes Mrs. Davis in sorrow, who "claim
the credit of practicing tolerance . . ." She rushed into
print to give the Council good advice:[24]

1. Attend Sabbath Services.

2. Do no shopping of any kind on the Sabbath day.

3. Do no work on the Sabbath day that can be done
at another time.

4. Every Sabbath read at least one chapter of the Bible
and memorize at least one verse.

5. "Look about on each Sabbath day for an opportunity
to do a kind deed or say a kind word to someone else."

She continued to advocate a more dynamic Judaism
in many of her articles which appeared in many parts of

the country. In 1889, the New York *Jewish Daily News* wrote of her: "Her lectures and writings have made her known throughout the length and breadth of the land."

She fought on many fronts. Among her letters is one from C. Arthur Pearson of London to whom she addressed an inquiry on the five-day week. He wrote her: ". . . I don't believe that anything whatever would be lost to the business world were Saturday a day of entire rest." The following year, on November 10, 1899, the New York *Jewish Daily News* reported an address she had recently delivered in which she urged: ". . . I would beg of you, fathers and mothers, to educate your daughters as well as your sons." A month later, she was writing in defense of Yiddish as a language. "Humor and pathos of a high order find expression on the Yiddish stage." She lectured widely on Zionism and received a very graceful letter from Rabbi Bernhard Felsenthal on one occasion. "I cannot refrain," he wrote on December 14, 1899, "from expressing to you my heartfelt thanks for the beautiful address on Zionism which you lately delivered here and which I found published in 'The Jewish Courier' . . . I think every one of your hearers or readers *must* appreciate this your address . . ." When an article of hers advocating Zionism was published in the *American Hebrew*, D. D. Morrison, Honorary Secretary of the Federation of American Zionists wrote to congratulate her "upon your splendid literary effort" and invited her to address their convention in June as one of a few "prominent speakers." Her contributions appeared with considerable regularity in Baltimore and New York as well as in Chicago and other Anglo-Jewish periodicals.

With the years, all of her efforts were intensified. She reported the National Conventions of the Council of Jewish Women and urged them again and again to keep the faith, to study Zionism and not to reject it out of hand. She was invited to help dedicate orphanages and old people's homes and her name appears with regularity on the board of directors' lists of countless philanthropic enterprises. In 1904, she was selected as one of the six outstanding Jewish women in Chicago, with Hannah Solomon and Julia Felsenthal among others. She was chairman of the Home Study Circles of the Council of Jewish Women. The reading of the Bible and especially of the Psalms was an important and invariable part of each session of these study groups. Nannie A. Reis had her own circle. One group, "The Zangwill Circle," was reading his *Dreamers of the Ghetto*. Mrs. Davis supplemented her Bible study courses with the works of Graetz and Leroy-Beaulieu.

In listing the organizations in which she was active since her arrival in Chicago in 1881, Mrs. Davis names sixteen, among them the National Women's League. In an autobiographical fragment we read:

> Winding in and out of this mass endeavor sometimes assisting, sometimes directing, always co-operating, have been our noble women, meeting every obstacle with faith and determination to overcome it. The task of the pioneers was difficult: to disarm prejudice, to educate, to produce cooperation, to bring about a better understanding were their aims. Did they succeed? Undoubtedly. Beginning with the C.J.W., where my earliest efforts were concentrated, followed by the formation of women's auxiliaries . . . and (naming other groups) . . . the Women's League [These were largely due to] "the self-sacrificing devotion of a small group of our women, those whose tact, ability, training, and education fitted them to bridge the gulf that separated the differing elements of our community."

Her work expanded and took on wider dimensions. She was a favorite speaker at countless meetings. Her name is signed to a call to form the American Jewish Congress on the 23rd of January, 1916. As President of the Conference of Jewish Women's Organizations in Chicago she was responsible for a petition addressed to President Wilson asking that a national day of mourning be designated for the victims of "brutal massacres and pogroms" in the Ukraine. Her successive birthdays—the seventieth, seventy-fifth, eightieth, eighty-fifth were not merely Chicago celebrations but received national attention. Rabbi Stephen Wise came from New York to her eightieth birthday party "to pay her tribute." There were 1,500 guests, including three daughters, five grandchildren and a great-grandson. In May of 1942, Rabbi Solomon Goldman installed a panel of National Women's League officers. Mrs. Benjamin Davis was named its National Honorary Vice-President. She led a full, rich, satisfying and graceful life. She died March 22, 1943.

Sociologists have endlessly addressed themselves to the phenomena of group life. They speak of "the simple loyalty or positive ethnocentrism which makes up residual Jewish identity . . ." They condemn "the rejection of the parvenu or vulgar quality of 'the culture of organizations' which marks Jewish life . . ."[25] They praise and salute its many accomplishments. Belonging implies a measure of financial security, ability to pay dues, to contribute to charity. It rests on leisure which is created by relative affluence. Professor Greenberg of Yeshiva University describes the ascent of Jews as "the greatest collective Horatio Alger story in American immigration history." Perhaps it was from his knowledge of such success stories and based on his acquaintance with Jews that Horatio Alger got his endless plots, variations of the Cinderella story. The formula: virtue and application and undeviating hard work rewarded by fame and fortune. Horatio

Alger was "a roly-poly little man, shy, and not at all forceful" who had given up the ministry for teaching. He was Benjamin Nathan Cardozo's tutor, and when Cardozo applied for admission to Columbia, the sole educational reference that he could give was that he had been privately tutored by Horatio Alger.[26]

Women have greater leisure than men and thus a greater need for identifying with groups. Homemaking is a lonely occupation. Their children grow up and leave home. Their husbands die. Clubs, committees, become channels of personal fulfillment. It is possible that American Jewish culture "lives off the residual capital of loyalties left from past commitments . . . An active search for identity is on . . ."[27] Each individual subject to inexorable laws, seeks to find—after the essential needs are met—a pattern, a rhythm, a way of life, an understanding of God and self, a meaningful relationship to inner and outer space. The phenomenon of discovery repeats itself endlessly in the lives of women. Strangers to each other "in a world they never made"—they fulfill themselves and their inner yearnings by activities which are endlessly alike. A few additional examples will suffice.

Whether our protagonists are in revolt against anonymity or react as Noras slamming doors on boredom and ineffectual existence, whether they are seeking self-fulfillment or paying off a debt to Providence for countless blessings, they assert themselves through group activities. Steadily the twentieth century has emancipated woman after her diligent groping for recognition in the nineteenth. "Modern gadgets have given her time, cosmetics have made her beautiful, clothes have made her chic, husbands have spoiled her, and education has made her equal. The American woman . . . has never had it so good."[28] Of all these bounties, American Jewish women have partaken in good measure. Both "conspicuous consumption and conspicuous leisure" have been theirs.[29] Yet their pleasures have been constantly tarnished by assaults upon their sensibilities of tragic events abroad. There was always a sense of "there but for the grace of God go I." They experienced both pity and fear. Only good works and philanthropy could assuage the impact of catastrophes which befell Jews in other parts of the world.

We have met women from the Eastern seaboard and women from the Midwest. Our next glimpse of women's groups activities takes us to the Pacific Coast.[30]

The discovery of gold in California in 1848 brought a vast influx of immigrants. Of the 80,000 people who were lured by the hope of making their fortune, only eight percent fewer than 5,000 were women. Of the earliest settlers, there were eight known Jews—seven merchants and a tailor. In 1900, one historian wrote of one of the earliest Jewish settlers in California: "Of the pioneer merchants of the 50's, Mr. Harris Newmark was the founder of a house still in existence. If any youth in Los Angeles would see for himself how honesty and strict attention to business commands success, let him visit the establishment of Mr. Newmark and his successors."[31] Because the earliest Jewish settlers were mostly single men, intermarriage was prevalent. Of seventeen early recorded marriages, there were four known intermarriages. "Some of the men," writes Turner, "kept mistresses, which sometimes (were) consummated in marriage. One Nathan Tuch married a full-bloodied Indian squaw, and when he died his wife had him buried in the Jewish cemetery."[32] A nonconforming immigrant, in the sense that he brought his wife and six children to Los Angeles in 1854, was Joseph Newmark. There is a portrait (undated) of the clan of Newmark, an impressive and dignified family to judge by aloofness of mien of the men and avoirdupois of the ladies and by their imposing costumes. The parents,

Joseph and Rosa Newmark, are displayed in photographs in the background. Their six children are grouped in congealed tribute in the foreground. Fortunately, a fine photograph does exist of Joseph and Rosa. In the Los Angeles *Herald Examiner* of April 12, 1964, there is a reproduction of a photo of Mr. and Mrs. Joseph Newmark. He has a serious, calm, reserved air. The high forehead, the ascetic mouth denote a man of intellect and restraint. Beside him there stands a simply garbed, very beautiful woman whose calm and dignity and gentleness are eloquent even after a hundred years. The caption reads: "City's first rabbi and his wife who helped build a Catholic college." The accompanying story, one of a series, titled "The Women Who Helped Shape Los Angeles," carries the headline "Rosa Newmark's Deeds Rose Above Religion."[33] In the "transforming of a pueblo into a megalopolis" all groups worked together. "And so it was with the Jewess who contributed toward the founding of the City's first Catholic university . . ."

"She was Mrs. Joseph P. Newmark (born Rosa Levy in London) who sailed with her six children from San Francisco where they had for several years made their home." They disembarked on "a gloomy day" in 1854. Rosa's husband was "genuinely religious and exalted in character, a man deeply entrenched in his faith . . . he became Los Angeles' first acting rabbi . . ." He was a founder of the city's Hebrew Benevolent Association. His wife Rosa was a founder of the Ladies Hebrew Benevolent Society several years later. "Although its founder, she would never accept an office in the group, but worked tirelessly in behalf of the charity until her death." Nurses were then unavailable. The Ladies' Society provided volunteer nurses and then helped in every way when death came. "Should any one wonder how the mother of six could pursue such an active schedule of charitable duties, that was due in part to another Los Angeles 'first.' The Newmarks had brought with them a Chinese servant . . . the first Oriental to come to Los Angeles." It is interesting to note that Rosa Newmark like her sisters all over the country at later times did not organize her Ladies' Society until all of her children were married and no longer living at home.

When the Bishop of Los Angeles proposed a Catholic college for their city, "the women at Rosa's suggestion and under her direction sponsored a fund-raising fair— the result of which was hundreds of dollars turned in for the education fund." When she died, her obituary notice in the Los Angeles *Star* read: "The community was greatly pained yesterday to hear of the death of Mrs. Rosa Newmark. . . . The venerable lady was very highly esteemed for her many amiable qualities . . . The funeral . . . was one of the most numerously attended . . . in Los Angeles. . . . The long line of carriages which followed the deceased to her last resting place bespoke the high estimate in which she was held, not only by her co-religionists, but by the entire community." Her life was like that of countless other Jewish women all over the land.

The biographies and autobiographies of these women contain striking similarities. They are independent of time and place. One recalls Sadie American, who boasted membership in one hundred organizations. Then a sketch of Mrs. Maurice Turner turns up. Although almost three generations separate them, we find them kindred spirits. Listed are thirty-six major activities in which Rose Turner is involved, beginning with the National Presidency of B'nai B'rith Women, including service to hospitals and to the blind, a cancer clinic, orphanage, art museum and symphony association. Turning from Los Angeles to Philadelphia we find in another woman's capsule biography, an almost identical history. Geography is not a factor. In

November 1965, a native of Philadelphia, Rose Bender, died at the age of 69. Her activities began when at the age of eleven she organized the first Young Judea Club in America. She was identified with every aspect of the Zionist movement, served on the national board of Hadassah, was twice a delegate to the World Zionist Congress in Geneva in 1939 and in Basle in 1946, promoted and aided the Technion in Israel and helped in vast financial undertakings responsible for the erection of academic and cultural buildings in Israel.

Here is a handwritten biographical sketch of a woman in her eighties. It was written in May of 1965 and is as beautifully executed as a medieval manuscript. It is the work of a native of Santa Barbara, Rachel Levy Kauffman, members of whose family were residents of San Francisco from 1851. Her parents "were descendants of an ancient French-Jewish family in Lorraine." She was born in 1872. Her father, like his forebears, was interested in viniculture. Rachel attended the public schools of Santa Barbara and then spent two years in France studying music, art and literature. On her return to California, she met and married in 1896, Jules Kauffman, a native of Alsace, France. In 1900, they moved to Los Angeles where her husband founded a bank which later merged with the Bank of America. They had one daughter, lived a busy active communal life, were active in the Wilshire Boulevard Temple. Writing in the third person, Mrs. Kauffman describes the many affiliations and organizational activities which filled sixty-five years of her adult life. She founded and became first president of her temple sisterhood. She was president of the State Federation of her temple Sisterhood. She too served as Board member of an orphanage and other philanthropic institutions. She was a founder of the National Council of Jewish Women, of Hadassah and B'nai B'rith on the Pacific Coast. But unlike others, she took an active role in non-Jewish activities. She belonged to and helped found a number of societies devoted to literature and art. She was a charter member of the Los Angeles Urban League, a founder and officer of the Alliance Française, president of the Community Art Commission of the City of Los Angeles, served on the Los Angeles Social Service Commission and proposed the creation of its Community Chest, and helped establish music and literature groups in her adopted city. During World War I, she was a vice-president of the French Red Cross. This does not exhaust her affiliations. But it does prove the possibilities of the creative uses of leisure by women.

Many more such case histories abound.

There is one unique West Coast document which deserves particular notice. It is a book published in 1965, written in Yiddish. Its author is now a 100 years old. She is bright, alert, does her own housework and gardening, and pursues a regular schedule of self-imposed tasks, one of which was her daily stint of writing her autobiography.

It took Rachel Anna Kositza almost eleven years to trace the story of her wanderings. Written in Yiddish, *The Recollections of a Woman of Byalostok* describes a life that was full of the sorrows of growing up in Czarist Russia, contains many incidents of her exploitation in factories by her own co-religionists, tells of the gruesome trans-Atlantic crossing, portrays the cruel and degrading aspects of poverty in the new world, with many graphic details of hunger, poverty, insecurity.[34] She describes a pious Jewish employer who not only underpaid his female employees but who waged constant campaigns against their virtue and chastity. The story ends happily with the serenity and peace of her own little home and garden in Los Angeles and with delightful vignettes of her recent years. Her inspiration has been Grandma Moses. But Rachel Anna has well earned her own laurels through the

pleasures of authorship. Her daughters rejoice in her
accomplishments. If there be a moral in an autobiography,
it is that if one lives long enough and laughs at life a
little, old age need have no terrors.

There was never a lack of able and endowed leaders.
The supply was inexhaustible. The mantles fell on many
shoulders. New leaders arose. One such woman was Dora
Spiegel, "gentle spoken, soft of mien, ideal of vision."
She was the childless wife of a busy surgeon. She found
her sublimation early in her married life. "Dora Spiegel
taught in her own home the first group of Jewish children
in New York City . . . She prepared the first Jewish blind
boy for the Bar Mitzvah."[35] Denied her own children,
she siphoned her maternal instincts to other people's children. "Dora Spiegel loved young people . . . In turn, young
people loved her for she imparted to them a love for
learning, for culture, for music, for the finer things of
life . . ."

Dora Spiegel tried to formulate her simple creed—and
perhaps succeeded when she wrote on "The Survival of
Judaism" as follows:

"I do not know the exact definition of religion. To me
it is a way of life, in all walks of life—in the community,
in the country, and in the whole world."

In countless ways the members of the National Wom-
en's League had kept faith with its founders. There was
always a deep and abiding loyalty and awareness of the
personality and the dreams for the good life of Mathilde
Schechter. Her wishes were a sacred charge to thousands
of women who had never known her. They still are today.
They associated her in time and in vision with Henrietta
Szold. In 1960 "A Double Centennial" was celebrated by
the National Women's League—that of Mrs. Schechter
and Mrs. Szold. They were memorialized in an article by
Mrs. Fanny B. Minkin.[36] "But they were more than mere

contemporaries. . . . Both were leaders. . . . Each founded a national organization bearing her imprint." Their biographies present a dramatic contrast. Mathilde Roth, orphaned at an early age, became a ward of the Breslau Jewish Orphan Home. Henrietta Szold daughter of Rabbi and Mrs. Szold of Baltimore, surrounded by love and warmth, was given intensive training by her scholarly father. Mathilde turned to teaching in Hungary and tutoring in England. Henrietta taught school in her native Baltimore. There but for their dedication to Judaism and the Jewish way of life all similarity ends. For Mathilde Roth met Solomon Schechter in London. Together they built a creative life. Henrietta Szold wrote her own unique, dedicated solitary chapter in history, an incandescent and heroic narrative.

The organizational lives of Jewish women may be summarized as a Book of Numbers. For Hadassah founded by Miss Szold claims a membership of over 300,000. The National Women's League is second with approximately 200,000 members. One may note also that the National Council of Jewish Women claims 100,000 members and B'nai B'rith Women 135,000 members. The twentieth century was in terms of women's organization a period of phenomenal growth.[37]

12

As Jewish women faced the tragic era which
began in the thirties, as their hearts reached out to the
victims of Nazi and Fascist hordes, they responded with
an outpouring of love and kinship, of desire to help and
assuage which was to unite them with other women who
read the newspapers and listened to the radio with the
same sense of horror and disbelief. The children's crusade
which rescued our little ones from certain death in Germany was led by Henrietta Szold of Hadassah. It knew
no spiritual or geographic boundaries. The women of
WIZO (Women's International Zionist Organization) in
every country of the world united in a moral crusade behind her. In Chicago, Pearl Franklin, Hannah Shulman
Sager, Bertha Berkman did not spare themselves. Their
days and nights, their personal possessions, their most
dedicated services were enlisted. In Los Angeles, Mrs.
Sieroty; in Boston, Mrs. Rubenovitz; in Minneapolis, Mrs.
Baron and Mrs. Brin; in Philadelphia, Mrs. Bender . . .
It was a total commitment, a complete surrender of self.

Each woman longed for the miracle which saved the life of Isaac and stayed the hand of Abraham. And the women whose parents and grandparents had come from Warsaw and Vilna and Byalostok reaffirmed their ties with lands they had never known and communities they had only heard about. In America, foster parents adopted children and housed refugees and helped the lucky ones who had managed to escape. They mourned the martyred millions as if they stood at the graves of their own kin.

Now a miracle took place, an event of historic significance to the stateless, homeless refugees. The State of Israel was proclaimed on the 15th of May in 1948. At long last a permanent address was available to the homeless. Had not one shelterless young couple in the refugee post war days whose child was born in an open field, named their infant Niemand? They explained the name to an American journalist, Marie Syrkin, saying that it was the only name they could give their child—for were they not themselves nobodies deprived of every human need, of all dignity?

As early as 1900 an eloquent poet had written:

> We only are desolate. Earth, cold and stern,
> Begrudges us fiercely the home that we found.
> We journey, but no one awaits our return,
> O, tell us I pray of you, whither we are bound.[1]

At last they knew, these frail, rejected and wounded refugees, whither they were bound. For the new State of Israel had proclaimed the unbelievable doctrine of the Return! Providence had relented at last.

The impact on American Jews was electrifying. One of America's most lyrical voices, that of Karl Shapiro, described his emotions in unforgettable lines:

> When I see the name of Israel high in print
> The fences crumble in my flesh; I sink
> Deep in a Western chair and rest my soul.

I look the stranger clear to the blue depths
Of his unclouded eye, I say my name
Aloud for the first time unconsciously.

Had not Emma Lazarus as far back as 1883 seen the
handwriting on the wall when she wrote: "There is something absolutely startling in the world's sudden awakening
to the probable destiny of Israel."

No single volume could possibly be large enough to
present in depth the history and the description of countless accomplishments of the many women's organizations
engaged in humanitarian endeavors, pursuing dreams of
a better society for all. Often one encounters similar goals
with the same protagonists serving under different banners. "Let your words be few," we read in Ecclesiastes,
". . . as dreams come with many worries, so the fool speaks
with many words." To speak with too many words, to
list too many organizations, to add luster to the known
and to rescue from total oblivion many of the unknown—
is not the purpose of this volume. It is for us to unroll
the scroll of history, to recall to life some of the forgotten
ones, to engage in the remembrance of things past, to
seek guidance for the shape of things to come. Brevity is
dearly bought. For there are events, traumatic and epic,
that need reexamination. There are biographies of noted
women that need to be stripped of clichés, there are many
stereotypes to be demolished. There are those who have
earned their laurels who need to be disinterred. There
are the anonymous Shunammites who should be saluted.
It is a spring of ever gushing waters. Our cup runneth
over.

Hadassah has had many endowed chroniclers. Henrietta
Szold's name is known to millions in many lands. We
need not gild the lilly.

Hadassah is the Women's Zionist Organization of America. It looks toward the land of origins—the land of the

Bible. It is native to the soil of America. For American
Jews have early evinced an interest in the dream of Zion
restored. So have a number of American Christians, like
Hannah Adams, the first American woman historian,
author of a number of books. Dogged by misfortune, ill
health, poverty, monotony, anxiety, and all the ill-starred
misadventures which attended her career, Miss Adams
wrote to a friend: "I next chose a subject in which I
thought it probable that I should not meet with any in-
terference. I formed the design of writing the *History of
the Jews* . . ." It was published in two volumes in 1812.[2]
But even as early as 1759 American Jews had assisted a
resident of Safed who had come to America to collect
funds for needy Jews in Palestine. Other itinerant fund-
raisers soon followed, bringing "fresh regards from Zion."[3]

By 1832 a society was founded for the raising of funds
for indigent Palestinian Jews "in a systematic, responsible,
and economic fashion, the first such group in America."
Mordecai Manuel Noah had already launched his gran-
diose plan for a Jewish colony on the "Niagara frontier."
Isaac Leeser preached Zionist sermons and exhorted his
readers in the *Occident* to help their co-religionists in
Palestine. Emma Lazarus wrote her "Zionides" and was
addressing American Jews in her "Epistle to the Hebrews."

After the Russian pogroms and the mass migrations to
America, the Hoveve Zion society came into being in
1884. This was in New York. But it was in Chicago, in
1896, that the first organized effort to answer Herzl's call,
took place. The responders, big and little, were East
European Jews in crowded, poverty stricken tenements.
The three little Jerusalimsky sisters like other children
used to accompany their father to those early Zionist
meetings. One of them, Bertha, as Mrs. Harry Berkman
(active in Hadassah) became the chronicler and custodian

of every scrap of historic paper, of letters from Herzl and
Nordau and Henrietta Szold.[4] Here countless women inspired by the age-old dream of a return to Zion of the
displaced Jews of the world were involved from their early
childhood in the work of an organization that dedicated
its purpose to the healing of the sick in Palestine, now
Israel; to the encouragement of a creative Jewish life for
American Jews and "to foster the Jewish ideals." It attracted women not for a year or a decade. When they
joined, it usually meant a commitment to the principles
of Hadassah and to meeting its needs, for the life of the
individual member.

They have wrought well. Hadassah's membership boasts
of more than 300,000 members in more than twelve hundred chapters in the United States. Health stations, infant
welfare stations, clinics and splendidly equipped hospitals
are the pride and the health safeguard of Israel today. The
Youth Aliyah program which organized children's crusades from Nazi-dominated lands has been a noble undertaking. The children whom Henrietta Szold led to the
Promised Land are now proud citizens of a new democratic state, manning its outposts with courage, contributing to the growth of the land with zeal. These truly are
Henrietta's children! Hadassah, jointly with the Hebrew
University established the only medical school in Israel.
Undaunted though saddened by the loss of its Rothschild-
Hadassah Hebrew University Hospital which since 1948
stood as a beautiful but desolate monument on Mt. Scopus
the organization built at Ein Kerem near Jerusalem another imposing institution. Its City of Healing is an awe-
inspiring sweep of modern buildings growing out of the
Judean hills. The Henrietta Szold-Hadassah School of
Nursing is the pride of countless donors, big and little in
many parts of the world. It is an expanding and ongoing
and continuing program stretching to meet new needs,

dreaming of ever new undertakings, such as the Kennedy Memorial Building, "so that Medical Center patients will not be disturbed by the tens of thousands of visitors arriving yearly." This memorial to John F. Kennedy will serve as a Tourist Reception Center where lectures may be given "on areas that cannot be visited."[5]

To single out from the more than 300,000 members a few who are to be noticed is patently inadequate. The great leaders are known and honored. Many of them are New York women—Irma Lindheim, Rose Jacobs, Tamar de Sola Pool. So we turn to three women in other parts of the land who will serve as prototypes for hundreds of thousands of Shunammites. Two are from the Middle West and one from California.

The two Chicagoans are Pearl Franklin and Dora Yavitz. The Californian is Bertha Sieroty, "whose dedication to the work of Hadassah was complete and all encompassing."[6]

Bertha Sieroty was born in Poland in 1890. When she was six her parents, Raphael and Esther Brown, came to San Francisco. There her father became an early worker in the Zionist ranks. Bertha and her two brothers grew up in a home where Jewish tradition and history were cherished. She married Adolph Sieroty of Los Angeles in 1917 and joined Hadassah the following year. "There were no lapses from 1918 until she passed away in 1944." Her husband was a highly successful merchant. The home in which the Sieroty family lived was one of the showplaces of Los Angeles. A huge and imposing mansion on Fremont Circle, it soon became the place where visiting Jewish lecturers were entertained and where many receptions and meetings in behalf of many causes were held as a matter of course. There one could meet and hear notables from every part of the world. Judge Morris Rothenberg, president of the Zionist Organization of

America, 1932-1936, came to visit there and to enlist new
members for the Zionist cause. It was one of the homes
where a woman historian was invited to speak for Hadassah in the same year, 1936. The Sieroty home was a household run with great decorum and a dignity and grace
which was innate and which never varied. Mrs. Adolph
Sieroty was like the chatelaine of a ducal estate in bearing
and manner.

"For many years she served as a National Vice-President
of Hadassah, and in Los Angeles on numerous boards
including Jewish Centers Association, the Bureau of
Jewish Education, the United Jewish Welfare Fund, the
Los Angeles Community Council, the Zionist Youth Commission, the Emergency Council for Palestine, the American Jewish Congress, etc." It was to her home that Henrietta Szold sent Ilse Warburg, herself a refugee from
Germany, in order to get funds for the transporting of
Jewish refugee children to Palestine.

"Her services to the great causes of her people were in
the spirit of selfless dedication and consecration."[7] She
and her husband were among the founders of Temple
Sinai of Los Angeles. She worked closely with Augusta
Kohn whose husband was Rabbi Jacob Kohn. They were
friends as well as co-workers in every good enterprise involving both the Jewish community and the philanthropic
and civic causes which flourished in Los Angeles, and in
other parts of California.

They wore many hats, did these dedicated women. For
we find them founding numerous organizations, adding
their time and talents to many causes devoted to rescue
and rehabilitation of Jewish refugees, preservation of
human rights and dignity, assuring immigrants an opportunity to become Americanized and acclimated, extending a sororal hand to those in their midst and those far
away.

A daughter writing her tribute to her mother well illustrates this social concern. In the June 1954 issue of Women's League *Outlook* is a sketch of Dora Yavitz. She was born in Jersey City, New Jersey, December 25, 1886. She and her husband Philip, having moved to an outlying section of Chicago at a distance from all synagogues, did what so many Jews did, established a synagogue in their home. Her daughter writes: "The first recollection I have of my mother's participation in Jewish and communal life came in 1919. There was no place to worship . . . A synagogue was organized in our home and opened to the community. Our bookcase became the Ark of the Torah. Our home became the scene of all activities." Eventually a synagogue was built. "Today the synagogue stands as a bulwark in the Conservative movement . . . My mother served as president of its Sisterhood and in numerous other capacities for many happy years . . . In 1938 she was asked to take the Chairmanship of the first National Convention of National Women's League to be held in Chicago."

Dora Yavitz belonged to 18 organizations, small and large. Some were local in scope. Others were well known both on the national and international level. She belonged to B'nai B'rith, HIAS, Hadassah, National Council of Jewish Women, American Jewish Congress, Round Table of Christians and Jews, local charities, an old people's home, orphanages and many other philanthropic groups. She died September 28, 1956.

She had, as did countless other Jewish women, a formula for service: Nothing that concerned her coreligionists was alien to her. Nothing that the community or the nation demanded of her was beyond the range of her involvement. She was typical of the Jewish "Book of Numbers" in America. She was counted and honored in her time. Yet as thoroughly as the tide obliterates footprints in the sand, she and her sister Shunammites have been erased from the tablets of history.

Both in the great Midwest and on the national scene of Hadassah there is another name deserving of attention. The memory of Pearl Franklin is to be kept green because of her good works, because of the total self-abnegation of her life, because she belongs to the tradition of the American Jewish spinster who forsook marriage and the normal satisfactions of life and because of an inner compulsion (almost like the taking of vows of celibacy), or the force of circumstances, she sublimated all personal hopes, spent all passions in the work of her chosen organization. In the Middle West and beyond, Pearl Franklin's name was synonymous with Hadassah.

"We Remember Pearl Franklin With Love and Reverance" was the heading of Chicago Hadassah tribute to Pearl Franklin. They recalled her with a measure of awe and devotion seldom encountered. They memorialized her with words and with a Pearl Franklin Wing in the Hadassah Medical Center at Ein Kerem near Jerusalem.

In reading a touching memoir written by her sister Lillian, in many editorials and other tributes one is moved by the impact of a strong and outgoing personality thoroughly oblivious of herself, enflamed with a zeal for others, involved and concerned and magnetic. Those who knew her and were counted as her intimate friends saw in her a sublimation and dedication to her cherished cause seldom surpassed. She was by profession a lawyer and a college teacher. Her students were her loyal disciples. They ultimately became her friends. She knew them, followed their careers, spurred them to graduate study, helped them find jobs, was informed of their romantic involvements, attended their weddings and celebrated all the rites of passage of their children as if they were her own. She was at ease with people of all sorts and all backgrounds. She loved to laugh. She could also feel great sorrow and shed tears for others. She was popular with both men and women. She was a spinster by choice. In figure and bearings she was matronly—and indeed she was a communal matriarch. She knew intimately all the great men and women of the Zionist movement and in Hadassah. Henrietta Szold, Tamar de Sola Pool, Rose Jacobs, Irma Lindheim were her close friends. Chaim Weizmann, Albert Einstein, Shmarya Levin, Nahum Sokolow enjoyed her presence, respected her mental endowments, her warm and hearty personality. She was courageous and unafraid of a rousing fight for principle. Her sister's narrative recalls one forgotten aspect of her life which deserves for sheer drama to be known.

"Thus Pearl became the President of the Chicago Chapter of Hadassah. She attended the ZOA Convention. Although most of the Hadassah women in Chicago were ignorant of the political undercurrents in the Zionist movement, things broke loose at the Convention. The struggle was between Weizmann and his adherents and Brandeis and his followers . . . Most of the National Board Members of Hadassah . . . were in favor of Brandeis. Consequently, Louis Lipsky, President of the ZOA, removed them from leadership. The women, furious, retaliated by leaving the ZOA and organizing as an independ group of the World Zionist Organization, which it has remained ever since. Pearl was largely responsible for this action and was elected National Vice-President with Alice Seligsberg as President."[8] This charming anecdote of Pearl's intransigence, her ability to take others with her, is unique in the annals of the relationship of women's groups to the masculine dominance of related groups. It has all the flavor and the spontaneity of the Middle West, whose accomplishments and leaders have been largely overlooked by the Eastern seaboard. It is of a piece with the courage and derring-do of a Hannah Solomon, an Ernestine Rose.

From the year of its founding until the present, Hadassah has followed an undeviating consistency of purpose. True to the call of its founder, loyal to its venerable tradition, it has hewed a program dedicated to healing and helping needy kin. It has made philanthropic history. It has earned respect. Its meetings are reported in far-flung areas of the world. In its issue of August 19, 1966 an Anglo-Jewish periodical highlights the deliberations of Hadassah's 52nd national convention in Boston. *The Jewish Observer and Middle East Review* of London reports the meeting which was attended by 2,000 delegates and guests. President Lyndon Johnson greeted Hadassah as a voluntary organization "which gives impetus to our nation's major objectives—that of helping people to help themselves." And Levi Eshkol, Prime Minister of Israel, greeted them with the warmth they had richly earned in their long and honorable years of service: "The name of Hadassah is written large across the panorama of modern Israel, bearing testimony to the magnificent record of creative achievement and inspired endeavor, which has consistently characterized your movement from its inception."

Interesting are the words of the President of Hadassah, Mrs. Mortimer Jacobson. They have a familiar ring. "The basic concern of a modern Jew in a free society is not whether his son will face anti-Semitism—not whether his son will be able to earn a living—but whether he will remain a Jew." To that end she urged the members to ensure a Jewish education for their children "as an important part of their way of life" and the daily practice of Judaism "so as to set an example for their children to follow."[9]

In the year 5727 (1966), Mrs. William Henning Rubin,

president of Chicago Hadassah, greeted the members of that chapter, on the occasion of the New Year, with these words which paraphrased the Boston program: "The great concern of educators and leaders is whether the American Jew will remain a Jew. The only remedy to this dilemma is a knowledge of our rich and priceless heritage, with the parents setting the example."

So there is a health program in Israel and an educational program in America. And the dream of a Baltimore-born Jewess is fulfilled.

A kindred group to Hadassah is Pioneer Women. It is the Women's Labor Zionist Organization of America. Organized in 1925 following a request from Rahel Ben Zvi in Palestine—later to become a First Lady of Israel— "to help build a well for a tree nursery in Jerusalem." It was a symbolic call to which seven women in New York responded. It now has 500 branches in the United States and affiliations in Canada, Mexico, England, France, New Zealand, Argentina, Australia, Brazil, Belgium, Chile.[10] Pioneer Women work with a kindred group in Israel Moetzet-Hapoalot. They list more than a thousand "installations" in Israel whose purpose is the rehabilitation of newcomers to Israel. These immigrants come from more than a hundred lands. To meet training needs for thousands of young people, there are seven vocational schools maintained in Israel. There are also five agricultural training schools. In addition the group maintains infant centers and kindergartens, day and night nurseries, orphanages and summer camps.

The program of Pioneer Women in America "is geared to the highest standards of service; fostering active citizenship, creative American-Jewish living; promoting Jewish education." In the United States there are literary figures, sociologists, leaders of the American labor movement

whom the group claims with pride. In Israel, there is
Golda Meir, one-time foreign minister now Prime Minister who long ago, in her American antecedent years served
as its first National Secretary. Rahel Shazar, First Lady
of Israel, noted author and lecturer, is another loyal member. Of the eleven women members in the last Knesset,
nine were members of the Israeli sister organization of
Pioneer Women. These groups, widely separated, have a
universe of discourse based on their involvement and
support of the labor movement and its ideology, in every
country in which they function.

Hadassah and Pioneer Women, both Israel-oriented,
have a common purpose with still another group—the
Mizrachi Women's Organization of America. It was
founded in 1925 and has grown to a network of 300 groups
with a membership of 50,000 women. "Today it is the
major women's religious-Zionist organization in the
United States . . ." The group maintains "an extensive
network of child-care, social service, and educational projects in Israel . . ."[11] In their notice of the Mizrachi
Women's philanthropies President Eisenhower and his
successors in office have paid tribute to their child-oriented
work in Israel. President John F. Kennedy wrote them:
"It is heartening to learn of the devotion and sense of
service which has helped to create children's villages,
homes, schools and settlement houses in Israel." He noted
that through their endeavors "hope and progress have
emerged from despair." The members of Mizrachi Wom-
en's Organization in the tragic year of 1963 voted to establish the John F. Kennedy Memorial Library a month
after his death.

In addition to the children's villages, vocational schools,
Teachers' Training Seminary, a Student House donated
to the Bar Ilan University, a very touching ceremony took
place in a community dedicated to the memory of one of

their founders: In October of 1965 they dedicated in the Bessie Gotsfeld Children's Village "the reconstructed ancient synagogue of Leeuwarden, Holland." Here on a Judean hill site once barren and desolate at Raanana are 250 verdant acres with newly planted trees where orphaned children from twenty-five countries are taught and cared for. It is gratifying to note that the graduates of this and other children's villages which they maintain "are in high demand." Together with the Mizrachi Women's Organization of Canada, they established the Haifa Community Center where nursery school children, adults and old people have social service programs provided for them. Recent immigrants are especially made welcome.

When in 1965, Mizrachi Women looked back on forty years of ceaseless crusades to expand their Israeli institutions they summarized their endeavors in these words: "It takes Faith to build a Land. It takes Faith to build a Person."

Of them it might well be written: WE KEEP THE FAITH.

In passing it is of interest to note that in 1955, yet another ultra-orthodox group came upon the scene. The world headquarters of the Lubavitch Center is in New York. "Women from all walks of life joined in concerted efforts dedicated to the propagation of Torah-true Judaism." Nshei Chabad, the women's arm of the Chassidim (Hasidim) "remains unique in that it does not engage in fund raising. Its sole aim is to bring the word of Torah-true Yiddishkeit (Jewishness) to an increasing number of Jewish women."[12]

Jewish women's organizations range from the Traditional Orthodox groups to the Conservative and Reform orientation. The differences are marked. So are the similarities. Just one year after the women of the most Traditional Jewish point of view, deriving their inspiration from Rabbi Menachem M. Schneerson who heads the Lubavitch Chassidic movement, had organized themselves into a religiously oriented assembly, a member of a Reform Congregation, the North Shore Congregation Israel of Glencoe, Illinois, injected a curious and unexpected note of consonance into the official publication of Reform Judaism, *American Judaism*.[13]

"The Essence of Jewishness—Two Views," is a study in contrasts. "What Makes Me A Jew?" asks Helen Davis Szold. She is, by the way, identified as being "distantly related to Henrietta Szold." Describing her American antecedents in which for three generations her family reveled, she discovers within herself areas of ideological and religious rapport which make her, "an American woman who looks like a *shikse* (gentile), and a Polish man with a long gray beard join hands across an ocean and continue to march down the centuries . . ." She quotes George Bernard Shaw's opinion that "The Jew was born civilized" and interprets it by these words: "I think Shaw meant that the Jew is born respecting himself and hence it is natural for him to respect the self of another, *and assume moral responsibility for both.*"[14] She glories in her faith and in the creation of the State of Israel. She is stirred by the prophetic teachings, "as a Jewess I can live no other way . . ." She concludes with these words: "This is what binds a woman as American as the Bill of Rights to an old man in Poland who never heard of it. And this, wherever you may find him on the face of the earth, is the Jew." There is immediate official rebuttal by the editor and a rabbi. But we are only concerned with the feminine narrative here.

Yet Mrs. Szold's affirmation is not the universally accepted point of view of women in the Reform movement. Perhaps there is in truth no universal point of view in

Judaism. *American Judaism* also opens its pages to a revealing feminine lament titled "The Void."

> My faith—
> How little it requires.
> No sacrifice
> Of my desires,
> No genuflection
> Or candle fires
> *My* faith
> (How often it inspires) . . . .
>
> My belief—
> How seldom it intrudes
> Upon my methods
> Or my moods,
> Upon my weekend interludes!
> *My* belief
> (How often it eludes) . . .
>
> My creed—
> How heavily does it lean
> On conversations at the green
> On contributions in between!
> *My* creed
> (How little does it mean) . . .[15]

There is no unanimity. There is great diversity here within the green pastures of the Reform Movement. It embraces both the holy and the profane. The latitude of democracy in religious practice!

The National Federation of Temple Sisterhoods was founded in the year before the first World War, 1913. It has carved a strong role in the Reform movement. Its chief activities being channeled through the more than 600 sisterhoods affiliated with 640 parent Reform congregations. Youth activities and seminars for religious school teachers claim its concern. In 1931 it became "the patron body" of the Jewish Braille Institute of America. It is also co-publisher of *American Judaism.*

In the *New York Times* of June 24, 1966, under the heading "Reform Judaism Aids Unchurched" the meeting of the Central Conference of American Rabbis is covered. It was held in Toronto.

A thorough survey was presented to the Conference of the status of the Reform movement in the Western Hemisphere which in all includes 670 Reform Congregations. An analysis of statistics of Jews in the United States shows that there are in this country 5.6 million Jews. Twenty to thirty per cent are affiliated with the Orthodox or Traditional groups. Forty per cent are divided between the Conservative and Reform branches. The rest are unaffiliated. It was proposed that Reform Temples "open the doors of the synagogue for the unchurched and unsynagogued" . . . It was recommended that they try to bring "the message and insights of Judaism to the unaffiliated Gentile."[16] So far there has been but little public interest shown by women in these plans. In addition to routine synagogue activities Sisterhood members show a creative interest in child welfare, in community projects, in interfaith contacts. Members are active on a national level, in White House conferences, in the work of the United Nations, in civic and patriotic undertakings.

Leafing through the announcements and descriptions of NFTS programs shows how wide are its interests and how eager the membership is to help both synagogue and community. A Sisterhood in Stamford, Connecticut, sponsors a Tutorial Educational Program. A Sisterhood in Downey, California, is engaged in Bible study. The group calls itself "Tea and Torah." Dr. Maurice Eisendrath is involved in a series of "Tea and Torah" sessions in Steubenville, Ohio. Volunteer teachers from Congregation Beth Elohim Sisterhood in Brooklyn, New York, have acted as teacher's aids, have visited homes of Negro families, have taught music, sewing, art and remedial reading in the public schools. In Chappaqua, New York, the Sisterhood has had monthly meetings called a "Dialogue Group" with Christian Church Women. The Temple Sholom Sisterhood of Chicago has a Play and Learn Project, also known as PAL which is a kindergarten for culturally disadvantaged children. This is a joint undertaking with Hull House. The Beth Hillel Sisterhood of North Hollywood, California was invited by the First Methodist Church of that city to display a Seder table in its "Days to Remember" exhibit. A Sisterhood in St. Louis—Shaare Emeth—has undertaken the enlarging of its Temple Library "as the outstanding library of Judaica in the city." A random sampling of women's activities which have enriched their communities.

As the catalogue of activities of Jewish women's organizations grows in length and scope, the impression is one of a spiritual continuum, of a united purpose unmarred by divisive fences, unspoiled by impenetrable curtains separating one religious group from another. Here, for example, is a poetic tribute to Martin Buber in the pages of *American Judaism:*

> All real living is meeting,"
> He said (this man destined to be
> In love with the world, from boyhood on),
>
> Turning from books to the simple Hassidic
> Heart-beat of life as holy joy
> And the rich world of *I and Thou*
>
> Where a shy need in persons asks
> And gives its morsel of bread, an answering
> Yes to the other . . .[17]

The common denominators of faith and mitzvoth (good

works) unites more than it separates the Jewish women of America.

"A force of unvarying direction, which is to the soul what gravity is to the body, ensures the cohesion of the group by bending all individual wills to the same end. That force is moral obligation." Thus Bergson.[18] That sense of moral obligation is the central thread on which the many Jewish organizations are strung. A purpose enflames a group. An individual may inspire it. If there be a universal truth in it, if there be a need, the cause endures. Women with time on their hands, women with a need to be fulfilled, involved, useful are caught up by the message, the personality. They ally themselves. They give themselves. They grow in the doing and the giving.

The birth of a philanthropic enterprise may be spurred by events that are described as "an act of God." It may be caused by the evil that is inherent in some men. It may be brought about by corrupt governments and decadent societies, or precipitated by indifference and moral laxity. It may grow out of the worship of false gods, out of obeisance to the golden calf, or the adulation of "the bitch goddess success." But where there are remediable conditions, where healing and therapy, and physical and moral sustenance can be mobilized and dispensed, there is also hope. Poets have wrestled with these problems, and philosophers.

> Read history; so learn your place in Time;
> And go to sleep: all this was done before . . .
> Read history: thus learn how small a space
> You may inhabit . . .
> Work boldly . . .
> . . . keep heart and face—
> Not to betray the doomed and splendid race
> You are so proud of, to which you belong . . .[19]

The posthumous voice of Rabbi Joshua Loth Liebman reminds us that "The task of human intelligence is not to fold our hands and sit by patiently and passively awaiting doom; it is rather to use our reason to find out what the circumstances are in which we will cooperate . . ."[20]

Among the circumstances in which American Jews were willing to cooperate were those that created organizations like HIAS and ORT. HIAS had two antecedent organizations from which it derived. The Hebrew Sheltering House Association which was founded in 1884 and the Hebrew Immigrant Aid Society, established in 1902. The Hebrew Sheltering and Immigrant Aid Society was founded in 1909 by the merging of the two groups. The term is a contraction of initials of the parent groups. Its purpose was to help Jewish immigrants en route to the United States. But the volume of immigrants swelled and as circuitous routes and new destinations became imperative, offices were opened in the far East and new homes for the immigrants were found in Canada and South America. Now it has merged with other social service agencies engaged in similar work and serves in the United States and Israel and other countries as United HIAS Service. Unlike other women's organizations that grew out of the needs to minister to immigrants, its women's division is small. New York has nine branches, Chicago seven. In Chicago, the Fannie D. Copeland HIAS Women's Auxiliary pays tribute to its Lithuania-born founder who until her death in 1938 was its dynamic leader, a woman of compassion and great sympathy for the immigrant whose life she had shared and whose plight she wished to better.

Of the sorrows, tribulations, indignities, extermination which the Jews experienced in Russia and other East European lands much has been written. Libraries are filled with the annals of horror. That Jews, men and women, reacted with total compassion and total generosity has been obvious. That some Christians reacted with equal horror and disbelief and heartbreak is often forgotten. American women like Hannah Adams, Julia Ward Howe, Frances Willard, Eleanor Roosevelt took these sorrows to heart. Joaquin Miller, Edwin Markham, Theodore Roosevelt gave unmistakable proof of their abhorrence of pogroms and imprisonment and libel and expulsion. In a long forgotten poem titled "The Jews," Edwin Markham spoke for his times and his generation and his fellow Christians.

They come out of the night of years with Asia in their
    blood,
Out of the mystery of Time that was before the Flood
They saw imperial Egypt shrink and join the ruined lands;
They saw the sculptured scarlet East sink under the gray
    sands;

And have they not had grief enough, this people shrunk
    with chains?
Must there be more Assyrias, must there be other Spains?
They are the tribes of sorrow, and for ages have been fed
On brackish desert-wells of hate and exile's bitter bread . . .
They built the walls of cities with no threshold for their
    own;
They gave their dirge to Nineveh, to Babylon their
    moan . . .[2]

It was in Czarist Russia in the days of darkness that ORT was born.

ORT—the Organization for Rehabilitation Through Training—is "the vocational training agency of the Jewish people." It was in 1880 that Samuel Poliakov, a Russian Jewish industrialist, petitioned Czar Alexander II for the right to establish a philanthropic fund for destitute Jews.

Having secured official permission a group of six men—of whom Poliakov was one and the noted philanthropist, Baron Horace de Günzburg was another—sent out a circular letter to announce the establishment of the fund and to ask for gifts. Gifts came in small and large amounts and the way was open for the creation of an organization dedicated to the spread of industrial and agricultural training. Its unwieldy Russian name was contracted to ORT and the English equivalent became the Organization for Rehabilitation Through Training.

The stringent laws under which Russian Jews were restricted and kept from learning useful trades and agricultural skills were for a brief time somewhat eased. The peddlers and artisans and small inn keepers had had no future, no hope of economic betterment. Then Alexander II was assassinated and pogroms and persecution and a reign of terror followed. ORT finally received a charter in 1906. Trade schools were again opened. Apprenticeships were established, scholarships were granted and loans were made available to trained artisans. The grim, bleak years of the First World War disrupted and dislocated and diminished the Jewish population. But ORT followed the refugees and the work of rescue and rehabilitation went on. "And then came the Russian civil war and more pogroms." Then a delegation of ORT leaders traveled to Western Europe and America. Help had to be found and that quickly.

In the United States, in 1922, ORT established a foothold. Classes were set up in the Western hemisphere wherever refugees were admitted. Canada and South America were hospitable to ORT ideology and to refugees alike. The United States gave its acceptance.

In Brooklyn, in 1927, Women's American ORT came into being. It grew from a tiny group to an organization of more than 65,000. Women's American ORT became

the largest ORT organization in the world. There are
branches in many lands. The women joined because they
believed in the dignity of labor, the importance of the
individual. They responded with whole-hearted warmth
to the plight of victims of two wars, to the displaced, to
the former inmates of concentration camps. Schools were
built in every part of the world, in Europe and in Africa
and in Israel, the place of the ingathering of the homeless
exiles and victims of oppression. Former professional men
and women, artists and musicians whose bodies had been
injured were taught other skills. Former surgeons operated
poultry farms. Former musicians learned how to weave.
Children of the African ghettos who had had no previous
schooling were taken into day and boarding schools, fed,
clothed, taught. Older men and women were re-educated.
Teachers from the ranks of refugees were sent to a Swiss
Training Institute and briefed on newer teaching techniques. Women's American ORT prides itself on these
activities and on being an active participant in communal
affairs in this country. There is continuing help and re-
education of the refugees who come to America or who
find their ultimate home in Israel.

Its slogan taken from "Eight Steps of Charity" formulated centuries ago by Maimonides has been over the
years the backbone of its philosophy: "The most meritori-
ous of all," said Maimonides, "is to anticipate charity by
preventing poverty, namely: to give our reduced brother a
considerable gift or loan, or to teach him a trade, thereby
establishing him in business and enabling him to earn
an honest livelihood and not be reduced to the dreadful
alternative of begging for charity. This is the highest step
in the Golden Ladder of Charities."[22]

To this goal the women of America who belong to
ORT are dedicated.

In the year 1917, the American Jewish Congress was

founded. Its purpose—to secure civil, political and religious equality for East European Jews and to protect the existing settlements in Palestine. A delegation headed by Judge Julian W. Mack and Louis Marshall attended the Peace Conference in Paris. Adjournment of the group after the conclusion of the Peace Conference, did not terminate the impetus of what was originally to have been a temporary organization. In 1922, Nathan Straus became President of the reconstituted group as a permanent organization. Stephen S. Wise and Israel Goldstein zealously dedicated themselves to the ideology and program of the American Jewish Congress which sought to fight the spread and evil machinations of the Nazi movement, which advocated the development of the Zionist ideology and spearheaded the fight for civil rights in the United States. In 1936, the World Jewish Congress was created, assuring its vigilance in the matter of Jewish rights wherever threatened. In the same year, in Chicago and in many other cities, the newly organized Women's Division of the American Jewish Congress, then six years old, ably led by Louise Waterman Wise, secured a foothold and began making a dynamic contribution to the many causes sponsored by the parent organization. Using the motto "a woman's place is in the world," they placed no limits on concern or goal.

From the beginning they saw in the striving for equality and social justice a common cause with all submerged groups. "In this country the Jewish woman has been able to work for a democratic society which would recognize no frontiers of creed or color or class . . . we have embraced the opportunity to participate in the struggles for fulfilling the American promise of full equality for all people . . . we were also enabled . . . to express our love for our religious and moral heritage."[23] In a "Salute to the Women's Division" in *Congress bi-Weekly* there ap-

pears an enthusiastic endorsement in tribute to its ideology, growth and world-wide enterprises:

> The Women's Division has also appealed to an in-
> creasing number of American Jewish women because it
> has displayed an unusual sensitivity to the problems
> that concern the welfare and security of the family,
> home and community. The Women's Division has
> viewed these problems in the broadest and yet the most
> intimate context. . . . It will undoubtedly chart new
> experiments in cultural and educational programs for
> the organization, and explore further ways of expand-
> ing and activating the membership to meet the chal-
> lenges that confront them as Jews and Americans.[24]

Louise Waterman Wise, married to Rabbi Stephen S.
Wise, was both founder and president of the Women's
Division of the American Jewish Congress. An artist by
vocation and a social worker by avocation she lent her
presence and her inspiration to this group until her death
in 1947. Her personality survived her death and the
women whom she led and inspired during her lifetime
have paid tribute to her memory in countless ways. A
concrete testimonial may be seen in an impressive building erected in Israel. The Louise Waterman Wise Youth
Hostel in Jerusalem which they built is "a cultural and
intellectual meeting ground for the youth of Israel and
young visitors from all parts of the world." Israel's Ministry of Education had asked that a youth house be
built. The Jewish National Fund provided the land. The
Women's Division of the American Jewish Congress built
this memorial to their own Louise "in memory of her
love of children, faith in Israel and devotion to democracy."

The American Jewish Congress has illumined the problems of Jewish life in countless ways. One of them is in

the series of "Dialogues in Israel." Women have taken
a small but significant role in these dialogues. Golda Meir
delivered a brilliant address titled "Unity in Diversity in
Jewish Life" on the occasion of the Third Dialogue.
Alluding to what united Jews in the past—their knowledge
of the Torah and acquaintance with Hebrew, she stated:
"What united us in the past is quite clear. The great worry
is—what will unite us now, in the present?"[25]

Then this former Milwaukee schoolteacher asked some
trenchant questions about the future of Jewish life in
America: "What is happening to hundreds and thousands
of Jewish students? What is the Jewish content of their
lives? What is their link between themselves and the
Jewish community in America, and what is their link
with Israel? . . . In response to these questions I have
heard few optimistic answers." Rabbi Joachim Prinz,
President of the American Jewish Congress, in answer,
stated "what Mrs. Meir said has left me in a state of
depression." He shared her misgivings and her pessimism.
For him the reality of American Judaism lies in its being
"a non-Hebraic Jewish community, of which a small number, an elite, will be taught and will voluntarily learn
to speak Hebrew . . . the rest will be what they are, Jews
in the United States, living and finding their Jewish fulfillment there as they do."

In the closing minutes of the Third Dialogue an
Israeli speaker referred to the fact that it was a woman,
Mrs. Betty Alderson, who had first broached the possibility of such a series of frank discussions between members of the American Jewish Congress and leaders of
Israel.[26] He concluded: "I find within American Jewry
a certain provincialism and parochialism . . . American
Jews live for the moment . . ." To remedy the situation
he suggested an American Jewish Peace Corps in Israel—
a form of a Return to Zion.

Perhaps the most concise summary of what the men and women of the American Jewish Congress hold most significant is "Coming to Terms With Being Jewish"—a headline which appeared in the *Jewish Observer and Middle East Review* on August 19, 1966, in summarizing the Fifth Plenary Assembly of the World Jewish Congress. They came to the conference as members "of a perplexed generation." They dealt with every facet and aspect of Jewish life in every country where Jews live or exist. They came to grips with the ever-present threat of assimilation. "To know and feel themselves part of the Jewish people—that was the need repeatedly expressed in one form or another, as real in the mighty United States community, and in the sovereign State of Israel, as in the small, isolated and insecure communities elsewhere."

High on the list of its insecure communities, as reported to the Women's Division by Mrs. Hilde Prinz, were Jews living in the Soviet Union and those in South America. To meet the urgent problems presented by the plight of Russian Jewry twenty-four major Jewish organizations met in conference in Washington. "The Women's Division conducted workshops, educational and protest meetings, and participated in the picketing of the U.S.S.R. Embassies in Washington and New York. This is an ongoing concern which will result in many more activities." Results were negligible. "The only possible reaction in Russia so far has been the permission of the government for the baking of matzot in some parts of the Soviet Union."

In South America "the general problem . . . is the threatening assimilation in a country which is largely Catholic and where intermarriage and conversion are daily occurrences. As a result of all this, there has been a constant flow of emigration from Argentina to other countries, notably to Israel. The World Jewish Congress which is very strong in South America supplies us with a great deal of information."[27]

In summary it is perhaps apt to quote from Dr. Joachim Prinz. He stresses the vital importance of "the courage with which we approach the issues that affect us as Americans and as Jews."[28]

In this gallant approach to current problems the women stand shoulder to shoulder with the men.

The interpenetration of religious ideology into the clubs and associations and philanthropies of American Jewish life is incontrovertible. Its ramifications are truly astounding. "There already exists a society of Orthodox Jewish scientists which is dedicating itself to the solution of problems created for Orthodoxy by modern technology."[29] The Jewish Labor movement is aware of this trend.[30] So each in its own fashion is every woman's group that has been discussed in these pages. That there is erosion and attrition in Jewish ranks is obvious. That women's groups are aware of it is patently clear. That their programs and educational seminars and workshops and study groups and publications deal with these problems is incontrovertible. Intermarriage and indifference, social mobility, wider acceptance on the part of the host culture are among the social factors at work. Against these trends is an army of women with banners. Their awareness and concern are unmistakable. Alone or with parent men's groups they confront their problem. In considering their strength and energy, their vision and dedication, there is an upsurge of optimism, a belief that there will always be a "remnant of Israel." To recognize depletion and to close ranks—that is part of every Jewish woman's organization program.

When B'nai B'rith was organized in America on October 13, 1843, there were some 25,000 Jews in America.

At that time "the spirit of the age was one of philanthropy," writes one of its chroniclers.[31] But social discrimination as well as charity was a major concern. European stereotypes and ethnic clichés had crossed the
Atlantic with the immigrants of all races and all backgrounds. "With the arrival of a sizable German-Jewish
immigration in the 1840's, this stable situation began to
change," writes John Higham, after noting that the
earliest Jewish immigrants in America had achieved acceptance in the communities in which they had settled.[32]
In 1843, Jews of America were aware of both social and
economic stratification within their own ranks. "They
lacked community consciousness and that is what the infant B'nai B'rith set out to teach them . . ."[33] Gradually
its role expanded and many aspects of Jewish life in
America and elsewhere were studied with a view of amelioration. It was many years, however, before the women
entered the ranks. In 1895, B'nai B'rith proposed the
formation of women's units as "auxiliary lodges." The
first women's auxiliary was established in San Francisco
in 1897. Mrs. Herman Gutstadt, wife of the president of
the San Francisco B'nai B'rith District No. 4, became its
first president. "We have no information as to Mrs. Gutstadt's activities during her presidency as there are no
records prior to 1909 . . . the women did not have their
own council until 1941—Judge Lenore D. Underwood of
San Francisco was the first president of the Women's
Supreme Council—and were not an autonomous organization until 1956 when B'nai B'rith Women became an
official national organization."[34]

So in point of time, the Women of B'nai B'rith is a
young organization. In point of accomplishment it has
made giant strides. They admit to long decades of frustra-
tion. "Was this but a man's world? Were Jewish women
to be consigned to the home? Was B'nai B'rith—and this

was the crucial question—to deny itself the vast potential for good work which lay dormant among the Jewish women of America?" So begins their official history.[35]

Their resounding answer has been provided in the activities of this group since its tenuous inception in the last years of the nineteenth century. In 1940 B'nai B'rith Women met in Washington with six Women's Districts represented and organized the Women's Supreme Council. Sixteen years later the B'nai B'rith Triennial officially created the National Organization of B'nai B'rith Women. They had arrived with this act of formal recognition. Their growth has been phenomenal. In 1940 there were 38,000 members. In 1956 there were 137,000 members.

What had they wrought?

They have chosen service to War Veterans as one of their major activities. "In hundreds of veterans and military hospitals, thousands of B'nai B'rith Women are providing . . . personal services which symbolize the tradition of Service, to which B'nai B'rith is dedicated." Among the youth services which they help support are B'nai B'rith Hillel Foundations, B'nai B'rith Youth Organizations and the B'nai B'rith Vocational Service. The Women of B'nai B'rith cooperate with many government agencies and share in every major national community enterprise as well as in major Jewish endeavors. In its list of "Community Dynamics" the Anti-Defamation League stands high. Adult Jewish education is fostered through "Ongei Shabbat," Sabbath study and prayer groups, through holiday observances and participation in B'nai B'rith Institute of Judaism. With their men they share in many philanthropies such as the Leo N. Levi Memorial Hospital, National Jewish Hospital, Bellefaire and the B'nai B'rith Center at Rochester, Minnesota.

In Israel, the "Women's Supreme Council originally assumed responsibility for the maintenance of the B'nai

B'rith Children's Home in Jerusalem as a permanent
project when the late Henrietta Szold, leader of Hadassah
in Israel referred the problem of Nazi-terrorized children
to B'nai B'rith leaders in Israel."[36]

A dramatic centennial was celebrated in October of
1965 and reported in the *B'nai B'rith Women's World*.
The men and women of that organization were looking
backward to a century of involvement and concern with
settlers in Palestine and Israel. In 1865 Sir Moses Montefiore, noted philanthropist, had appealed for funds to
help cholera victims in Palestine. An immediate donation
from B'nai B'rith was the answer. "But money contributions have not been the only kind that the organization
and its members have made. Some of the highlights of the
long and fruitful association now entering its second century, are described in these pages." These services are
both significant and touching because they show insight
and imagination in philanthropy. For example, thirty
shelters for hitchhiking soldiers to protect them from the
sun were presented by B'nai B'rith Women during the
war for Independence. There are two B'nai B'rith-founded
communities in Israel—Moledeth B'nai B'rith and Ramat
Zvi. There are community buildings dotting the land and
community centers flourishing and trees planted by B'nai
B'rith Women casting welcome shadows over once barren
ground. There are students at the Hebrew University and
at Technion and at the Weizmann Institute who are sub-
sidized by their scholarships. Since 1948, children vic-
timized and emotionally disturbed by their Nazi torturers
have been sheltered and rehabilitated in their Children's
Home. At Beit Vegan there are now seven modern buildings, for they outgrew the original Jerusalem buildings
in 1955. And the B'nai B'rith members of the United
States and Canada rejoice in the newly formed B'nai
B'rith lodges in Israel. There the Henrietta Szold Lodge

operates a kindergarten thus honoring the great American leader of the children's crusade. In Jerusalem a great Martyr's Forest Shrine keeps the memory of our *kedushim* forever green.

This is a record of sublimation. The loneliness with which all women contend is channelled into countless therapeutic activities. In service to others women have discovered that growth of self is possible. Their other-directed activities have wrought many changes in personality, in intuitive understanding, in knowledge. The discovery of the needs of others has united these women both in action and in the profession of their faith. "The gradual withdrawal from worship and religious study on the part of the male creates a void which must somehow be filled; women represent the logical group which can bridge the gap." So writes an American Jewish sociologist.

So in the cherishing of their ancient tradition, in keeping alive ancestral memories, in developing a sense of social concern, in the mandatory performance of Mitzvoth (good deeds) the American Jewish Woman and her sisters in other lands—have zealously and passionately kept the faith.

13

One day as Elisha was journeying in the land of Shunem—so reads the Bible—he passed the house of a woman "who urged him to eat some food. So whenever he passed that way, he would turn in there to eat food. And she said to her husband, 'Behold now, I perceive that this is a holy man of God, who is continually passing our way. Let us make a small roof chamber with walls, and put there for him a bed, a table, a chair, and a lamp, so that whenever he comes to us, he can go in there.' "[1] Elisha called this good woman "the Shunammite" and availed himself of the food and shelter she provided.

The Shunammite is an anonymous woman as are many of our protagonists working alone or in association with others. That, by and large, is the story of the Jewish woman in America. It is a saga of the simple housewife involved in her family, in her community, in her country. It describes her secret oblation to Judaism in the days of earliest settlement in South America and Mexico when to be discovered in Jewish observance meant to be turned over to the agents of the Inquisitors. The earliest Jewish women in America are known to us because of this grim record.

The narrative unfolds. A part of the story has been aptly called "Portraits Etched in Stone,"[2] for carved in granite are the records of the virtues and the sorrows, the fruitfulness or virginity of countless women forever at rest in ancient cemeteries—"God's Acres." Slowly, very slowly, they begin to speak for themselves in letters to their husbands and to their children, in diaries they sometimes kept, in fragmentary acts of theirs which others recorded, in the outpouring of grief in which husband or orphan describes the loss and the anguish of life without the lost ones. Their inventories of household goods, their last wills and testaments mention their treasured possessions. So in our mind's eye the candlesticks gleam and the mirrors reflect them and their books and spectacles tell us how some of their leisure hours were spent. It is at first a family-centered life they led. But always there is room for the widow, or the little children orphaned, or the stranger who weary as was Elisha passed their doors and for whom the Shunammite and all the Shunammites who came after her provided food and shelter and unfailing hospitality.

That was the ancient Jewish tradition and the women observed it and kept the faith.

But there was also the beloved new land. Wide its verdant prairies. Magnificent its rivers. Long vistas, physical and spiritual. New concepts, new freedoms, new attitudes sprang up. Voices unencumbered by prejudice and hate eloquently proclaimed a new doctrine. Democracy was born and was cherished and nurtured here. The moral climate was as free as the wide and unfenced horizon.

Once in the earliest days of the Jewish settlement in the New World when secret Jews wanted to warn each other of danger from Inquisitors, they would say, "Take one step at a time—for the *matzoth* is fragile." Now the bread of affliction which they had known for centuries and the fragile matzoth they had carried for so long, could be replaced by a more sustaining diet—less bitter, less fragile. They could recite a hundred benedictions daily. Their blessings multiplied and the land was good and many of its people of all faiths were their brothers, fellow-Americans.

America was made up both of strong men and women and of those who were frail. Pioneers of staunch faith. Adventurers unafraid of dark impenetrable forests and women who followed their men over mountain trails and long interminable green acres and through the arched hills which erupted over the land. There were Indian traders among them whose homes were outposts with synagogues for their co-religionists and for themselves. Such a household was presided over by Joseph Simon, father of Miriam Simon Gratz and grandfather of Rebecca Gratz. Or like the cabin of Meyer and Rachel Hart who were among the first eleven families to settle in Easton, Pennsylvania.

There were men and women who followed *le Juif*, Elias Stultheus, into the Louisiana country when it was still under the French flag. There were the early settlers of Charleston and Savannah and Boston and New York and Newport. There were the mothers of soldiers who fought in the Revolutionary War and their sweethearts and wives. And women who followed every other war with fast-beating hearts, for their sons or husbands were involved in all of them.

America is the saga of the silent women, the anonymous ones, dispensing hospitality as Jews have ever been commanded to, as the nameless Shunammite served Elisha. And of the articulate women who rose through talent or compassion or inner vision to the very heights of greatness. Rebecca Gratz, beautiful, gentle, compassionate, rejecting marriage to cling to her faith, leaving a record of a life dedicated to good works. Emma Lazarus at the docks of New York Harbor staring with tear-welled eyes beholding the outcasts of Europe fleeing the terror of pogrom and persecution. Lillian Wald climbing steep tenement stairs, imperiling her life to nurse the sick and aged through raging epidemics. Henrietta Szold, gentle scholar, founding Hadassah, leading a new children's crusade to the Promised Land. Mathilde Schechter, guiding an army with banners, women dedicated to reclaiming Judaism, its folkways and mores from the erosive forces which were depleting the ranks. Jessie Sampter singing her songs in a new-old land. Louise Waterman Wise, the essence of compassion and humility, boldly championing the cause of democratic equality for all people. Tamar de Sola Pool, bag in hand, flying to Cyprus to spend Passover with refugees confined in barbed wire cages like animals in a zoo. An immigrant woman, Anna Rosenberg, rising through sheer ability and indomitable loyalty to be Assistant Secretary for Defense. A Milwaukee, Wisconsin, schoolteacher, Golda Meir, becoming the Foreign Minister and finally Prime Minister of a reborn nation, Israel.

The list is long and greatly to be cherished. The story of the Jewish woman in America is in a sense also the record of commitment. For it is women joining together in unions and on the picket lines, in bands of volunteers answering innumerable calls for time and energy, in schools for immigrants and playschools for little children; in clubs and societies and associations for the improvement and amelioration of the handicapped and underprivileged and the deprived; a vast army of dedicated and aroused and inspired women marching to an inner melody, marching to a song which only the dedicated and consecrated votary can hear.

This narrative describes the "organization" woman, one who is committed to a cause, enlists in a total way. She pays her dues and attends meetings and earns funds for special projects. She is aware of the pressure of world events and the demands made on all citizens to meet every national need, every humanitarian campaign. She knows the importance of education on every level. If she has not herself had the advantages of higher education, she has learned where adult education classes are held and how to enroll in them. She develops special skills as they are called for. She is learning and teaching. She is involved and committed.

Very little attention has been paid here to "the lotus eater," the woman who leads a charmed life, emancipated from financial and economic problems, detached from the rank and file, indifferent to all claims on her. She may be found enjoying her "conspicuous leisure" on cruises, in resorts, in country clubs, on shopping sprees, on the couch of a psychoanalyst. She is a refugee from self, an escapee from boredom. She has slammed the door on her past. She embarks with others like her on an endless search for deliverance from life. In a penetrating book, *The Human Situation,* by W. Macneile Dixon, we read:

"And how wide, how grotesquely wide of the mark are they who indulge in childish and insensitive chatter, babbling for the hope of a future existence as a petty, personal desire, born of selfishness . . . The story of humanity becomes the story of a long procession of sufferers, for whose sufferings no justification is offered, of poor souls intellectually and morally confounded, who entered existence blind to any reason for their coming and will leave it blind . . ."³

Decidedly the idle babblers, the human driftwood traveling de luxe, are unaccounted for here. They exist. But we do not know their numbers, nor do we chart their meanderings. For them as for ourselves, we say with the Psalmist

> For I am thy passing guest,
> A sojourner like all my fathers . . .⁴

There are imperishable moments in the life of Everyman and Everywoman. One not to be forgotten moment is when the walls of their own home encompass the family, surrounding it with protective shelder, shutting out the world and creating a place, quiet and impregnable, a unit separate from all the world. Another supreme moment is experienced when with their group and through sacrifice and joint effort, they share in the erection of a shelter for their faith, a monument to their heritage, a meeting place to which they may go to refresh their souls, to offer thanks, to seek expiation, to reaffirm their faith, to find solace in bereavement, joy in the celebrations, or peace of mind when problems are overwhelming and seemingly insoluble. Together with their co-religionists they erect a dwelling in which their faith resides and is honored, in which the Eternal Light forever burns, in which they may commune with God.

In the annals of America, the Jews have built sanctuaries for their faith for more than three centuries. These are the landmarks in time which comfort the builders and sustain their succeeding generations. Within Judaism men have been the builders and prime movers of congregational life. This has been largely true of the Christian

churches of this land also. But there comes a time when
women discover that they "have a heritage in religion to
regain, develop, and carry forward."[5]

What is the Jewish woman's place in the life of the
communal religious structure? It begins traditionally with
physical separation. Behind latticework fences or curtains,
women sit in balconies. The prayers and ceremonies that
take place below are offered by their men. In the balconies
only the sibilation of the devout and the rustling of clothing and the rising and sitting down betrays their presence.
That is the way of the Orthodox practice and it may be
observed at Shearith Israel and similar congregations in
this country, at Bevis Marks Synagogue in London and at
the Spanish and Portuguese Congregation in Amsterdam
and in many other places where the Traditional or Orthodox practices are perpetuated. In Israel one need only
visit the section known as Mea Shearim to be aware of
the deep hold these ancient folk ways still have on their
communicants.

At the opposite end of the spectrum there are Jewish
houses of worship which for size and grandeur and vast-
ness and soaring vistas and stained glass windows and
reverberations of organ music and chants and decorum
resemble great cathedrals. Adaptation and acculturation
have had their way. "In the past," writes Mordecai Kaplan,
"Judaism helped the Jew to live at his best . . . It gave
him the key to eternal life hereafter . . . it prescribed a
way of life for him, an ideal and a discipline . . . Can
Judaism do as much for the modern Jew?"[6] The answer
is involved and complex. There are spiritual values and
earnest devotions and "good Jews," to use a phrase of
Kaplan's, to be found everywhere. For if "being a Jew
should commit one to a specific standard of goodness"[7]—
then we are bound to recognize that such a commitment
exists wherever Judaism is practiced. By men. By women.
It existed in every worthwhile project and undertaking

in which women banded together for the common good. It was present in Emma and Josephine Lazarus, daughters of Orthodoxy, brought up under the benign influence of Shearith Israel Congregation. It was found in no smaller measure at Temple Sinai in Chicago where Hannah Solomon had learned the tenets of Reform Judaism. There are "Paradoxes of Religious Belief," writes Professor Milton Rokeach of Michigan State University, in discussing "the Golden Rule versus the rule of exclusion."[8] "Brotherhood and bigotry are intertwined in all religion," he quotes from Gordon Allport. Certainly in the lack of rapprochement of the extremes in Jewish ranks, in the deliberate lack of concord, we find areas of social distance which should be bridged. We need to have "dogma tempered with humility." We need to espouse a wide tolerance and put into practice the techniques and usages of mutual respect. Judging from the ease with which women are able and willing to work together within disparate ideologies, judging by the proliferations of women's groups in which the same women are involved, despite differences in background and synagogue or temple membership, we are safe to generalize that the causes unite them more than the barriers separate them. In every woman's purse are membership cards which proclaim this doctrine. They give their allegiance to the amelioration of conditions that are socially undesirable. They are ready to follow any leader who inspires them to transcend the limitations of exclusiveness, who points the way to concepts of social progress, of peace, of the elimination of racism and poverty. The country club and the kibbutz may have nothing in common but their mutual admiration of a Henrietta Szold or a Golda Meir. Is it possible that "the weaker sex" is pointing the way to the stronger?

What had they wrought in twentieth-century America, these "organization women?" There were changes in the

structural patterns of their community. In the years of
mass migration, the new immigrants had tried to repro-
duce in the areas of first residence a mirror-image of the
European *shtetl* as they had known it. Women soon became aware of the attractions of middle-class life of those
who had had several generations to enjoy the harvest of
their parents' labors in America. The early peddlers were
now department-store owners, tycoons, professional men
and women. The earlier East European *shtetl* mirror-im-
mage was supplanted by portraits of prosperous Jews living in areas of second residence or most comfortably established in the suburbs. The earlier pull from within rested
on nostalgia, on memory, on faith. The pull from without was based on creature comforts, material possessions,
status symbols, professional training for children. Among
parents, ambition vied with memory. Among children,
ambition led to separation from immigrant parents, to
assimilation and to gradually increasing intermarriage.

The religious life of the Jew reflected these changes.
German Jews belonged to Reform temples. East European
Jews who practiced Judaism faithfully were the Orthodox.
Among the Russian and Polish Jews were many newcomers who had thrown off all religious affiliation while
still in Europe and were avowed atheists and agnostics
who substituted Utopian hopes for a Great Society and
loyalty to the labor movement for the old reliance on
religion. What was needed for the believers was a bridge
between Reform and Orthodoxy. That bridge became
the Conservative movement. "A distinguishing aspect of
the Conservative Movement," writes Moshe Davis, "continued to be its ability to unite the diverse elements within itself."[9]

This recognition of diversity in Jewish ranks has been
noted by sociologists and historians in South America and
in Canada as well as in the United States. "There are

two contiguous trends emanating from this problem—*return* and *withdrawal*."[10] Dr. Davis stresses the relative ease of "withdrawal" in a free society. He adds: "In Canada, where official government figures on intermarriage are available since 1921, the rate of mixed marriages has increased from 6.2 per cent in the period 1936-1940, to 9.6 per cent during the Second World War, then to about 16 per cent in 1960 . . . Estimates for Argentina vary from 15-20 per cent." All surveys show this trend of increasing intermarriage. "A study of Washington's Jewish community (81,000) broke down the rate of intermarrying Jewish men by generations: 1.4 per cent for the foreign-born, 10.2 per cent for the first generation of American-born, 17.8 per cent for the second. At the rate for the college-educated members of the last group was a startling 37 per cent. Moreover, the Jewish birth rate has remained stable in the last 40 years, while the rest of the nation's has been generally rising."[11] These statistics were not viewed dispassionately by the Jewish women in the Western hemisphere. They regarded intermarriage as a threat to group survival—and a personal blow to family preservation and continuity. While this constitutes "withdrawal" from Judaism, there is evident a noticeable trend toward conversion to Judaism on the part of the formerly Christian mates. It may be noted that in Los Angeles there are two full-time schools for the instruction of converts to Judaism. Yet "The old tree is still somewhat suspicious of the new wood."[12]

The status of women in traditional Judaism has been another factor spurring withdrawal, according to sociologist Marshall Sklare.[13] The historic position of women, he states, has been "the most disruptive force" . . . in the ranks of Orthodoxy. The Conservative group recognized this and took corrective measures. This is particularly important because men "do not evince the same

degree of religious interest as of old." Sklare states that
women are reputed to have "a special affinity for religion"
and that more than half of those regularly attending Friday evening services are women.[14] That is one of the
reasons why in the opinion of experts, Conservatism is
the fastest growing of the three movements within Judaism
"which in the future decades may well be *the* regnant
form of American Judaism."[15]

Women may be numerically stronger at services but
they still have a long way to go to achieve equality and
recognition. Eloquent Christian voices have made the
same complaint. Pearl Buck, writing on "America's Medieval Women," has this to say: "It seems to me that
women are very badly treated in America. A few of them
know it, more of them dimly suspect it, and most of
them, though they know they ought to be glad they live
in a Christian country where women are given an education, do not feel as happy in their lonely hearts as they
wish they did. The reason for this unhappiness is a secret
sense of failure, and this sense of failure comes from a
feeling of inferiority, and the feeling of inferiority comes
from a realization that actually women are not much
respected in America."[16] Ashley Montagu, who claims to
have thought about this subject for some thirty years and
who finally wrote a book titled *The Natural Superiority
of Women,* admits that "Women have been conditioned
to believe that they are inferior to men . . ." The remedy:
". . . woman has now to emancipate herself from the myth
of inferiority . . ."[17] He pleads that "the liberation of
women means the liberation of man."[18] And that is a
goal to be greatly desired. More recently, Andrew Sinclair has contributed a forthright study, "the most com-
prehensive account yet published of the American woman's steady and persistent drive toward equality . . ."[19]
Yet it must be emphasized that such advances as women

have made in their status as Jews have come about indirectly and not as a feminist crusade for recognition of their claims to equality. Women were searching for meaning, for direction, for a viable relationship with God. If they had a natural bent for religion it grew out of a meaningful quest for understanding, for insight into the nature of things. So Henrietta Szold could write to Rose Jacobs: "I had thought in the remote days of my youth that one attained to serenity and wisdom with old age. What do I find in *my* old age? Vagueness, eternal wonder at the meaning of things, inadequacy to the daily tasks, anything but tranquillity."[20]

Lily H. Montagu, in "The Expression of My Personal Faith," a part of her book, *The Faith of a Jewish Woman,* writes in the same vein. "I believe in God as the God of truth . . . It matters infinitely what we think and believe, for thought and belief *do* affect conduct. We know that some of the best Jews the world has produced have been unlearned and that learning and the love of truth are not necessarily the same thing . . ."[21] It is a quest and not a crusade that we encounter again and again in what the women feel about their search for God. Men have echoed these sentiments again and again. "The frontier of American Jewish survival is still the synagogue," writes a Reform rabbi.[22]

We see women against the framework of world and national events. We study them within specific economic and social settings. We observe them as they bend before the winds of acculturation and accommodation, reconstructing their outer lives and manners to conform with those of their neighbors in the host culture. We see them diminished by status-striving or enlarged by noble goals. But always in our desire to get at the core of the matter we come back to the individual woman, to her basic isolation, to her inner loneliness, to her quest for purpose in her own life, to her deepest needs which lead to self-understanding and self-fulfillment. Some women find fulfillment in the world outside. Others find it in solitary prayer and in meditation and in contemplation. Faith looms large in some lives. It is totally absent in others. The articulate women we have portrayed were those who could seize on their inner light and let it shine before the world. The anonymous ones gave us but one clue to their inner-directed lives—the measure of their good works, the ability to submerge self in others' needs, the eloquence of a day-to-day nobility as seen in deeds, in action. Of prayer, humility and compassion—often overlooked and ignored by those around them—yet dominating lives and exalting and magnifying them.[23] It is their answer to the call of God.

"The Ability to Answer," is what Heschel identifies with the act of prayer.[24] "Prayer is *our* humble *answer* to the inconceivable surprise of living. It is all we can offer in return for the mystery by which we live. Who is worthy to be present at the constant unfolding of time?" Leo Baeck approaches the subject as a kindred spirit to Heschel. His section on "Gratitude and Prayer" in *This People Israel* states: "The blessings permeated life with a sense of constant gratitude. Thankfulness becomes an element of existence."[25] And Heschel: "It is gratefulness which makes the soul great." And Buber asks: "How can we become what we are?" He insists on the act of self-recognition. "Let us recognize ourselves: we, in whom, and in whom alone, that mysterious affirmation and negation of civilization—affirmation and negation in one—was implanted at the origin of our existence, we are the keepers of the roots."[26]

Certainly some women have been "the keepers of the roots," the visionary souls who dreamed of the preservation of a priceless heritage, of a peculiar treasure with which they were entrusted. In one of his penetrating commentaries in *The Jewish Prayer Book,* Rabbi Joseph H. Hertz has an illuminating footnote on the role of woman in religion vis-à-vis God: "God's is more than a father's love. That is sometimes hard and confined to the successful child. Not so a mother's. With an instinct that is almost divine, she feels that the erring child, the unfortunate child has the greatest need of love. And such is God's love."[27]

For inwardness or *Kavanah* is not limited to men. There are women endowed with a peculiar grace, with a delicacy of perception and insight, with a nobility of soul, with an intuitive knowledge of what to do with their loneliness which equals that of the great seers whose lives have been dedicated to its pursuit.[28] "*Kavanah* is not readily translatable into a single equivalent English word," writes Evelyn Garfiel in *The Service of the Heart.* "It connotes intention, devotion, dedication . . ."[29] It is at the heart of the state of prayer—an indwelling, an immanence, an essence of unity with the Divine. It is a state of contemplation. It is also service which expresses man's awareness of the goodness of God. "A *Mitzvah* requires *Kavanah,*" states the Talmud.[30] Maimonides stated that "Prayer without *Kavanah* is not prayer . . . if one has prayed without *Kavanah,* he must pray again with *Kavanah.* If his mind is upset and his heart troubled, he should not pray until he calms down . . ."[31]

This transcendent gift is found in many of the protagonists of this book who have been singled out by name and by achievement. It abides also in the anonymous ones, in the silent ones, in those who fulfill themselves in gratitude, in sublimation, in Mitzvoth. "Hasidism . . . retained the Kavanahs as a means of illumination of the soul. . . . Reform Judaism sought to return to the simple ideas of Kavanah as expressed in the Bible and rabbinic literature.

In its view Kavanah means sincerity in worship, the union
of word and thought, deed and intent, whereby the soul
is directed to its heavenly source."[32] Rabbi Leo Baeck, an
heroic symbol of martyrdom in our time, says: "We live
in a darkness surrounded by mystery . . . behind every
certainty there stands a concealment, behind every clarity
a new mystery is revealed." "The inner serenity of this
people," he writes in another section of *This People Israel,*
rests on prayer and "Prayer also gives the will to the
way."[33] It is the way of *mitzvoth* in action.

Even the existentialist agrees. "Judaism . . . shares with
Existentialism a sense of the responsibility that we all
must bear, and it is indeed an awesome responsibility; a
sense of freedom that we must exercise in making our
choices in difficult situations, and it is indeed a dreadful
freedom. . . . We move out of the poverty of a restricted
individualism to a sense of identity, first with other Jews,
and then with the whole of mankind."[34]

The literature of other faiths glows with these concepts.
In the biographical and autobiographical works of Quak-
ers. In the insights of European and especially English
mystics. In *The Cloud of Unknowing.* In Blake and Kahlil
Gibran and Evelyn Underhill. As for Jews, they find in
the Prophets "the idea of a special covenant binding together Yahweh and Israel . . . they penetrated to the
fundamental problems of moral responsibility, and offered conceptions of righteousness and ethical greatness
that have appealed to men of similar quality in all centuries since . . . they were men of mystic responsiveness,
in whom new insights broke with suddenness and such
apparently supernatural cogency that they could not be
taken as ordinary intellectual achievements but were
inevitably regarded as revelations of divinity."[35] This
sense of mission, of universal concern, of mystery and
fulfillment is a shared pool of experience. It is found in

the lectures Martin Buber delivered in his lifetime before audiences in nonsectarian universities. It is heard today in the words spoken by Professor Heschel at Leland Stanford University in 1963, *Who Is Man,* discussing such subjects as "Solitude," "Preciousness," "Indebtedness."[36] *"As sheer being man dissolves in anonymity . . ."* he avers. And we recall the anonymous women of our narrative in total agreement. Baeck and Heschel, separated in religious ideology, are in constant accord when it comes to the analysis of the ineffable in human life, of the sources of inspiration and creativity. Baeck speaks of ". . . the miracle in which the artistic spirit awakens . . ." Heschel, as if continuing the discussion adds: "The sort of creativity is discontent with mere being, with just being around in the world . . ." To which Baeck responds: ". . . the created man, begins as if by a miracle to be creative."[37] Heschel: "Consciousness of the self comes about in being challenged, in being called upon, in the choice between refusal and response." Baeck: "Life and thought directed to God, *kavanah,* had become one here." In this way, the Jews achieve inner serenity, he adds. M. Esther Harding in her book *The "I" and the "Not-I"* recalls that the anthropologist Levy-Brühl was the first to describe an experience which he aptly called "participation mystique."[38] A professor who lectured on religion at Oxford University, G. Stephens Spinks, in describing types of prayer states: "Mystical prayer is the prayer of communion and has its own techniques of meditation, contemplation, and the suppression of self."[39] He also introduces a Russian term used by Berdyaev—*sobornost*—as ". . . a community in which all men come together without compulsion or an imposed uniformity in the oneness of the Divine."[40] It was such an ethical concept which Rabbi Israel Lipkin of Salant, "the Salanter," stressed in his *Musar* movement. "Rabbi Israel believed that mutual *Musar* meditation

would inspire a man to the most lofty thoughts . . . In the
Musar conventicle a man may divest himself of all wordly
concerns; there he will learn the transiency of mundane
affairs."[41]

Long ago the Psalmist sang, "in the great congregation
I will bless the Lord." In that "Great Congregation"
women's voices have joined their men and their hymns
of praise and prayer reverberate in the corridors of time.

In a strangely revealing collection of essays titled *Why
I Am Not a Christian,* Bertrand Russell states some universal truths, emotions and doubts. He reaches conclusions
that are applicable to all adherents to faith as well as to
nonbelievers. For the human situation does not exclude
anyone. *"The good life is one inspired by love and guided
by knowledge,"* he writes.[42] In one of his essays titled "A
Free Man's Worship" he wrote in a mood "not unlike
what religious people call conversion." He "became suddenly and vividly aware of the loneliness in which most
people live, and passionately desirous of finding means
of diminishing this isolation."[43]

If there be a unifying thread in this narrative of the
emerging impact of the Jewess on America, one independent of time and of place, it is the desperate sense of
isolation which a woman experiences in a household from
which her dear ones have gone. The walls are blotters
absorbing sounds of all her yesterdays. She drowns in
silence. Her work-accustomed hands are still. She is no
longer needed. She wanders through her empty rooms
recalling other days, other times, other needs. All unready,
she has been retired from life, changed from a participant
to a spectator. Her mood has been beautifully stated:

I have let all the members of my household go their ways;
All those close to me have long since scattered,
And everything—within the heart and throughout nature—
Is filled with the loneliness of always.[44]

This is the mood of the spinster whose life resounds to the sounds of other people's laughter. Of the childless woman whose arms ache with the passion of the unfulfilled. Of the widow whose life's companion has been wrested from her and who must plod her lonely way alone. Of the mother who lived vicariously through her children and who is no longer sustained by their triumphs and their need of her. Fortunate are those whose faith upholds them and who live in quiet resignation until they are released. But even for those and for their unsustained sisters—the empty hours must be filled. There are social needs to be met. There are wrongs to be righted. There are those who need to be comforted and healed. So the "organization woman" is born. Let no one underestimate the work of their hands. They are the builders. And the tools that they use are the tools they have always used—a loving heart and willing hands.

And they build "with the stones that other builders rejected."

To every writer as he nears the end of a book there comes a devastating moment of truth. Then the unused materials and the discarded scrawls and the boxes of notes filled in many libraries become so many accusers. What is to be done about the many biographies of women of note and significance? They have not been used because of the quiet demands of the anonymous ones to be heard. What about the many other organizations whose work has had one's personal allegiance? Why are they unrecorded? Can one assume that the organizational charter of one group resembles that of many others? That the members of all groups have certain basic drives, goals and needs that are like the tools of an anthropologist universally applicable? Why should the faceless protagonist be the chosen heroine? Why should a single act of faith illumine

the historical scene with its effulgent light? Why should
the long climb from anonymity to self-discovery and self-
fulfillment become as difficult as climbing the steep side
of Mt. Hermon?

Every woman needs to cast a shadow. She may be as
nameless as the Shunammite whose good works earned
her immortality. She may have written words etched in
bronze and cherished by millions. The involved woman
has a threefold loyalty: first, identification with her Creator; second, loyalty to those who preceded her and led
her to the green pastures of self-fulfillment; third, loyalty
to her own self. Always she is leading an inward life and
an outward life—God-directed or group directed. The creative soul is the involved soul. The enduring philosophy,
the glorious vision, the total oblation is hers.

The subject is limitless. The variations on the theme
are endless. Women have wrought wondrously. Their
accomplishments are stunning. They stand on the threshhold of time where past and future meet. Each woman
is both heiress and apprentice. Within her hands are the
strands of history. She marches to the song of yesterday
and hears the brave hymn of a new tomorrow.

Notes

CHAPTER 1

[1] Ware, Caroline F. ed., *Cultural approach to History*, 119.
[2] J. S. Bixler, "Shall We Let the Ladies Join Us," in *American Scholar*, Vol. LV., No. 4.
[3] Theodor H. Gaster, *The Holy and the Profane*, p. 169.
[4] R. Learsi, *Israel*, 287.
[5] Quoted by Freyre, *op. cit.*, 36. See also extensive references in Lebeson, Anita Libman, *Pilgrim People*, esp. to the work of Solidonio Leite, Da Influencia do Elemento Judaico no Descobrimento e Commercio do Brasil (Seculos XVIe XVII) . . .
[6] Freyre, *op. cit.*, xxv.
[7] Robert Gordis, *The Root and the Branch*. p. 25.
[8] Arnold Wiznitzer, *Jews in Colonial Brazil*, p. 5. Also called *Gaspar Judeo*.
[9] *Ibid.*, p. 7.
[10] *Ibid., Jews in Colonial Brazil*, pp. 10–11.
[11] *Ibid.*
[12] Arnold Wiznitzer, *The Records of the Earliest Jewish Community in the New World*. New York American Jewish Historical Society, 1954.
[13] Wiznitzer, *The Records of the Earliest Jewish Community in the New World*, 22.
[14] *Ibid.*, 26, 29.
[15] Introduction to E. M. Shilstone's *Monumental Inscriptions in the Burial Ground of the Jewish Synagogue at Bridgetown, Barbados*, 1956.

16 Shilstone, *passim.*
17 *Op. cit.,* p. 146. The year is 1774.
18 Wiznitzer, *Jews in Colonial Brazil,* pp. 14–15 ff.
19 *Ibid.,* Wiznitzer, pp. 15, 19.
20 *Ibid.,* pp. 166–167.
21 *Ibid.,* p. 148.
22 *Ibid.*

CHAPTER 2

1 See Isaac S. Emmanuel in *American Jewish Archives,* April, 1962, pp. 32–68.
2 J. R. Marcus, *Early American Jewry,* I, p. 40.
3 Pool, *op. cit.,* p. 161.
4 *Op. cit.,* p. 169.
5 *Ibid.,* 175–176.
6 *Ibid.,* p. 177.
7 Martin Buber, *At the Turning,* New York, 1952, pp. 25–26.
8 The latest translation from the original Yiddish by Beth Zion Abrahams, New York, 1963.
9 Marvin Lowenthal, *The Memoirs of Glückel of Hameln,* New York, 1932.
10 Kobler, *Her Children Called Her Blessed,* p. 137. See also Edinger, Dora, *Bertha Pappenheim. Freud's Anna O.* English Edition, Highland Park, Ill., 1968.
11 Quoted by Abraham I. Katsh in "Hebraic Foundations of American Democracy" in Dagobert D. Runes, *The Hebrew Impact on Western Civilization,* p. 11.
12 See Moshe Davis, "Jewish Religious Life and Institutions in America," in *The Jews,* edited by Louis Finkelstein, Vol. I, pp. 354–453.
13 Pool, *Portraits Etched in Stone,* p. 181.
14 Salo W. Baron, in *Great Ages and Ideas of the Jewish People,* p. 392.

CHAPTER 3

1 Jacob R. Marcus, *Early American Jewry,* Vol. I, pp. 58 ff.
2 Marcus, *op. cit.*
3 This invaluable source as well as other manuscripts quoted here may be found in a fascinating collection of "Primarily Hitherto Unpublished Manuscripts," *American Jewry Documents,* Eighteenth Century, *passim,* edited by Jacob Rader Marcus with many notes appended to each document. See esp. pp. 12–14, 37.
4 Marcus, *op. cit.,* p. 49.
5 AJHS Publications, XLIX, p. 54.
6 Lebeson, *Jewish Pioneers in America,* pp. 178 ff.
7 Marcus, *American Jewry Documents,* pp. 74–79.
8 AJHS *publications,* vol. XLIX, No. 1, p. 37.

9 Nina Davis, Translator, *Songs of Exile by Hebrew Poets,* Philadelphia, 1901.

10 Aaron Levy, *Founder of Aaronsburg. Studies in American Jewish History,* No. 1, American Jewish Historical Society, 1951.

11 Joseph L. Blau and Salo W. Baron, *The Jews of the United States 1790–1840, a Documentary History,* Vol. II, p. 516.

12 *American Jewish Historical Quarterly,* Vol. LIV, No. 3, March 1965, pp. 243–277.

13 Malcolm H. Stern, "The Sheftall Diaries: Vital Records of Savannah Jewry (1733–1808)," in *AJHS Quarterly,* March 1965.

CHAPTER 4

1 Blau and Baron, *The Jews of the United States,* 1790–1840, Vol. III, pp. 701–702, 965–966.

2 See *ibid.,* p. 702, for refusal to accept a Miss Mervin as a bona fide convert.

3 Blau and Baron, *op. cit.,* pp. 678–680 and 980, (a bona fide convert).

4 Lebeson, "Hannah Adams and the Jews," in *Historia Judaica,* October 1946, pp. 113–134.

5 *Ibid.*

CHAPTER 5

6 Marcus, *American Jewry Documents—Eighteenth Century,* pp. 75-76.

7 Blau and Baron, *op. cit.,* Vol. I, p. 5.

8 *Ibid.,* p. 12.

9 Albert M. Hyamson, *The Sephardim of England,* London, 1951, p. 146.

10 *Ibid.,* p. 149.

11 *Ibid.,* 159.

12 Thomas J. Tobias, "The Cemetery We Rededicate," in *AJHS Quarterly,* Vol. LIII, No. 4, pp. 352 ff.

13 This account is largely based on Elzas, *The Jews of South Carolina,* 1905, and the research work and published articles by Anita L. Lebeson. Also a mournful tribute is paid to the late, brilliant young man, Morton Patla, of Charleston, who typed all of her poems for the author.

14 Quoted in full in Elzas, *The Jews of South Carolina,* pp. 181–184.

15 The writer interviewed both Mrs. Halsey and her husband and learned much about "Miss Penina."

16 A Freudian interpretation suggested by the psychoanalyst, Dr. Minna Libman Emch.

17 Wolf and Whiteman, *The History of the Jews of Philadelphia from Colonial Times to the Age of Jackson,* p. 239.

18 See *American Miniatures, 1730–1850,* edited by Harry B. Wehle,

Curator of Paintings, The Metropolitan Museum of Art, New York, 1937, p. 40, ". . . there is Rebecca Gratz with her compassionate mouth and her serious, intelligent brown eyes . . ."

[19] *Op. cit.,* p. 238.

[20] David Philipson, *Letters of Rebecca Gratz,* p. xx. See also Moshe Davis "Mixed marriage in Western Jewry," in *Jewish Journal of Sociology,* Jerusalem, 1969 reprint.

[21] Philipson, *Letters of Rebecca Gratz,* xvii, *passim.*

[22] *Op. cit.,* I, p. 205.

[23] Morais, *Eminent Israelites,* pp. 109–112. Lady Burdett-Coutts was a great friend of Charles Dickens.

[24] Philipson, *Letters of Rebecca Gratz,* pp. 83–86.

[25] *Op. cit.,* pp. 83–86.

[26] Morais, *Eminent Israelites, passim* and pp. 149 ff.

[27] *A Biographical Dictionary of Early American Jews.*

[28] Grace Aguilar, *The Women of Israel,* II, pp. 117.

[29] Wolf and Whiteman, *Jews of Philadelphia,* pp. 372–372 and p. 115. See also Anita Libman Lebeson, "The Forgotten Centennial," *Congress Weekly,* December 28, 1953.

[30] This is based on a thorough and exhaustive study of the *Occident* and specific volume and page references are not given, but are available. All quotes here and elsewhere have been carefully collated.

[31] Yuri Suhl, *Ernestine Rose and the Battle for Human Rights,* p. 10.

[32] *Ibid.,* p. 28.

[33] Quoted by Suhl, *op. cit.,* p. 84.

[34] *Ibid.*

[35] *Ibid.,* p. 153.

[36] *Ibid.,* p. 101.

[37] *Ibid.,* p. 282. See also Andrew Sinclair, *The Better Half,* Harper & Row, 1965, pp. 87–89 and 198.

[38] Suhl, pp. 220–224.

[39] *Ibid.,* pp. 274–275. *See also* Sinclair, Andrew, *The Better Half. The Emancipation of the American Woman,* pp. 87 ff.

CHAPTER 6

[1] *Encyclopaedia Britannica.*

[2] Based on the three-volume *Autobiography of Carl Schurz;* Claude M. Fuess, *Carl Schurz, Reformer;* Wayne Andrews, editor of *The Autobiography of Carl Schurz,* New York, 1961. Also from notes of Dr. Dora Edinger, a research librarian.

[3] Fuess, pp. 142–143.

[4] *Ibid.,* pp. 218–219.

[5] Lebeson, *Pilgrim People,* pp. 351ff.

[6] Cyrus Adler and Aaron M. Margalith, "American Intercession on

behalf of Jews in the Diplomatic Correspondence of the United States, 1840–1938," *AJHS Publications*, xxxvi (1943) ; *Virginia Magazine of History and Biography*, xxv (1917).

7 Lebeson, *op. cit.*, p. 357.

CHAPTER 7

1 This autobiographical fragment of Philip Cowen appears in *Autobiographies of American Jews*, edited by Harold U. Ribalow.

2 *The Cambridge History of American Literature*, Vol. III, pp. 121ff.

3 Ably edited by Ralph L. Rusk, Professor of English, Columbia University, in 1939.

4 *Ibid., passim.*

5 *Ibid.*, p. 35.

6 Rusk, p. 31.

7 *American Hebrew*, April 25, 5644.

8 Rusk, editor, *Letters to Emma Lazarus*, pp. 9–10.

9 Marnin Feinstein, *American Zionism*, pp. 17 ff.

10 *Ibid.*, pp. 17–19.

11 H. E. Jacob, *The World of Emma Lazarus.*

12 Rusk, *Letters to Emma Lazarus*, p. 30.

13 Rusk, *op. cit.*, pp. 30–31.

14 See Henrietta Szold's brief but dependable sketch in The *Jewish Encyclopedia*. See also H. E. Jacob, *The World of Emma Lazarus.*

15 From the biographical sketch of Josephine Lazarus, *passim.*

16 *Josephine Lazarus, passim.*

17 Charles A. Beard and Mary R. Beard, *Basic History of the United States*, p. 116.

18 *Ibid.*, p. 119.

19 Wolf and Whiteman, *History of the Jews of Philadelphia*, p. 198.

20 Wolf and Whiteman, *op. cit.*, pp. 198–199.

21 Marcus, *Memoirs of American Jews 1775–1865*, Vol. I, pp. 29 ff.

22 *Letters of Rebecca Gratz*, pp. 14–15.

23 Marcus, ed., *Memoirs of American Jews*, Vol. I, p. 251. The writer has used original manuscripts in Charleston, S.C.

24 Morris U. Schappes, *Documentary History of the Jews in the United States*, pp. 137 ff.

25 *Ibid.*, p. 138.

26 Morris and Commager, *Encyclopedia of American History.*

27 *Op. cit.*, p. 245.

28 Quoted by Wolf and Whiteman, *History of Jews in Philadelphia.*

29 Morris and Commager, *Encyclopedia of American History*, p. 517.

30 Letters of Rebecca Gratz, p. 28.

[31] Morris and Commager, *Encyclopedia of American History*, p. 519.

[32] Schappes, *op. cit.*, pp. 324 ff and 625 ff.

[33] Schappes, *op. cit.*, pp. 401–405.

[34] *Encyclopaedia Britannica* and Letters of Rebecca Gratz, pp. 211–212.

[35] Stuart E. Rosenberg, *The Jewish Community in Rochester, 1843–1925*, pp. 8 ff.

[36] *Ibid.*

[37] Morris and Commager, *op. cit.*, p. 444 ff.

[38] Guido Kisch, *In Search of Freedom*, p. 26.

[39] *Ibid.*, p. 31. Quoted by Professor Kisch.

[40] Morris and Commager, *op. cit.*, p. 448.

[41] I. J. Benjamin, *Three Years in America, 1859–1862*, 2 Vols., translated by Charles Reznikoff. See Chapter IV, pp. 85–92.

[42] *Ibid.*, p. 85.

[43] Benjamin, *op. cit.*, p. 108.

[44] Julia B. Heller (1857–1926), *Some of Her Writings, passim.*

[45] Marcus, *Memoirs of American Jews*, Vol. III, pp. 50, 70.

[46] *Ibid.*, p. 324.

[47] *Ibid.*, p. 326.

[48] *Ibid.*, pp. 326–327.

[49] *Ibid.*, pp. 326-348.

[50] *Ibid.*, pp. 168–169. His portrait is in Charleston, South Carolina, in the Halsey home.

[51] S. R. Brav, "The Jewish Woman, 1861-1865," *A. J. Archives*, Vol. xvii, pp. 37–39.

[52] Lebeson, *Pilgrim People*, 228.

[53] Brav, *op. cit.*, p. 47.

[54] Korn, *American Jewry and the Civil War*, pp. 99–103.

[55] Korn, *op. cit.*, pp. 101–102.

[56] *Ibid.*, p. 103.

[57] Quoted by Korn, p. 104.

[58] *Ibid.*, p. 106.

[59] Korn, p. 107. See also Anita L. Lebeson in F. Kobler, *Her Children Call Her Blessed: A Portrait of the Jewish Mother*, pp. 176–179.

[60] Lebeson, *Recall to Life: A History of Chicago Jewry*, 1961.

[61] Brav, *The Jewish Woman, 1861–1865*, p. 98, *passim.*

[62] Quoted by Brav, *op. cit.*, pp. 61–63.

[63] *Ibid.*, pp. 65–67.

[64] *Ibid.*, p. 69.

[65] Korn, "Factors Bearing upon the Survival of Judaism in the Ante-Bellum Period," *American Jewish Historical Quarterly*, Vol. LIII, pp. 341 ff.

[66] David and Tamar de Sola Pool, *An Old Faith in the New World,* pp. 249 ff.

[67] *Ibid.*

[68] Heschel, *op. cit.,* p. 15.

[69] Guido Kisch, *In Search of Freedom. A History of American Jews from Czechoslovakia, passim.* See esp. p. 33.

[70] *Ibid.*

[71] *American Hebrew,* Vols. 15–18, May 18, 5643—May 2, 5644.

[72] Ribalow, *Autobiographies of American Jews,* pp. 33–34.

CHAPTER 8

[1] James, Edmund J., Editor, *The Immigrant Jew in America,* passim.

[2] See also Sherman, *The Jew Within American Society,* p. 60ff, and Golden's Preface to the 1965 edition of Hutchins Hapgood's *The Spirit of the Ghetto,* first published in 1902.

[3] James, *op. cit.*

[4] James, p. 4.

[5] *Two Hundred and Fiftieth Anniversary,* p. 231.

[6] Jacob Lestschinsky, in *Jewish People—Past and Present,* Vol. IV, p. 55.

[7] *Ibid.,* p. 59.

[8] David and Tamar de Sola Pool, *An Old Faith in the New World,* pp. 359 ff.

[9] Lebeson, *History of the Jews in the United States in Jewish People,* Vol. IV, p. 20.

[10] Pool, *op. cit.,* p. 361.

[11] *Ibid.,* p. 369 ff.

[12] Hutchins Hapgood, Preface, by Harry Golden, p. xii.

[13] Hapgood, *op. cit.,* p. 79.

[14] *The Jewish Prayer Book,* pp. 345–346.

[15] P. M. Raskin, quoted by Hertz, *Prayer Book,* p. 344.

[16] Hapgood, *op. cit.,* pp. 84–85.

[17] Pomrenze, *op. cit.,* pp. 113–136.

[18] *Ibid.,* p. 122. Italics mine.

[19] *American Jewish Historical Quarterly,* Vol. LIII, June, 1964, pp. 431–433.

[20] James, *The Immigrant Jew in America,* p. 5.

[21] Lebeson, editor, *History of Chicago Jewry, passim.*

[22] Pomrenze, "Aspects of Chicago Russian Jewish Life," pp. 132–133. See also Tom Brooks "The Terrible Triangle Fire" in *American Heritage,* Vol. VIII, Number 5, pp. 54 ff.

[23] *Ibid.,* p. 126.

[24] Max L. Baym, in *Publications of American Jewish Historical Society,* Vol. xxxvii, p. 17ff. "Emma Lazarus' Approach to Renan."

25 Moshe Davis, *The Emergence of Conservative Judaism,* p. 11.

26 B. W. Korn, "Factors bearing upon the survival of Judaism in the Ante-Bellum Period," *Am. J. Historical Quarterly,* Vol. LIII, p. 345.

27 Emma Felsenthal, *Bernhard Felsenthal, Teacher in Israel,* p. 250.

28 Rabbi Freehof of Temple Rodef Shalom in Pittsburgh is Honorary Life President of the World Union for Progressive Judaism and has contributed many works to the interpretation of Judaism and the Reform Movement. Quoted from an article in *American Judaism,* Fall, 1965.

29 Theodore N. Lewis, "Portrait of Reform's Founder," in Congress bi-Weekly.

30 J. G. Heller, *Isaac M. Wise, passim.* There are literally dozens of passages referring to women. P. xiii for above quote.

31 Heller, p. iv.

32 Heller, *op. cit.,* p. 271.

33 *Ibid.,* p. 580.

34 Malek Ravitch, "Song on the Seas to My Mother-Tongue."

35 Heller, *op. cit.,* pp. 583–584.

36 "On the Position of Women," in Heller, pp. 568–569.

37 *Ibid.,* p. 570.

38 Heller, *op. cit.,* p. 571.

39 Milton Steinberg, *The Making of the Modern Jew,* pp. 176–177.

40 See *Commentary* for February and July, 1966, for a fuller discussion.

41 Mordecai Waxman, editor. *Tradition and Change. The Development of Conservative Judaism,* p. 7.

42 Arthur Ruppin, in *Jewish People—Past and Present,* Vol. I, p. 349.

43 *Ibid.,* p. 354.

44 Quoted by Maurice Samuel in "Russian Jewry: Flowering and Frost," in *Congress Bi-Weekly,* June 20, 1966.

45 *Ibid.*

46 H. L. Meites, *History of the Jews of Chicago,* p. 133.

47 Emma Felsenthal, *Bernhard Felsenthal,* 76–78.

48 Robert Gordis, *op. cit.,* p. 78. Several books have recently been added to the growing library dealing with the Conservative Movement to which the reader is referred: Moshe Davis, *The Emergence of Conservative Judaism;* Herbert Parzen, *Architects of Conservative Judaism;* C. Bezalel Sherman, *The Jew Within American Society,* p. 192 ff.; Robert Gordis, *Jewish Tradition in the Modern World,* Syracuse Univ., 1965; Mordecai Waxman, editor, *Tradition and Change;* Eli Ginzberg, *Keeper of the Law: Louis Ginzberg.*

49 Agus, *Jewish People* Vol. IV, pp. 131 ff.

50 Gordis, *Conservative Judaism,* pp. 19 ff. See also Lebeson in the

Joshua Bloch Memorial volume, published by the New York Public Library, 1960.

⁵¹ Correspondence quoted in Parzen, *ibid.,* pp. 26–78.
⁵² *Builders of the Conservative Movement,* p. 21.
⁵³ C. Davidson, *Out of Endless Yearnings,* pp. 58–59.
⁵⁴ *Op. cit.,* pp. 64–65.
⁵⁵ Mary Antin, *The Promised Land, passim.* For quote see pp. 355–356.
⁵⁶ *Ibid.,* pp. 357–358.
⁵⁷ Psalm 18.
⁵⁸ Introduction to *My Portion,* p. ix.
⁵⁹ *Op. cit.,* p. 71.
⁶⁰ R. Kohut, *My Portion,* pp. 180–182.

CHAPTER 9

¹ Louis Rosenberg, *Canadian Jewish Population Studies* No. 2. "The Jewish Population of Canada; A Statistical Summary from 1851 to 1941," p. 5.
² Quoted by Louis Rosenberg, author of above study.
³ *Universal Jewish Encyclopedia* vol. II, p. 651.
⁴ In a long article on Canadian history in the *Universal Jewish Encyclopedia,* the work of one woman is singled out—Mrs. A. J. Freiman.
⁵ R. Kohut, *My Portion,* p. 184.
⁶ *Ibid.,* p. 199.
⁷ Lebeson, in *Early History of Zionism in America,* pp. 155–190. See also Dr. Judah Rosenthal, *The Settlement of East European Jews in Chicago, 1860–1880.* Also, "Aspects of Chicago Russian Jewish Life, 1893–1915" in *Chicago Pinkas,* pp. 113–136.
⁸ Pomrenze, *Aspects of Chicago Russian-Jewish Life, 1893–1915,* pp. 117 ff.
⁹ Joel S. Geffen, "America in the first Hebrew Daily Newspaper: *Ha-Yom* (1886–1888) in *American Jewish Historical Quarterly,* March, 1962, pp. 149–167.
¹⁰ Philip P. Bregstone, *Chicago and its Jews,* quotes from Lebeson, *Jewish Pioneers in America.* See his section "Noteworthy Celebration," pp. 39–40.
¹¹ *Ibid.,* pp. 40–41.
¹² *Ibid.*
¹³ Bregstone, pp. 44–45. (Italics added.)
¹⁴ Thanks to a niece of Michael's, Mrs. Alfred S. Alschuler, Sr., of Highland Park, Ill., the family papers were made available to the writer.
¹⁵ Morris A. Gutstein, *A Priceless Heritage,* p. 327.
¹⁶ *Ibid.,* pp. 327 ff.

[17] The writer knew her and heard her speak.

[18] H. L. Meites, *History of the Jews in Chicago*, p. 179.

[19] Lebeson, *Jewish Pioneers in America*, pp. 9–10.

[20] Heller, *Isaac M. Wise*, pp. 571–572.

[21] Heller, *op. cit.*, pp. 571–572. See also pp. 476, 547. See also Bregstone, *Chicago and Its Jews*, pp. 38–46.

[22] See "On Remembering Ray Frank Litman" by Anita Libman Lebeson in Simon Litman, *Ray Frank Litman: A Memoir*.

[23] *Ibid.*, p. 4.

[24] *American Jewess*, 1898, pp. 19–21. This periodical was published from Nov. 4, 1895, to March 18, 1899.

[25] These letters were made available to the author by Professor Simon Litman.

[26] Lebeson, "On Remembering Ray Frank Litman," an Epilogue to her husband's biographical Memoir, pp. 193–202.

[27] Franz Kobler, editor, *Her Children Call Her Blessed*, pp. 182–194.

[28] For seven years, the years of Nazi horror, the writer served as chairman of the Service for Foreign-born Committee of the National Council of Jewish Women in the Chicago area and as a member of the National Committee. The National Council of Jewish Women rescued tens of thousands of distinguished men and women, Nobel Prize winners and anonymous victims by securing sponsors for them, helping them emigrate, finding new homes for them in the United States, Mexico, and Canada and other havens in the Western world.

[29] Rebekah Kohut, *My Portion*, pp. 243–244.

[30] *National Council of Jewish Women*, p. 14.

[31] *Ibid.*, p. 39.

[32] *Ibid.*, p. 47.

[33] *Ibid.*, p. 24.

[34] *Ibid.*, p. 122.

CHAPTER 10

[1] The above is based on personal knowledge, on a study of the Minnesota Historical Society summaries, on conversations with Mrs. Rachel Brin Helstein, her daughter who lives in Chicago. It also includes seven years as volunteer chairman of the Chicago Service for Foreign Born Committee of the National Council of Jewish Women, during the time that Mrs. Brin was president.

[2] Leon Huhner, *Essays and Addresses*, "The Jewish Woman in America," pp. 32 ff.

[3] Hirsch, *My Religion*, pp. 168–186.

[4] Alschuler, *op. cit.* Based also on many conversations with Rose Alschuler.

[5] Alschuler, *Bits and Pieces*. This was written in August, 1916.

[6] Heschel, *Man's Quest for God,* p. 76.

[7] *Ibid.,* p. 75.

[8] Proverbs 7:4

[9] Lucy Freeman, *Farewell to Fear,* New York, 1969.

[10] Proverbs 9: 1, 6.

[11] *American Jewish Historical Society Publications, XLIX,* Sept. 1959.

[12] Another roll of honor is found in the Universal Jewish Encyclopedia. Listed are many women who made signal contributions to the larger community without identifying with the group which had been their point of spiritual origin.

[13] Sherman, *The Jew Within American Society,* pp. 40–41.

[14] Women's International Zionist Organization.

[15] WIZO in Israel, December 1953, p. 14.

[16] L. Rosenberg, *A Study of the Jewish Community in Canada,* 1931–1961.

[17] Sherman, *Jew Within American Society,* p. 161.

[18] Margaret B. Crook, *Women and Religion,* p. 45.

[19] *Ibid.,* p. 48 (Numbers 12:2) .

[20] Psalm 68:12. Professor Crook uses here the English Revised Version of 1885, an altogether more beautiful translation than the Standard Revised Bible.

[21] Jacob Zausmer, "In the Footsteps of the Generations." I am indebted to Mr. Abraham Berger of the Jewish Division of the New York Public Library for sending me the Xerox copy of this article and to Mr. Hermon Lebeson for graciously translating it.

[22] *American Jewess,* July, 1896.

[23] Andrew Sinclair, *The Better Half: the Emancipation of the American Woman,* pp. 29–30, 37, 58–64, 198, 200.

[24] *Ibid.,* p. 53.

[25] Emerson, "Fate", p. 26.

[26] Lebeson, *History of Chicago Jewry,* p. 9.

[27] Lebeson, *History of Chicago Jewry,* p. 10.

[28] Lebeson, *History of Chicago Jewry,* p. 15.

CHAPTER 11

[1] Henri Bergson, *The Two Sources of Morality and Religion,* p. 255.

[2] Tamar de Sola Pool, "Henrietta Szold," p. 323.

[3] Quoted in Simon Noveck, editor, from an essay by Tamar de Sola Pool, "Henrietta Szold," in *Great Jewish Personalities in Modern Times,* p. 323.

[4] *Ibid.,* p. 325.

[5] Personal Memoir of Sarah Elkin Braun, addressed to the writer.

[6] Tamar de Sola Pool, *op. cit.,* p. 342.

[7] See Mordecai Waxman, *Tradition and Change*, pp. 111–127.

[8] *Ibid.*, pp. 112–113. Italics mine.

[9] Described by Mrs. Elias L. Solomon who was present.

[10] Solomon Schechter, *Studies in Judaism*, Second Series, p. 148 ff.

[11] *Ibid.*, pp. 149–152.

[12] *Ibid.*, p. 154.

[13] *Ibid.*, pp. 163–180.

[14] *Ibid.*, p. 126 ff.

[15] Quoted with permission of Mrs. Solis-Cohen who supplied this material.

[16] Excerpt from Bulletin of the Conference of Jewish Women's Organizations, dated January 1951:

Mrs. Jacob Kohn Honored

... Mrs. Kohn came to Sinai from New York in September, 1931, and has endeared herself to everyone who has had the privilege of meeting and knowing her. Her interests are so numerous that space does not permit the mention of all of them. Mrs. Kohn represents Conference on the Bible Section of the L. A. Federation of Women's Clubs, where Jewish as well as non-Jewish women come to her for advice and counsel. Together with Mrs. Solomon Schechter she helped organize the National Women's League of the United Synagogue, of which Mrs. Kohn was the first president, and she is now holding the office of Honorary Vice President. She is one of the thirteen women who worked to found the National Hadassah Organization.

She has served for many years with the Sisterhood of Sinai. It was through her efforts and assistance that the book, Home Beautiful, was conceived. Mrs. Kohn is now serving on the Board of Directors for the Council of Jewish Women, and keeps an active interest in the work of Conference. We wish her many more long years of good health to carry on her good deeds.

[17] From data submitted by Rabbi Jacob Kohn.

[18] L. Rosenberg, *Two Centuries of Jewish Life in Canada.*

[19] Phyllis Lee Peterson, "The Jew in Canada," reprinted from *Maclean's Magazine* and sent to the writer by the American Jewish Congress of Canada.

[20] Photostat of a clipping in the files of Mrs. Benjamin Davis, undated.

[21] *Harper's Bible Dictionary:* "Shunammite."

[22] The notebooks, papers, scrapbooks, official documents of Mrs. Benjamin Davis were made available to the writer by Mrs. Cherrie Krueger, her daughter.

[23] All of these quotations are from the personal papers and scrapbooks of Jeanette (some of her papers spelled it Jeannette) Isaacs Davis.

[24] *Chicago Israelite*, May 1897.

[25] I. Greenberg, "Adventure in Freedom—or Escape From Freedom

—Jewish Identity in America," *American Jewish Historical Quarterly,* vol. LV, No. 1, September, 1965, pp. 5–21.

[26] Lebeson, *Pilgrim People,* p. 469 ff.

[27] I. Greenberg, *op. cit.,* pp. 20–21.

[28] "The Feminine Tragique," in a *Saturday Review* critique of *After Nora Slammed the Door,* July 11, 1964, p. 32.

[29] Thorsten Veblen, *The Theory of the Leisure Class.*

[30] See Justin G. Turner, "The First Decade of Los Angeles Jewry: A Pioneer History (1850–1960), in *American Jewish Historical Quarterly,* vol. LIV, No. 2, December 1964. It is an important contribution to American history. The footnotes and bibliographical references are exhaustive. Based also on other nonpublished data made available to the author by Justin Turner.

[31] *Ibid.,* p. 125.

[32] *Ibid.*

[33] Photostat courtesy of Justin G. Turner.

[34] This work was translated by Hermon Lebeson.

[35] *Outlook,* May, 1948, p. 8 ff.

[36] In an article by Fanny B. Minkin.

[37] The *Outlook* is published by National Women's League, edited by Mrs. Zillah Kohn.

CHAPTER 12

[1] M. Rosenfeld, "On the Ocean," translated from the Yiddish by Alice Lucas, *Jewish Quarterly Review,* vol. XII, p. 91.

[2] Anita L. Lebeson, "Hannah Adams and the Jews," in *Historia Judaica,* vol. VIII, No. 2, pp. 113–134.

[3] Marnin Feinstein, *American Zionism—1884–1904.*

[4] These Bertha Berkman very kindly permitted the writer to have full access to, together with countless photographs and memorabilia and many precious recollections of the founding of Hadassah and her meetings with Henrietta Szold and other pioneers of the Zionist Organization and Hadassah.

[5] *Hadassah Magazine,* June 1965.

[6] This biography was sent in by Mr. Justin G. Turner of California.

[7] The quotations are from a biographical sketch sent by Justin Turner to the writer. Also based on personal knowledge of Mrs. Sieroty, Miss Pearl Franklin and Mrs. Yavitz.

[8] Memoir by Lillian Franklin in manuscript.

[9] *Jewish Observer and Middle East Review,* August 19, 1966.

[10] Based on manuscript summary submitted to the writer.

[11] The complete file of these data on Mizrachi Women's Organization of America, was assembled for the writer by Leah Mishkin, Librarian and Curator of the Hebrew Theological College of Chicago.

[12] Their bilingual magazine *Di Yiddishe Heim* and manuscript data secured by the Curator of the Library at Hebrew Theological College, Mrs. Leah Mishkin.

[13] *American Judaism,* January, 1956. Vol. 5, No. 3.

[14] *Op. cit.*

[15] Claire Levi, *American Judaism,* January, 1956.

[16] *New York Times,* June 24, 1966, p. 22.

[17] Jacob Trapp, *"Martin Buber"* in *American Judaism,* Vol. XV, No. 2. Winter, 1965–1966.

[18] Henri Bergson, *The Two Sources of Morality and Religion,* 255.

[19] *Collected Poems of Edna St. Vincent Millay,* pp. 730–731.

[20] Joshua Loth Liebman, *Hope for Man,* p. 43.

[21] Edwin Markham, *Collected Poems,* pp. 24–25.

[22] "The Highest Step," the Story of Women's American ORT.

[23] American Jewish Congress, National Women's Division 1965 Convention Report.

[24] *Congress bi-Weekly,* March 15, 1965, pp. 3–4. Samuel Caplan was for many years its brilliant editor. He died May, 1969.

[25] *Congress bi-Weekly,* November 9, 1964.

[26] *Ibid.,* p. 65.

[27] Report to National Women's Division of American Jewish Congress, March, 1965.

[28] Joachim Prinz, "Facing Our Jewish Task," in *Congress bi-Weekly,* May 11, 1964.

[29] Theodore Friedman and Robert Gordis, editors, *Jewish Life in America,* p. 33.

[30] Bezalel Sherman, "Secularization and Religion in the Jewish Labor Movement" in Friedman and Gordis, *op. cit.,* pp. 109–127.

[31] Maurice Bisgyer, editor, *This Is B'nai B'rith.*

[32] John Higham, "Social Discrimination Against Jews in America, 1830–1930," Publication of the American Jewish Historical Society, pp. 1–33.

[33] *This is B'nai B'rith,* 28.

[34] From a report to the writer submitted by Adele Nusbaum, Director of Public Relations, B'nai B'rith Women.

[35] "The Women of B'nai B'rith," in *This Is B'nai B'rith,* pp. 94 ff.

[36] *This is B'nai B'rith,* p. 98.

[37] Marshall Sklare, *Conservative Judaism, an American Religious Movement,* p. 86.

CHAPTER 13

[1] 2 Kings: 4.

[2] David de Sola Pool, *Portraits Etched in Stone.*

[3] W. M. Dixon, *The Human Situation,* p. 424.

[4] Psalm 39.

[5] Margaret B. Cook, *Women and Religion.*

[6] Mordecai Kaplan, *The Future of the American Jew,* p. 343.

[7] *Ibid.,* p. 348. See section titled "The Good and the Beautiful in Jewish Life."

[8] Milton Rokeach, in *Trans- action,* Jan.–Feb., 1965, pp. 9–12.

[9] Moshe Davis, *The Emergence of Conservative Judaism,* p. 326.

[10] Moshe Davis, "Centres of Jewry in the Western Hemisphere: A Comparative Approach." Reprinted from *The Jewish Journal of Sociology,* vol. V, No. 1, June 1963, London. Italics added.

[11] *Time,* "The New American Jew," June 25, 1965.

[12] *Time,* June 25, 1965.

[13] Marshall Sklare, *Conservative Judaism,* p. 86 ff.

[14] *Ibid.,* p. 88.

[15] *Op. cit.* See also pp. 83–84 and 109–128.

[16] Pearl S. Buck, "America's Medieval Women," *Harper's Magazine,* August 1938.

[17] Ashley Montagu, *The Natural Superiority of Women,* pp. 23, 24.

[18] *Ibid.* p. 26.

[19] Andrew Sinclair, *The Emancipation of the American Woman.* See also review in Panorama, Chicago *Daily News,* July 10, 1965.

[20] Kobler, *Her Children Called Her Blessed,* p. 272, February 17, 1934.

[21] Lily H. Montagu, *The Faith of a Jewish Woman,* pp. 65–66.

[22] Rabbi Balfour Brickner, "A Blueprint for Jewish Survival," in *American Judaism,* vol. XIV, No. 1, Fall, 1964.

[23] See Samuel H. Dresner, "Prayer, Humility and Compassion" in *Judaism,* Vol. 3, No. 1.

[24] Abraham Joshua Heschel, *Man's Quest for God,* pp. 4–6.

[25] Leo Baeck, *This People Israel,* pp. 220, 243, 257, 398–399.

[26] Martin Buber, *At the Turning,* pp. 25–26.

[27] Rabbi Joseph H. Hertz, *Daily Prayer Book,* p. 1097.

[28] *Kavanah* (variously spelled) is discussed in the *Universal Jewish Encyclopedia,* vol. VI, pp. 346–348.

[29] Garfiel, *op. cit.,* pp. 137–138.

[30] Quoted by Garfiel, p. 138.

[31] *Universal Jewish Encyclopedia,* VI, p. 347.

[32] *Ibid.,* p. 348.

[33] Leo Baeck, *This People Israel,* "The Meaning of Jewish Existence," pp. 257 and 399.

[34] Typescript of a lecture by Professor Abraham Kaplan on "Existentialism and Judaism" delivered at the Oscar Hillel Plotkin Library, 1964.

[35] Edwin A. Burtt, *Types of Religious Philosophy,* p. 21.

[36] A. J. Heschel, *Who Is Man,* pp. 33, 44, 94, 107. Italics mine.

37 Heschel, *Who Is Man*, pp. 95, 106. Baeck, *This People Israel*, pp. 399, 257.

38 Harding, *op. cit.*, p. 38.

39 G. S. Spinks, *Psychology and Religion*, p. 128.

40 *Ibid.*, p. 178.

41 M. Glenn, *Salanter*, p. 34.

42 Bertrand Russell, *Why I am Not a Christian*, p. 56. Italics added.

43 *Ibid.*, p. 104 ff.

44 Boris Pasternak, from his poem "Autumn."

Index